Bridges Burning

Bridges Burning

✦

America's Challenge of the 21st Century

William K. Tell, Jr.

iUniverse, Inc.
New York Lincoln Shanghai

Bridges Burning
America's Challenge of the 21st Century

iUniverse books may be ordered through booksellers or by contacting:

iUniverse
2021 Pine Lake Road, Suite 100
Lincoln, NE 68512
www.iuniverse.com
1-800-Authors (1-800-288-4677)

ISBN-13: 978-0-595-38431-0 (pbk)
ISBN-13: 978-0-595-67620-0 (cloth)
ISBN-13: 978-0-595-82807-4 (ebk)
ISBN-10: 0-595-38431-5 (pbk)
ISBN-10: 0-595-67620-0 (cloth)
ISBN-10: 0-595-82807-8 (ebk)

Printed in the United States of America

Contents

Acknowledgement

There are several people I would like to thank who have helped me these last several years during the writing of this book. First, I would like to thank Donald Sutherland whose commitment to this project has been unwavering. Donald has a keen sense of today's issues and his exploration and research of these topics give the writing of this book greater texture and balance. I would also like to thank my long-time assistant, Agnes Brady, whose dedication to keeping my hectic life organized has been unsurpassed. Her attention to detail and assistance in my well-being for over 25 years is greatly appreciated. My daughter Catherine came to work for me five years ago as an extra set of eyes for this project. She and I do not always see the world through the same set of glasses but I thank her for putting aside these differences and appreciate her honest and helpful insights. I would like to express thanks to Edward Romer who is responsible for the dynamic cover design. Finally, I would like to thank my family and friends who have encouraged me to keep moving forward with this project, this has meant a lot to me.

—Bill Tell

Preface

Great nations must face the undeniable reality that their position in power can not last forever; decline is inevitable. Interestingly, a great nation's decline may occur precisely at the moment in time when it feels most healthy and invincible and this may be in part a result of cultural and institutional decay. Historians Will and Ariel Durant describe cultural decay as, "Caught in a relaxing interval between one moral code and the next, an unmoored generation surrenders itself to luxury, corruption and a restless disorder of family and morals."[1] Arguably, the U.S., at the end of the 20th century displayed these characteristics. And, at the beginning of the 21st century, Americans are at risk of losing the beliefs, ideals and traditions central to sustaining a healthy democracy and are threatened by a modern culture that places its values away from traditional democratic values. A crisis of vitality is emerging that goes to the heart of America's character and strength.[2] This dilemma raises doubts about America's continuing success as a world leader and could weaken the strength of the U. S. democracy in itself.[3] American citizens must be promptly made aware of this dangerous internal challenge to their country if it remains on its present course. They should also understand that if their fellow citizens are not tempered by institutional education and cultural reforms, substantial adverse consequences for their nation's future could follow.

The role that U.S. citizen's play and the degree of their individual commitment to engage in political participation and appropriately guide their country's policymakers is crucial. The chapters herein set forth in greater detail the crucial future role that America's citizens must play in response to the corrosive changes that have taken place since the 1960s in the U. S. culture and the dangerous decline in the educational quality of its citizens that threatens the fundamental democratic values and culture adopted by America's Founders. In these circumstances, this book provides a realistic but hopeful framework by which U.S. citizens can learn to understand, adopt and contribute to implementing the educational and cultural reforms needed to regain and sustain American preeminence. Preservation of the freedoms and opportunities to which prior generations of American citizens have become accustomed are at great risk in the 21st century as globalism and clashes between cultures and religions become more frequent and dangerous.

The ultimate success in the 21st century of a democratic republic depends on a healthy culture, strong institutions and involved citizens. This was the underpinning of America's unique founding model built around the twin engines of democratic governance and free market capitalism. Weak institutions will lead to unfavorable outcomes that can undermine a nation's culture, governance and economy. This in turn will inflict injury on both citizens and institutions. At some threshold these interrelated impacts will combine to create a vicious downward spiral of irreversible institutional decline. The major indicators showing U.S. citizen performance over the last 25 years already provides many reasons for concern.

In the above context, it is important to analyze the impact and meaning of the 2004 U.S. Presidential election which demonstrated the willingness of American citizens to remain engaged even when the nation faced a great and dangerous global challenge. This important analysis is set forth in significant detail in Chapter 2. It can quite likely be carried forward in future Presidential elections. During the interim it is hoped that our readers will contemplate and communicate the analysis and ideas set forth herein.

—William K. Tell

1

America's Great Challenges in the 21st Century

"Those who cannot remember the past are condemned to repeat it."

—*George Santayana*

The Rise and Fall of Great Powers

We often hear the phrase "past performance is no guarantee of future results." The history of the rise and fall of great nations clearly confirms this adage. Today, more than ever, the United States in the 21st century faces a fate similar to Rome in the first century BC or England in the 20th century as the proliferation of a global economy, international terrorism and a politically weakened educational system threaten the U.S.'s position as the world's only super power capable of carrying out this needed role.

A broader examination of history provides sobering evidence that no great power has ever been able to permanently overcome history's cycles. These cycles continue to bring regular waves of challenge—some internal, some external—crashing onto the shores of great powers and often unleashing events that signal their decline.

History: Not Just Linear

The challenges in the 21st century, so far, to the United States' economic and military preeminence are consistent with past experiences of other former great powers. Throughout the ages, no great power has ever discovered the proverbial

1

"Fountain of Youth" which would enable it to permanently retain or regain pre-eminence. However, there is a certain amount of optimism that there might be grounds for an important American exception. As the U.S. enters into this period of challenge, an understanding of what led to past declines and the desire to avoid some of the same pitfalls may help to soften, or even reverse this inevitable course.

Currently, the U.S.'s economic and military preeminence can not insulate America from history's cyclical nature nor ensure its position of preeminence. U.S. citizens must be fully prepared to carry out the active and important role of addressing the responsibilities bestowed upon them to defend their unique democracy and maintain The U.S.'s position as a global leader.

Some of the world's most prominent past and present historians have contended that history's cycles are an immutable reality, largely beyond the control of human society. Historian Arthur Schlesinger, Jr., explained that, "A true cycle…is self-generating…War, depressions [and] inflations, may heighten or complicate moods, but the cycle itself rolls on, self-contained, self-sufficient and autonomous…"[4] More than two thousand years ago, Greek historian Thucydides advised, "the accurate knowledge of what has happened will be useful because according to human probability similar things will happen again."[5] In his seminal work, *A Study of History*, Arnold Toynbee concluded that, "Certainly, in the movement of all these forces that weave the web of human history, there is an obvious element of recurrence."[6]

William Strauss' and Neil Howe's *The Fourth Turning* describes history's cyclical rhythms in terms of four "turnings" which construct a complete historical cycle:

- The "First Turning:" is an age of strengthening institutions and weakening individualism.

- The "Second Turning:" is a time of spiritual upheaval when new values and challenges occur to the existing civic order.

- The "Third Turning:" is an era of rising individualism and weakening institutions where the old civic order decays.

- The "Fourth Turning:" is a decisive period of secular upheaval where the old civic order is replaced with a new one.[7]

Strauss and Howe's analysis suggest that Anglo-American history has witnessed five such cycles since the Wars of the Roses (1459–1487): 1) the Reformation, 2) the New World, 3) the Revolutionary War, 4) the Civil War, and 5) the

Great Power eras. Each of these has been marked by a distinct crisis with events culminating in a climax. The crisis events generally precede the climax by roughly 10–20 years. Rapid advances in technology, improvements in transportation, economic globalization, and the increasingly rapid dissemination of information may well shorten the future intervals between climax events.

In its current cycle, the U.S. experienced the "First Turning" during the 1950's and 1960's when the nation became globally confident and institutionally muscular. The "Second Turning" occurred from the mid-1960s through the mid-1980s and was defined by a change in the culture that began to redefine American norms and values. The "Third Turning," began in the mid-1980s. Strauss and Howe estimated that the "Fourth Turning" would arrive around 2005,[8] however, the events of September 11, 2001 may have triggered this period sooner than expected.

The U.S. over the last thirty years has been experiencing what Strauss and Howe describe as an "unraveling era." The best-known unraveling decades (the 1550s, 1660s, 1760s, 1850s, and 1920s) bring to mind risk-taking, bad manners, and a sobering of the social mood. "These decades produced few strong leaders or enduring public works but many artists, moralists, enterprisers, and reckless celebrities of enduring fame, people whom we remember for what they did alone, not in groups. Unraveling eras reflect a social mood that becomes newly personal, pragmatic, and insecure," according to Strauss and Howe.[9]

Cycles can be viewed on a larger scale as well, as described by historian Sir John Glubb whose study of great empires gives an interesting description of the life cycle of an empire. In his treatise, *The Fate of Empires and Search for Survival,* empires appear to have durations of approximately 250 years[10] after which they are vulnerable to particularly severe challenges. He cites examples including Assyria (247 years), Persia (208 years), Greece (231 years), the Roman Republic (233 years), the Roman Empire (207 years), the Mameluke Empire (267 years), the Ottoman Empire (250 years), Spain (250 years), and Britain (250 years).[11] Rome, because it went through two highly distinct stages is divided into those two phases. From his research, Glubb concluded that empires go through common stages—growth, peak and decay.[12] Against the framework of this research, the United States already appears to have gone through the "growth" stages (the Ages of Pioneers, Conquests, and Commerce) in which power and wealth are created and is now in the peak phase. In this penultimate stage, although the so-called "virtues" vital to a nation's growth are still in evidence, beneath the surface there is decay.[13] Whether America's cultural changes that evolved beginning in the 1960s provided the kind of decay Glubb had in mind is a matter that will be judged by future historians. Glubb's research, however, offers us another reason to prepare for the kind of great challenges which America will confront in the 21st Century.

"The impact of modernity, the beliefs, ideals, and traditions that previously were central to Americans and to American democracy—whether religious or civic, such as "Americanism"—are now losing their compelling cultural power," [14] warns author Os Guinness. "This crisis is not a crisis of legitimacy, like that of the Soviet Union, but a crisis of vitality that goes to the heart of America's character and strength. It therefore threatens to pose questions not only for America's continuing success and world domination, but for the vitality of democracy in America itself." [15]

If this internal challenge remains unrecognized and thereby not tempered by institutional and cultural reforms, substantial adverse consequences for the nation's future could follow. A continuing examination of the cycles of history can help explain why a nation should be aware of the experiences of past great powers and be prepared to understand and act on the importance of maintaining its internal institutional strength. Unfortunately, there is little if any education and instruction of these complex but critical factors in America's needed education of its citizens in these high priority areas.

Timing of the Period of Decline

Every nation's rise to power is followed by a period of decline leading to a significant diminishment in power, and in some instances, its outright destruction. Frequently the inescapable decline begins when nations or empires are at the height of their power when such a decline often would be considered unlikely. Citizens in a democracy should avoid being lulled into a false sense of security or complacency. Instead they should be well-prepared to embrace and carry out their responsibilities which will be set forth in the following chapter.

Donald Kagan and Frederick W. Kagan wrote in an insightful article, "Peace for Our Time?" of the British Empire in 1919 after World War I,

> Having just played a decisive role in winning the most devastating war yet fought, Great Britain stood at the height of its military power. Its armed forces were of unprecedented size, and the invention of the tank had given it a commanding technological lead over any potential rival. Such rivals were, at the moment, nowhere to be seen. England's archenemy, Germany, lay destroyed and helpless and, under the terms of the Versailles Treaty, subject to a rigid disarmament regime. Russia, an enemy of even longer standing, had collapsed

into bloody civil war and was even less likely than Germany to pose a challenge for the foreseeable future. In the Far East, England faced no European competitors, while Japan, the only indigenous power of significance, was a British ally. France and the United States, the most powerful states in the world after England, were so closely bound to it in friendship that war with them was unthinkable. Britain's leaders reckoned that no major conflict lay on the horizon for at least ten years.[16]

Although no major war did occur within a decade, the seeds for the decline of British power had germinated and were growing. By the end of the 1930s, British power had declined markedly relative to that of a resurgent Germany. Soon, Great Britain was embroiled in WWII which almost resulted in its destruction. Through sheer courage Great Britain fought on and with allied help, eventually prevailed. However, by the time World War II ended in 1945, Great Britain was no longer a dominant global power. At the beginning of the 21ˢᵗ century, the United States appears to have assumed a role not dissimilar from Great Britain at the end of World War I. The September 11, 2001 terrorist attacks, however, quickly shattered the notion that the United States had entered a perpetual paradise of peace and power.

Why Great Powers Decline

Although the September 11, 2001 attacks may mark a challenge it may not necessarily mark the beginning of a permanent decline of U.S. power or influence. But it is important that U.S. citizens understand the dynamics behind a decline which may prove useful in helping the U.S. navigate any future circumstances that could create openings for such a decline. Historical change can take a long period of time to reach its conclusion or it can take place rather quickly. In some instances there have been interim periods of recovery followed by further periods of decay with an overall long-term trend favoring and extending decay. Citizens must learn to recognize this and act in ways to diminish the effects of such a decline.

On the surface, given that no state or empire yet has found the magic formula for lasting greatness, it would appear likely to hold true that today's great powers can inevitably crumble with time. A more careful examination of the past, however, reveals a somewhat more hopeful scenario: None of the great powers that heretofore ultimately faded from preeminence have resembled the unique American democratic form of republican government based on citizen empowerment.

In general, there are six principal causes that have contributed to the demise of great powers: (1) corrosive internal weakness (political and cultural); (2) citizen failure to prevent growing institutional weaknesses; (3) an over-reliance on elite, autocratic rulers without checks and balances; (4) an insular worldview and policies; (5) the rise of a new power that supersedes previous powers in might and influence, and; (6) an invasion often precipitated by internal weaknesses that have made such invasions possible and their success likely.[17] When combined, these factors can create failures in legitimacy[18] that, in turn, causes the affected societies to unravel.

The United States' democratic political system has provided strong institutions, a system of checks and balances and a citizen's role that limits the risk of over-reliance on elite rulers. The nation's founding culture with its emphasis on individual freedom and citizen responsibility have provided the fertile soil in which schools and the media could provide the necessary education, information and understanding to limit the risk of its citizens having an insular worldview or policies that likely could result from such a perspective. However, this system needs to be maintained with the citizen prepared and willing to bear the greatest responsibility of playing skillfully the important caretaker's role.

The Egyptian, Babylonian, Roman, Persian, British, and Soviet Empires were subjected to one or more of the above-noted causes of decline. The Egyptian Empire at the height of its wealth experienced a sustained period of moral decline that was followed by revolution and overall decay. The Babylonians experienced a cultural decline followed by internal strife. The Romans had their Senate abolished by Emperor Septimus Severus with the help of the army, and then were beset by rampant misgovernment, followed by civil war and general unrest. In his account on the rise and fall of the Byzantine Empire, Charles Diehl notes, "More serious even than political demoralization, social demoralization was one of the main causes of Byzantium's decline and fall."[19] The British—and later the Soviet Union—found themselves overextended by large overseas empires that they could not effectively administer, coupled with the rise of rival powers in Europe and the burgeoning United States that dismounted them from their global supremacy.[20]

The vitality of a nation's culture is also a significant factor in determining a country's destiny. Historians Will and Ariel Durant, in explaining the fall of past empires and great powers, have asserted that cultural decay and decline of values can further hasten a nation's downfall. They observed such a pattern of cultural decay in *The Lessons of History*, "Caught in a relaxing interval between one moral code and the next, an unmoored generation surrenders itself to luxury, corruption and a restless disorder of family and morals, all but a remnant clinging desperately to old restraints and ways."[21] Arguably, the U.S. at the end of the 20th Century was headed down this path while increasingly finding its fate and fortune more and more tied to that of distant reaches in the world.

In his book, *Winning the Future*, former House Speaker Newt Gingrich suggests that there are five issues that could threaten the nation's future if not addressed. First, is the threat that Islamist terrorists or rogue states could acquire or launch weapons of mass destruction. Second, American culture could deteriorate to the point that God will be driven from American public life. Third, he warns that the nation's citizens could lose their sense of patriotism. Fourth, he suggests that failing schools and weakening scientific and technological leadership could impede the country's progress. Fifth, the nation's aging population could lead to crippling fiscal burdens.[22]

As discussed above, internal decay and overextension can lead to a nation's decline from preeminence. An example of this is the challenges that will arise as the U.S. population ages. The number of older and retired citizens is expected to grow substantially faster than the working-age population. Considering that the United States has a "pay-as-you-go" public pension and senior citizens' health arrangement under which current tax revenue is used to finance the payments made by both programs when there are no investment instruments aside from treasury bills, notes, and bonds that are employed for the financing of these programs, these demographic changes could dramatically increase the federal fiscal burden in the absence of major reforms. Such an elevated fiscal burden and taxes on citizens could lead the United States to become fiscally overextended at a time when it's national security and critical global, commitments, and conflicts also are requiring increased federal funding. Such an increased burden could also stifle economic growth, lead to a decline in the standard of living and create an unwillingness of taxpayers to adequately fund their nation's security.

According to projections from the U.S. Census Bureau, the elderly population (ages 65 and older) in the U.S. is expected to increase nearly 50 percent during the 2000–2020 period.[23] At the same time, the population aged 55–64 who will be moving toward retirement years will rise 40 percent while those ages 14–24 that will be poised to replace them in the workforce will increase by just 0.5 percent.[24] From 2020–2050, there is expected to be increased growth in those ages 14–24 with that segment rising about 25 percent.[25] However, it is not likely to be enough to offset the rapid rise in the population age 65 and older, which is projected to increase by another 60 percent.[26]

Shifting Demographics

The above demographic trends underway in the U.S. already have resulted in a dramatic decline in the ratio of the working-age population and the aged population. In 2000, that ratio stood at 5.1:1.[27] By 2020, it is expected to have declined to 3.7:1 and then 2.7:1 by 2050.[28] To remain financially sound in these circumstances, the Social Security and Medicare systems require that the ratio of workers, who fund the programs through payroll taxes, and beneficiaries, remains relatively constant. Even if the entire working-age population participated in the labor force, this deterioration in the ratio of the working age population relative to the aging population would be increasingly problematic over time. However, not all of the working age population actually enters into the labor force or is employed.

With the aging of the American population, the workers-to-retirees ratio has begun to fall. In 1980, there were 4.3 workers for every person age 65 and over. In 1990, the figure fell to 4.2 but rose again to 4.3 by 2000. However, barring larger-scale demographic changes pertaining to increased immigration (which raises policy challenges of its own) or an increased birthrate, the figures are anticipated to drop to 4.2 in 2010, 3.3 in 2020, 2.6 in 2030, and then 2.4 in 2050.[29]

This deterioration in the workers-to-retirees ratio is expected to impose what could become a crippling financial burden on Social Security and Medicare. Annual Social Security spending will likely soar from a projected $526.6 billion in 2005 to $2.372 trillion by 2030 and $20.879 trillion in 2080 according to the Social Security Trustees' intermediate assumptions.[30] The latest report from the Medicare and Social Security trustees reveals that, barring changes in law and financing trends, Medicare will likely go bankrupt by 2020. In addition, it will likely begin running chronic deficits starting as early as 2012.[31] By 2024 Medicare's expenditures are projected to surpass those of the Social Security program and reach nearly 14 percent of GDP by 2078.[32] Overall, if Medicare is included, total combined spending could explode from a projected $706 billion in 2005 to $3.366 trillion in 2030 and $38.781 trillion in 2080.[33]

With respect to Social Security and Medicare, the Congressional Budget Office (CBO) warns, "When the future resource requirements of the two programs are shown year by year as a share of GDP, they more than double by 2075, rising from 6.9 percent of GDP today to a projected 16 percent in 2075."[34] To cover this yawning gap in finances, payroll taxes would need to be increased by more than 25 percent or some combination of changes in program benefits and tax hikes would be required.[35] Such a tax hike, however, would likely constrain economic growth or even worse, which could in turn generate other fiscal consequences.

But there may be another approach that avoids this dilemma and it is a policy approach that U.S. citizens should consider carefully. U.S. citizens could consider an approach that emulates the partial privatization of Social Security that was implemented in Britain more than a decade ago. Today, in contrast to its Western European neighbors, Britain faces only limited financing gaps within its public pension system.

In February 2005, President Bush introduced a Social Security reform proposal[36] that would establish personal retirement accounts in which workers could eventually deposit up to 4 percentage points of their payroll taxes. Initially, the contributions would be capped at $1,000 per year in 2009 but this cap would increase by $100 per year plus an adjustment for the growth in average national wages. If such a proposal were adopted, the transformation of Social Security into a partially private program with personal retirement accounts, the United States would join some 20 countries worldwide that have made private retirement accounts part of their national pension system.[37]

Nevertheless, changes to major benefit programs such as Social Security are highly controversial. Therefore, it is incumbent that American citizens are informed and knowledgeable about the reality of the long-term challenges brought about by the demographic changes now occurring. The enormous fiscal burden created by the needs of the Social Security and Medicare systems can expose the nation to significant risk factors and divisiveness that should be studies and anticipated in order to develop plans for mitigating future impacts.

Immigration

Another issue contributing to internal U.S. fiscal decay is the near absence of a cohesive policy for managing and financing immigration. Increased immigration presents sizable benefits but also brings substantial costs and societal problems for the United States and its citizens. A disclosure illustrates the possible perils of an unmanaged approach to immigration growth can be instructive and most helpful.

The United States in 2006 is in the midst of some of the highest levels of immigration in the nation's history. During 1990–99 a record 9.8 million immigrants came to the United States.[38] By 2002 there were an estimated 9.3 million undocumented immigrants (illegal aliens) in the United States[39] with this segment of the population growing by an estimated 250,000 persons annually.[40]

Mexicans accounted for 57 percent of the undocumented immigrants in 2002 and those from other Latin American countries comprised 23 percent of the total; 10 percent were from Asia, 5 percent came from Europe and Canada, and 5 percent from the rest of the world.[41] These robust immigration trends—legal and illegal—present clearly the all-important question: "Can the United States continue to successfully assimilate such large numbers of new residents?" If not, what would be the projected fiscal and foreign policy costs?

The related issue of assimilation also reaches to the heart of the priority area of challenge i.e., largely unmanaged immigration, which can significantly impact the nation's culture. Among those who have expressed such a concern is conservative commentator Patrick Buchanan, who warned in 2002, that "Uncontrolled immigration threatens to deconstruct the nation we grew up in and convert America into a conglomeration of peoples with almost nothing in common—not history, heroes, language, culture, faith, or ancestors. Balkanization beckons."[42]

Whether or not that observation is overly pessimistic does not take away from the importance of the nation's culture and the need to ensure that immigrants can assimilate in a fashion that the best of the nation's culture, namely its traditions of individual liberty, assimilation, and civic responsibility, can be sustained. A nation's culture is an important determinant in its destiny. Thomas Sowell, senior fellow at the Hoover Institution, observes, "[T]he skills, habits, and values which constitute the cultural endowment of a people usually play a powerful role in shaping the kinds of outcomes experienced by that people."[43] Immigrants can be an invaluable source of beneficial cultural capital but also a source of adverse cultural costs. Sowell explains that "a rapid accumulation of cultural capital—usually possible only by borrowing from the cultures of others, at least initially—has...produced dramatic economic and social changes." Nonetheless, he also notes, "intergroup differences present not only an opportunity for cultural interchanges and economic advancement, but also for negative consequences, ranging from social frictions to the spread of disease to the disintegration of whole societies."[44]

Additionally, some now argue the country's former capacity for assimilating new immigrants has also been weakened by a dramatically skewed immigration pattern (with a single ethnic group accounting for a disproportionate share of immigrants) that has evolved.

Former National Intelligence Council Vice Chairman Graham Fuller warned that the United States "may be building toward the one thing that will choke the melting pot" with the possible emergence of "an ethnic area and grouping so concentrated that it will not wish or need, to undergo assimilation into the mainstream of American multi-ethnic English-speaking life."[45]

Globalism: An Interconnected World, Seeking Technological, Economic, Political and Cultural Transformation

At the beginning of the 21ˢᵗ century, the United States has many economic and political interests flung across the far reaches of the globe. The technology-driven phenomenon that spawned these initiatives and their long-term dynamic is the ongoing trend of globalism. Although not a new phenomenon, it represents one of history's more remarkable economic, political, and cultural transformations. Moreover, although globalism has economic origins and the expansion of trade has often been described almost synonymously with it, globalism is broader than the flow of goods and services across national borders or economic relations alone. Its interconnected ramifications also touch almost every aspect of wealth transfers, culture, governance, and society.

Because wealth creation is inherently unequal, globalism has given new life to the capitalism vs. social justice debate. Columbia University Professor Jagdish Bhagwati writes of the anti-globalization movement's younger elements, "Far too many of the young see capitalism as a system that cannot meaningfully address questions of social justice. Many of these youthful skeptics seem unaware that socialist planning in countries such as India, which replaced markets system-wide with quantitative allocations, worsened rather than improved unequal access. Such socialism produced queues that the well connected and the well endowed could jump, whereas markets allow a larger number of people to access their targets. Capitalism is a system that, paradoxically, can destroy privilege and open up economic opportunity to many—but this fact is lost on most of the system's vocal critics."[46]

The impact of globalism also raises questions about the purpose and effectiveness of governments. Daniel Yergin, in his 1998 book, *The Commanding Heights*, identified globalism as a powerful force for change. "A new reality is emerging. [Globalism] is not a process but a condition—a globality, a world economy in which the traditional and familiar boundaries are being surmounted or made irrelevant."[47] Yergin argues that the shifts taking place are of a magnitude that is reshaping the world and outstripping the ability of its governments to prevent or even manage change. In his view, free markets could ultimately wrest control of the proverbial "commanding heights" (vital economic areas) from governments. This change would bring its share of enormous benefits but would not be without its great risks.

Yergin makes the case that the key political test for this new global reality will be whether market economies will be able to deliver in terms acceptable on such factors as economic growth, employment, and increased standards of living. Its impact on the environment and national identities will also be important.[48] The aftermath of the September 11 terrorist attacks reaffirms that the state is not likely to become irrelevant anytime soon. In areas of national security, a key area of responsibility that American Founders delegated to the national government, there will be a need to retain a sufficient degree of strength and influence to protect the nation against such non-market threats as those posed by international terrorism.

Increasing cross-cultural contacts through commerce and travel, globalization can help feed the evolution of cultures and also breed the risk of clashes of cultures and religions. Such effects can, if they are not managed effectively by those under their influence, promote destabilization of societies. Today, in the Middle East and Islamic world, one sees a gathering internal struggle between champions of liberal Islam and those who promote an austere fundamentalist version. This dynamic is one of the major forces driving the current threat posed by such terrorist organizations as Al Qaeda. More details are provided in Chapter 4.

Globalism comes with benefits and costs. The benefits from higher living standards, increased incomes, expanded opportunity, enhanced personal enrichment through travel and contact with peoples/cultures are substantial. The trade benefits, underpinning globalism, include the promotion of competition and innovation, expanded economic growth creating better jobs and wages at home and abroad, and a strengthening of the rule of law as trade depends on property rights, contract law, and increased economic freedom.[49] However, even as the global marketplace proves important to wealth creation, it also sows the seeds of discontent among groups and nations left behind and whose "costs" need ongoing examination. Some trade-offs and drawbacks could well be the unfolding crises of today and tomorrow. Not surprisingly, Columbia University professor of economics, Jagdish Bhagwati argues, "[G]lobalization must be managed so that its fundamentally benign effects are ensured and reinforced. Without this wise management, it is imperiled" [50] even, as he asserts, on average, globalization reduces poverty, decreases the use of child labor, improves the welfare for women, and does not lead to a destructive "race to the bottom" when it comes to real wages, labor standards, and environmental quality.

In order for citizens to be better prepared for the future complex challenges that will confront them, a brief survey of the principal challenge posed by globalism, aside from the widely acknowledged risks of income and economic inequality, is in order.

Conflicts between Non-Western and Western Cultures

One of the major implications of the trend toward globalization is the bringing of countries and cultures into greater contact with one another. While such contacts can promote economic and social development, they can also breed resentment and resistance among those who seek to preserve what they perceive to be the historical integrity of their countries and cultures. In the latter case, the risk of conflict between Western and non-Western cultures can be magnified. This dynamic is a generator of the war on terrorism as Osama Bin Laden decries the "immorality and debauchery" that has spread among the American people.[51]

Harvard University professor Samuel Huntington observes that issues that are "the classic ones of international politics"[52] can have the effect of widening cultural divides. Such items include:

1. The relative influence in shaping global developments and the actions of global international organizations such as the UN, IMF, and World Bank;

2. The relative military power, which manifests itself in controversies over non-proliferation and arms control and in arms races;

3. Economic power and welfare, manifested in disputes over trade, investment, and other issues;

4. People, involving efforts by a state from one civilization to protect kinsmen in another civilization, to discriminate against people from another civilization, or to exclude from its territory people from another civilization;

5. Values and culture, conflicts over which arise when a state attempts to promote or to impose its values on the people of another civilization;

6. Territory, in which core states become front line participants in fault line conflicts.[53]

Huntington argues that since the end of the Cold War, "Global politics began to be reconfigured along cultural lines"[54] and "the central and most dangerous dimension of the emerging global politics would be conflict between groups from differing civilizations."[55] He defines civilizations as "societies sharing cultural affinities"[56] and being "the highest cultural grouping of people and the broadest level of cultural identity people have short of that which distinguishes humans from other species."[57] He then goes on to enumerate seven distinct civilizations: the Sinic (Chinese), the Japanese, the Hindu (Indic), Islamic, Orthodox (centered in Russia), Western, and the Latin American (an offspring of European civilization that evolved along its separate lines).[58]

For as many as two decades, there have been hints that a conflict was beginning to stir. "There are unmistakable signs," Mohammed Sid-Ahmed, a leading Egyptian journalist observed in 1994, "of a growing clash between the Judeo-Christian Western ethic and the Islamic revival movement, which is now stretching from the Atlantic in the west to China in the East."[59] "In the 1980s and 1990s the overall trend in Islam has been in an anti-Western direction. In part, this is the natural consequence of an Islamic Resurgence and the reaction against the perceived 'gharbzadegi' or Westoxication of Muslim societies," Huntington adds.[60] Overall, this was not a coming conflict between religions but a broader one between civilizations. "Colonialism tried to deform all the cultural traditions of Islam. I am not an Islamist. I don't think there is a conflict between religions. There is a conflict between civilizations," a Tunisian lawyer noted.[61]

There was even some speculation that the "conflict" could spill onto American soil. Richard Betts, director of National Security Studies at the Council of Foreign Relations warned in 1998, "[The most] worrisome danger [is] that mass destruction will occur in the United States, killing large numbers of civilians. The primary risk is not that enemies might lob some nuclear or chemical weapons at U.S. armored ships or battalions, awful as that would be. Rather, it is that they might attempt to punish the United States by triggering catastrophes in American cities. But retaliation requires knowledge of who has launched an attack. Today some groups may wish to punish the United States without taking credit for the action."[62] The July 2004 report of the National Commission on Terrorist Attacks upon the United States (the "9/11 Commission") revealed, "The 9/11 attacks were a shock, but they should not have come as a surprise. Islamist extremists had given plenty of warning that they meant to kill Americans indiscriminately and in large numbers. Although Usama Bin Ladin himself would not emerge as a signal threat until the late 1990s, the threat of Islamist terrorism grew over the decade [1990s]."[63]

Given its fundamental nature, namely the assertion that the campaign of terrorism is about religion, this conflict will likely pose great danger to the United States for a sustained period of time. Worse, whereas, during the Cold War, the former Soviet Union could be trusted to understand and appreciate the ramifications associated with the old policy of mutually assured destruction in which a nuclear first strike would lead to a retaliatory strike that would destroy the other side. Those involved in the September 11, 2001 terrorist attacks actually intended to commit suicide for their cause. Death, for this ideological terrorist movement, is no obstacle. Their willingness to target civilians for death and destruction suggests that these groups seek the indiscriminate destruction of their foes, regardless of whether they are military personnel or civilians. All said, the United States and its allies will also need to develop means to mitigate cultural divisions that could be exploited by their terrorist enemies.

Huntington believes that ongoing demographic changes could fundamentally alter the world's balance of power. "Quantitatively, Westerners…constitute a steadily decreasing minority of the world's population. Qualitatively, the balance between the West and other populations is also changing. Non-Western peoples are becoming healthier, more urban, more literate, better educated," writes Huntington.[64] These shifts will serve to diminish the power of the West relative to that of the rest of the world as well as relative to that of the world's various civilizations, particularly the Asian ones.

Should the power of the West (and the United States) decline relative to that of the other major civilizations, this weakness could invite increased aggression on the part of other civilizations or, more likely, those claiming to advance such civilizations, as have often been the case when other great powers have suffered from growing internal decay.[65] In part, this is already happening with respect to the Al Qaeda terrorist group and its ideological allies.

U.S. citizens must be prepared to analyze the sacrifices and tradeoffs required to sustain their nation's power and the consequences of a loss of such power when it comes to policymaking, whether it is generated in areas related to the federal budget or a broader U.S. foreign policy.

The Expanded Role of U.S. Citizens in the 21ˢᵗ Century

At the opening of the 21st century, the U.S. is the world's principal superpower and directly confronted by a new global quasi-religious ideological struggle that is driving the global war on terrorism. In such an environment, it is also essential that U.S. citizens be sufficiently educated and informed to participate fully and effectively in the country's political process as envisioned by its Founders. Great nations, if they lose their self-discipline and moral values, can lose their social and cultural standards, and undergo internal decay. As has been the case with the U.S.'s prior epic challenges, the role its citizen's play, the sacrifices they are capable and willing to accept and the level of their commitment to the needed political participation in helping guide their country's policymakers chart the course needed will prove decisive.

This chapter set forth the historical, political, fiscal and global environment in which the United States and its citizens in the opening decade of the 21st century find themselves. The following chapters articulate the crucial and challenging role American citizens must play to preserve and protect the nation's culture, prepare for the global changes taking place. This book will also provide a framework for analysis by which America's citizens can be prepared to participate fully in supporting their country in carrying out the tasks required to sustain and protect their freedoms. Each generation must be asked to protect and preserve for the future of their country.

2

Freedom and Democracy in the U.S. Confront an Expanding Autocratic World

The newly-independent American colonies' experiment in democracy was launched over 200 years ago at a time when there were significant doubts as to its long-term feasibility. Earlier experiments in democracy saw governments mutate into tyrannies that devoured the freedoms which a democracy was formed to secure. The Roman Republic withered as its increasing autocratic power became vested in the office of a single ruler. Ancient Athens lacked a Senate to curb popular passions that sometimes fueled tyranny. At the time the U.S. Constitution was drafted several centuries later, there had been no republic that had endured for long in the absence of a Senate. Based on a keen understanding of human nature, particularly the human temptation to accumulate power, America's Founders put in place an elaborate system of checks and balances which granted citizens the ultimate responsibility to oversee the entire governance architecture, which Alexander Hamilton compromised to be, "The ingredients which constitute safety in the republican sense are a due dependence on the people, and a due responsibility."[66] As Hamilton saw it, freedom and responsibility were intertwined and the role of the citizen with regard to this principle would be crucial to sustaining a democratic republic.

The Civic Role for America's Citizens Envisioned by the Founders

Over three centuries ago, America's Founding Fathers launched one of the boldest political experiments in the history of mankind. The Declaration of Independence asserted that a democratic government would become empowered through delegation of authority and consent from its citizens, who would use their limited powers to protect their freedoms and secure their rights to life, liberty and the pursuit of happiness:

> We hold these Truths to be self-evident, that all Men are created equal, that they are endowed by their Creator with certain unalienable Rights, that among these are Life, Liberty, and the Pursuit of Happiness—That to secure these rights, Governments are instituted among Men, deriving their just Powers from the Consent of the Governed, that whenever any Form of Government becomes destructive of these Ends, it is the Right of the People to alter or to abolish it, and to institute new Government, laying its Foundation on such Principles, and organizing its Powers in such Form, as to them shall seem most likely to effect their Safety and Happiness.[67]

To be successful, citizens were expected to be both informed and engaged. Having just fought a war for independence and gained the basic freedoms of "life, liberty, and the pursuit of happiness" in the process, America's early citizens had a vested stake in the outcome of the experiment. The machinery put in place by the Founders and the responsibilities conferred upon the citizen were expected to help ensure that the new form of democratic governance would survive the test of time and surmount the inevitable challenges that would arise as a product of human nature from time to time.

At the beginning of the 21st century, changes in America's culture, challenges confronting some of its key institutions (education and media), and a degree of apathy threatened to impair the ability of contemporary American citizens to carry out their role as set forth by the Founders.

The first American colonists arrived in search of the freedom necessary to create their own destiny and thereby sought sufficient liberty under which they could govern themselves. After the American Revolution, the thirteen colonies entered into the Articles of Confederation that permitted them to function as largely autonomous entities cooperating with each other, rather than acting as a single nation. Under this arrangement, however, a series of political and economic problems soon plagued the new nation. Some states grew increasingly hostile toward others; the Continental Congress was weak and ineffective, and hints of rebellion seemed to be brewing.

The original thirteen colonies were fiercely independent-minded. With the war for independence still fresh in their minds, the young nation's citizens feared an overly strong central government. Yet, rather than strengthening the Articles of Confederation, the nation's leaders proposed a new constitutional charter for a federal form of government with a president, Congress, and Supreme Court. To some, the idea of a national president coupled with a national Congress seemed eerily familiar to the former rule by a British King and Parliament. The proposed new Constitution was drafted on the assumption that the future success of the nation would rely upon the ability of citizens to carry out their important role and responsibilities. Such an early and unprecedented empowerment of the citizen was an extraordinary basis for a new government.

The *Federalist Papers*, written by John Jay, James Madison, and Alexander Hamilton explained that the provisions and objectives in the proposed Constitution would require the new government to protect the liberty of the people, ensure their right to own property, and enable citizens to carry out their lives with freedom in the pursuit of happiness as established in the Declaration of Independence. Citizens would be provided by their government with the necessary protection to preserve their freedoms and carry out their duties of citizenship.[68] Likewise, the government would abide by the principles of the rule of law, honor a system of checks and balances and be limited and subservient to the people.[69] Governmental power was intended to be vigorous in its assigned areas of responsibility,[70] but such authority would only be extended to those matters where it was deemed necessary to promote the public good and "to guard as effectively as possible against any perversion of such power to the public detriment."[71]

For more than two centuries, U.S. citizens have generally understood and accepted their civic responsibilities as set forth by the nation's Founders in building and sustaining a successful and stable civil society. These basic responsibilities include adhering to the rule of law, fostering the well-being of family and community, upholding the ideals of Federalism and safeguarding freedom. However, during the 20th century a shift began to take place, in which citizens began to envision a larger role for the federal government. The dangers and risks of this new set of governance relationships are set forth in Chapter 3.

Forming a More Perfect Union

At the time the U.S. Constitution was drafted, many doubted whether the republic it would create could endure. Initially, there was serious doubt as to whether the new constitution would ever be ratified by the states. However, after considerable effort by its advocates, the Constitution was ratified. It has since become one of the nations most important and inspiring works.

These Founding principles were created with the awareness that there were historical precedents that saw popular governments frequently evolve into tyrannies. The Founders, therefore, identified several reasons and strategies to prevent any such transformation to tyranny. First, weak constitutions or poor enforcement of strong ones aided such an evolution. Second, a person or group of persons accumulated disproportionate power and then used it to hinder the freedoms of weaker parties, where a substantial loss of freedom was the end result. As noted in Chapter 1, the successes of earlier democratic societies were inevitably weakened by the problems associated with the duality of vices and virtues contained in human nature. Even though "republican government presupposes the existence of these qualities in a higher degree than any other form,"[72] there is the danger that some of these virtues may be undermined. For example, if a decidedly smaller share of citizens chooses to participate in the political process, the depth of leadership available to the country would diminish.

America's Founders understood the importance of giving citizens the power to guarantee accountability from their government through regular elections. The Founders believed this would foster a common cause between the nation's leaders and the citizens by whom they were elected to serve.[73] Unfortunately, today this important right (freedom to choose one's leaders) and responsibility (the role of bringing accountability to the government) has been fulfilled by far less than half of the United States' citizens in the most recent elections.

The Founders also recognized that a system of checks and balances would be essential in helping prevent any one individual or branch of the government from amassing too much power and thereby gaining the capacity to threaten the overall democratic system. "[T]he great security against a gradual concentration of the several powers in the same department consists in giving to those who administer each department the necessary constitutional means and personal motives to resist encroachments of the others."[74] Strict adherence to the principles of federalism were viewed as an effective bulwark against the rise of a large, powerful and intrusive federal government, as well as provide a force to constrain the passions and excesses of majority rule.

In Federalist No. 51, James Madison explained the benefits of federalism. He observed, "In a single republic, all the power surrendered by the people is submitted to the administration of a single government; and the usurpations are guarded against by a division of the government into distinct and separate departments. In the compound republic of America, the power surrendered by the people is first divided between two distinct governments, and then the portion allotted to each subdivided among distinct and separate departments. Hence a double security arises to the rights of the people. The different governments will control each other, at the same time that each will be controlled by itself."[75] The Founders realized that a constitutional framework alone could not preserve the important personal freedoms that properly belonged to the nation's citizens. They understood that family values and guidance, community participation and education would have to play a complementary role and that free and empowered citizens are the principal defenders of democracy. James Madison wrote of this relationship between the constitutional machinery and broader culture and values that permeated society is "[T]he genius of the whole system; the nature of just and constitutional laws; and, above all, the vigilant and manly spirit which actuates the people of America—a spirit which nourishes freedom, and in return is nourished by it."[76]

Putting the Citizens in Charge

The Founders envisioned an engaged and informed citizenry that would be expected to act as both change agents and stabilizers of society. According to that vision, empowered citizens would have to be active participants, not passive bystanders in civil society and that they would need to supply the energy and flexibility required to meet challenges as they would invariably arise. They also would be the custodians responsible for sustaining the essential basic values and virtues upon which the Founding principles were based.

In that context, James Madison wrote in *Federalist No. 46*, "[T]he ultimate authority, wherever the derivative may be found, resides in the people alone..."[77] In *Federalist No. 49*, he observed, "[T]he people are the only legitimate fountain of power, and it is from them that the constitutional charter, under which the several branches of government hold their power, is derived...."[78] And In *Federalist No. 51*, he explained that citizen participation in exercising authority is the most significant safeguard against tyranny or repressive government.

Without strong citizen guidance and support, governments alone cannot achieve successful democratic outcomes. One of the most important responsibilities of citizens includes ensuring that the federal government carries out its role energetically and effectively and within the limits of authority granted by the U.S. Constitution.

The Government's powers were to be vigorous in the assigned areas of responsibility, but limited to those matters deemed necessary to promoting the public good in order "to guard as effectively as possible against a perversion of the power to the public detriment. 'The specific powers that were conferred to the new federal government were: 1) Providing security against foreign danger; 2) Regulating trade and commerce with foreign nations; 3) Maintaining harmony and proper commercial intercourse among the States; 4) Promoting and supporting miscellaneous objects of general utility; 5) Restraining the States from undertaking certain injurious acts; and 6) Providing for giving due efficacy to all these powers with 'security against foreign danger' being 'an avowed and essential object of the American Union.'"[79]

Citizens were expected to hold their government accountable to its limited but robust responsibilities. Voting is one of the important means by which citizens in a democracy can voice their wants and needs. Assisting in the election process as poll watchers and election inspectors to protect the integrity of the electoral process is another avenue of participation. Citizens can also make themselves available for public service, by running for office or by maintaining an ongoing dialogue with their elected representatives and making their views known through public opinion polls.[80]

Alexis de Tocqueville's *Democracy in America* notes that, "Any discussion of the political laws of the United States must always begin with the dogma of the sovereignty of the people," adding, "[I]n America the sovereignty of the people is neither hidden nor sterile as with some other nations, mores recognize it, and the laws proclaim it; it spreads with freedom and attains unimpeded its ultimate consequences…"[81] The Founders placed their trust and confidence in citizens to lead their lives in a free, responsible manner. No nation had ever placed such a responsibility on its people before. De Tocqueville notes, "The Revolution in the United States was caused by a mature and thoughtful taste for freedom, not by some vague, undefined instinct for independence. No disorderly passions drove it on; on the contrary, it proceeded hand in hand with a love of order and legality."[82]

The assertion that basic citizens' rights permit many peoples and backgrounds to meld into one American nation with a common vision is "…a defining feature of the United States that, from its very beginning, has been a nation shaped by intention and by ideas," writes Os Guinness, Senior Fellow of The Trinity Forum. "One of America's greatest achievements…has been to create, out of the mosaic of religious and cultural differences, a common vision for the common good—in the sense of a widely shared, almost universal agreement on what accords with the common ideals and interests of America and Americans."[83] The Founders understood this potential of their design:

> Different interests necessarily exist in different classes of citizens. If a majority be united by a common interest, the rights of the minority will be insecure. There are but two methods of providing against this evil: the one by creating a

will in the community independent of the majority that is, of the society itself; the other, by comprehending in the society so many separate descriptions of citizens as will render an unjust combination of a majority of the whole very improbable, if not impracticable...The second method will be exemplified in the federal republic of the United States.[84]

William Tyler Page's "The American's Creed" vividly defines the idea of citizenship on which America's Founders based the Constitution:

I believe in the United States of America as a Government of the People, by the People, for the People; whose Just Powers are Derived from the Consent of the Governed; a Democracy in a Republic; A Sovereign Nation of many Sovereign States; A Perfect Union, One and Inseparable; Established upon those Principles of Freedom, Equality, Justice, and Humanity for which American Patriots Sacrificed their Lives and Fortunes. I Therefore Believe it is My Duty to My Country to Love it; to Support its Constitution; to Obey its Laws; to Respect its Flag; and to Defend it Against All Enemies.[85]

For more than two centuries, these unifying principles have made it possible for U.S. citizens to help the nation forge ahead for the common good of its people.

The Link Between Citizens and Institutions

The ultimate success of a democratic republic depends on a healthy culture, strong institutions, and involved citizens. A democratic society, by definition, depends on the actions and energy of its citizens.

Citizens act through their institutions—civic, political, and economic. A successful political democracy, combined with free market capitalism depends on strong, effective civil institutions and a healthy culture. This is the underpinning of America's unique model, which is built around the twin engines of democratic governance and free market capitalism.

Taken separately, both systems are inherently antithetical. The democratic system of governance is based on principles of equality. Free market economies are based on market discipline and efficiency which yields unequal results. However, the nation's political and social institutions, which include the legal system, the media, primary and secondary education and higher education, effectively absorb the creative tensions generated by these two concepts, helping mold a sense of shared commitment to a country in which all persons have equal opportunity to participate politically, obtain education, and to fully realize the fruits of their talents and abilities. This consensus tempers the centrifugal forces that might otherwise tear American society apart or at least impair its ability to prosper.

At the heart of this institution-based system are the citizens who carry out society's work with the civic and social institutions as their vehicles for action. With dedicated participation from citizens, these institutions are vibrant cells that process history's repeated challenges and translate its opportunities into social and economic progress. Without citizen participation, though, the institutions become hollow cells ravaged by the forces of the internal culture and political change, unable to respond effectively to the challenges and opportunities that continually arise and their attendant pressures on the social compact. Then, even a preeminent and mature democratic society could be placed at risk to the seemingly inevitable decline that all past great powers have experienced.

The democratic institutions through which citizens participate to create and sustain their social compact are interrelated and impact each other. When the institutions are healthy, they have an ability to create synergies that magnify the benefits that could be realized from each of the institutions operating alone. Likewise, when one or more of the institutions are weak, they have a deleterious impact on one another. For example, a strong education system can help produce citizens who will better safeguard a legal and justice system conducive to economic prosperity and social good. Nearly twenty years ago, Stanford University's Thomas Bailey noticed, "Various polls have consistently shown that the lower one goes down the educational scale into the sub-eighth-grade group, one finds more provincialism, more isolationism, more militarism, more jingoism, more indifference to foreign affairs…more demand for high tariff barriers and other instruments of economic non-cooperation…"[86] Recent surveys have found that just 11percent of American high school seniors are competent in geography and that high schools do not prepare American students to understand international affairs even as the United States faces substantial and complex global challenges.[87] Noel Lateef, President and CEO of the Foreign Policy Association warns, "If this situation persists, some 70 million Americans today who are age 15 and under may not even be able to identify major global issues, let alone understand, analyze and participate in addressing these issues."[88]

Through the major institutions, the citizens create, transform, and sustain society's external environment. This environment is heavily influenced by cultural, governmental, and economic factors. Public policy and the performance of the economy have a profound effect on the citizens and their institutions. Strong institutions can beget a culture of success where initiative, hard work, risk-taking, and individual responsibility are encouraged resulting in favorable public policy outcomes such as minimal regulation, low taxes, and beneficial legal protections. This enables citizens to pursue their economic opportunities and protect their basic liberties, and sustained economic growth, including innovation and entrepreneurship that fuels wealth creation and the development of new products and services that make life better for all.

Weak institutions, on the other hand, can lead to unfavorable outcomes that undermine a nation's culture, governance, and economy. Simultaneously, a weak culture, poor governance, and an anemic economy, can inflict injury on the nation's citizens and institutions. For example, if it becomes a norm of society that education is unimportant, a less competent citizenry would arise and such a citizenry will have a significant, adverse impact on all of their country's major institutions and its culture, government, and economy. At some threshold, the interrelated impacts upon weakened governance institutions a corroded culture on the citizens and country's weakened economy combined could launch a vicious downward spiral of irreversible decline. Earlier, in Chapter 1, it was noted that internal political and social decay and institutional weakness have been among the prominent factors that have driven the decline of earlier great powers.

Additional Challenges and Responsibilities Confronting U.S. Citizens in the 21st Century

Given the ongoing war on terrorism and the momentous global political, economic, technological, and cultural changes sweeping U.S. society and the world, a vital question is whether U.S. citizens in the 21st century are capable of playing the critical and complex role required of them by their country's founding principles. The answer needs to be "yes." This lesson of history must not be overlooked by U.S. citizens in preparing for their country managing impacts of the 21st century.

When one reviews the major indicators of today's U.S. citizens' performance, however, there are compounding reasons for concern. These measures include voter turnout, trust in the federal and state government's performance of the country's other leading institutions, membership levels of the citizens in civic and voluntary organizations, and the effectiveness of their public discourse.[89] All of these indicators are key components for constructing and evaluating the performance of U.S. citizens and how well they are prepared to carry out their responsibilities as needed and expected in the years ahead.

It was encouraging during the 2002 mid-term national elections that voters displayed awareness of the important issues and external threats facing their country in the global war against terrorism and a domestic economic recession. U.S. citizens, also, quickly became prepared to accept and support the leadership of President Bush in declaring and conducting war against global terrorism and Islamic jihad and stimulating the U.S. economy.

The 2004 Presidential Election and Continuing Challenges for the U.S. Citizen

The 2004 national election demonstrated that America's citizens remained willing to be engaged when the nation faces great and dangerous challenges. Voter turnout had been declining throughout much of the later parts of the 20th century with some studies indicating that American voters were not as well-informed as they should have been[90], the 2004 election, however, demonstrated otherwise.

Aside from the perennial "pocketbook" issue of the economy and jobs, U.S. voters in 2004 pointed to two additional issues as being most important to them. On the domestic front, the major issue cited by voters was moral values. On the international front, terrorism was most often cited as the most important issue.[91] Chapter 3 discusses the state of the nation's culture and the evolution that has taken place since the 1960s. It will also provide an historical context for the building-blocks of the modernist culture over which many voters became concerned. Then, Chapter 4 will provide a detailed analysis of the dynamics driving the global war on terrorism and will outline approaches that could prove instrumental to the U.S. in addressing the long-term threat posed by international terrorism and Islamic Jihad.

When it came to voters choosing between moral values or terrorism as the issues that they felt were most important, decisive majorities chose to re-elect President Bush. When it came to people who attend Church services weekly or more frequently, President Bush won decisively. The same held true both for Protestants and Catholics.[92] In short, those who are most strongly committed to their religious values voted one way, while those who appeared to be less committed voted another. Married people with children also voted strongly for President Bush. This suggested that those in family arrangements saw issues quite differently from those who were either single or in alternative arrangements.[93] These differences hint at a cultural divide and are discussed in the next chapter.

Another indication of the growing cultural divide is that some pundits immediately dismissed the importance of moral values in the 2004 election. *New York*

Times syndicated columnist Bob Herbert complained that the issue of values "has gotten out of control" and that the issue is "overrated."[94] However, a number of Democratic Party leaders who have experienced success in the "Red states"—those going for the Republican Presidential candidate, often consistently over a long period of time—have reaffirmed the judgment that values did matter to their states' voters.

Indiana Governor Evan Bayh stated of the Democratic Party following the election, "We need to be a party that stands for more than the sum of our resentments. In the heartland, where I am from, there are doubts. Too often, we're caricatured as bicoastal cultural elite that is condescending at best and contemptuous at worst to the values that Americans hold in their daily lives."[95] Virginia Governor Mark Warner echoed those sentiments and warned that a shift farther to the Left by the Democratic Party, as some have advised, would be "a recipe for disaster."[96] Michigan Governor Jennifer Granholm appealed to her fellow Democrats to develop a message that is "strong and strongly pro-work, pro-responsibility, pro-duty, pro-service, pro-child, pro-seniors...And not to be afraid of saying God...And not to be afraid of saying that this is a country that is based upon faith."[97]

James Q. Wilson, chairman of the American Enterprise Institute's Council of Academic Advisers noted that the idea that American politics dealt, in part, with moral issues in 2004 was not a new phenomenon for the nation. "American politics has frequently been gripped by moral issues," Wilson observed shortly after the election, "It is one of the aspects of our history and culture that makes us different from most European democracies."[98] Wilson also argued that some of the harsh criticism directed toward Christian fundamentalists was misplaced explaining, "research shows that organizations of Christian fundamentalists are hardly made up of fire-breathers but rather are organizations whose members practice consensual politics and rely on appeals to widely shared constitutional principles."[99] In other words, by their reliance on "consensual politics" and their appeals to "widely shared constitutional principles," Christian fundamentalists are performing exactly the kind of role that the Founders expected of the nation's citizens as described earlier.

Voters cited terrorism as the most important issue supporting President Bush's 86percent–14percent margin.[100] Nevertheless, those who were very worried about terrorism and likely believed that the war on terrorism was not making satisfactory progress tended to support Senator Kerry by a 56 percent–44 percent margin. This supports the idea that fear of terrorism may have, at least in part driven such decision-making among those who were very worried about terrorism, and those who saw the pre-election Osama Bin Laden tape as being very important, favored Kerry (53 percent–47 percent). The remainder—those who considered the Bin Laden tape as somewhat important or not too important—favored the President.[101]

Over the past 40 years, opinion surveys indicated that, on average, public cynicism has been on the increase. By the end of the 20th century, more than half the people surveyed had "just a little" confidence or "none at all" in the Government's ability to solve problems, and a sizable majority felt that government creates more problems than it solves. Even as trust and confidence in the government was falling, it was also diminishing with regard to such areas as religion, the media, and the nation's public schools.[102] In the 2004 election, by a 49 percent–46 percent margin, voters did not want the government to do more to solve the nation's problems.[103]

There are a number of factors that may be currently contributing to public cynicism. First, since the end of the 1970s, U.S. public trust in government has held below 50 percent and even under 30 percent from time to time. Another contributing factor is public distaste for "careerism" in politics whereby elected leaders establish careers almost exclusively dedicated to politics. "Careerism poses…problems for representative democracy,"[104] notes John Samples and Patrick Basham of the Cato Institute. "Once in office, careerist legislators pay less attention to the needs and wishes of their constituents. Moreover, careerist elected officials became a political class attentive to their own interests."[105] Finally, political scientists John R. Hibbing and Elizabeth Theiss-Morse reveal, "Many people do not find politics intrinsically interesting. They express no desire to reengage with the political process. They do not follow most political issues because they do not care about most issues. As a result, they want someone else to take care of the political sphere for them."[106]

Shortcomings in the U.S. educational system may, in the longer-run, hinder citizens' ability to fully perform their crucial role in an effective fashion. Indeed, some believe that these deficiencies are already taking a toll. New York University Professors Diane Ravitch & Joseph Viterritti explain:

> Ever since the late nineteenth century, Americans have relied upon government schools as a principal purveyor of deeply cherished democratic values. For many generations of immigrants, the common school was the primary teacher of patriotism and civic values. Many came to see the common school as the guarantor of the nation's promise of democracy and freedom. At the end of the twentieth century, however, there was widespread concern about whether the schools were continuing to fulfill that role…In the 1980s and

> 1990s many public schools embraced diversity as their mission at the cost of civic assimilation. In doing so they taught children to identify with their own ancestral heritage rather than a common stock of American ideals. The rise of multiculturalism as an ideology directly conflicted with the public school's once-prized mission of civic assimilation…A national assessment of students' knowledge of civics and government released by the U.S. Department of Education in 1999 showed that most American youths have a weak grasp of the principles that underlie the U.S. Constitution and lack a basic understanding of how government works…Nor have schools done a very effective job of instilling or nourishing the values that form a disposition toward responsible citizenship.[107]

"A majority of the young are growing up in homes whose parents don't vote; their schools don't emphasize civics, citizenship and current events…and the values climate they have grown up in emphasizes consumerism, self-seeking and hostility to government," Curtis B. Gans, director of the Committee for the Study of the American Electorate explains[108]. However, a hypothesis can be made that as democracies mature toward an advanced stage, voter participation falls from earlier highs. George Mason University Professor of Public Affairs, Hugh Heclo, notes that the U.S. is not alone in having suffered from falling voter turnout. He observes that "Declining voter turnout is a worldwide trend among the established democracies, notably since the end of the 1970s. This appears to be the result of a generalized decline in political parties' ability to mobilize voters."[109] Whether or not maturation, the substantial economic gains that had been attained by the end of the 1970s, the changing cultural values that arose in the 1960s, among other factors have contributed partly or wholly to this phenomenon remains to be seen.

Nevertheless, the "maturity argument" cannot fully explain the dynamics driving U.S. voting behavior. "Voting just doesn't engage a lot of people. They don't like to follow campaigns. They find the process unintelligible," adds Ruy Teixeira, author of *The Disappearing American Voter*.[110] This observation suggests that a changing culture and education may have helped drive Americans' diminishing appetite for voting. 2004 saw a marked rise in turnout, but 2004 also differed from recent elections in that the Campaign had a decisive issue in terrorism. If such an issue did not exist or was of a more subtle nature, it remains to be seen whether voters would have responded as they did in 2004.

This troubling phenomenon is, in part, the result of an educational system and culture, which for over 30 years has not been founded on the basis of citizen needs and the new global responsibilities and dangers facing the nation's citizens. Apathy has become one of the leading characteristics that define the American public. Whether or not the 2004 election marked the beginning of a recovery remains to be seen. However, a brief look back at the closing years of the 20th century can help citizens better understand its dynamics, which generated an increasing ideological and cultural movement toward apathy and autocracy.

In a November 1, 1998 *New York Times Magazine* feature story, Nicholas Lemann described the United States' political consensus as "a kind of one-way libertarianism" where the average citizen has no obligation to the country, but believes "the government has a very serious obligation" to that citizen.[111] Lemann concluded that U.S. citizens lacked the commitment to contribute their time and money on larger projects in the broader national interest. He characterizes this condition as "a consensus right now not to have a consensus about what the country as a whole should be or do" and concludes that if consensus "means a working agreement about what we as citizens owe one another and the country as a whole, then we don't have one."[112]

For over sixty years the role of the federal government has grown to become more centralized and expansive. "Historically, unchecked centralization has been the enemy of liberal democracy," observes *Foreign Affairs* managing editor, Fareed Zakaria.[113] As the citizenry shrunk from its basic civic responsibilities, the void was filled by special interest groups and an arrogant intellectual elite[114] who sought to replace America's unique founding principles with their myopic social-ized vision of utopia, the antithesis of a democratic civil society. "The politics of narrow self-seeking interest groups is only a little removed from the morality of every-man-for-himself," writes historian Daniel Boorstin.[115] This political process, while a democracy in theory, is actually becoming more like an oligarchy in substance.

Were they alive today, the nation's Founders would likely have been shocked and dismayed by the long-term trend by which America's citizens appeared to have evolved into disinterested bystanders with many of their freedoms usurped by the federal government. The nation's Founders expected that the citizenry would be the strongest defenders of the founding principles that have made their freedom and prosperity possible. "It ought also to be remembered that the citizens who inhabit the country...will stand ready to sound the alarm when necessary, and to point out the actors in any pernicious project," Hamilton asserted.[116]

How could he or any of the other Founders have thought any differently? The colonies had just fought a war to preserve their individual freedom. They had no doubt that the citizens could be counted on to tenaciously safeguard the fruits of their trials, and that their nascent republic would protect all that they had fought, sacrificed, and died for. The Founders believed and expected that almost everyone would participate. To reject the minimum responsibilities conferred on citizens by the U.S. Constitution would be to compromise and place at risk the unique political system that protected their rights and freedoms. From this perspective, the apathy currently pervasive among many America's citizens today is much more dangerous than idle laziness. It is the ultimate expression of a selfishness that threatens to destroy the nation's uniqueness. And once that distinctiveness is lost, America could become vulnerable to the forces that impacted other great powers, such as the Roman Republic, which led to their final phase of decline as discussed in the preceding chapter.

Informed, engaged, and responsible U.S. citizens empowered under the founding principles of democracy set forth in the Declaration of Independence and reaffirmed in the Constitution are the critical component of America's success and will continue to determine the shape of its future. The formation of future U.S. foreign policy in the dangerous 21st century world of nuclear proliferation and Islamist terrorism, and the role that will be played by the United Nations. Professor of Social and Political Ethics at the University of Chicago, Jean Bethke Elshtain explains, "With citizenship comes accountability for individuals. With statehood comes a measure of accountability for polities...The internal infrastructures of particular civil societies are connected to their counterparts in other societies in many ways. Civil society of this international sort is not possible without the domestic civic peace provided by states. If states do not afford ordinary civic peace, there is no civil society, hence nothing to connect to externally. It is that simple. States in which there is a democratic deficit, so to speak, are states denuded of flourishing civil society." [117] Elshtain also asserts:

> American citizens, due to the United States' place in the world, have an even greater role to play on the global stage...As we have learned to our dismay, all too often international 'peacekeepers'—they are never called soldiers—are obliged by their rules of engagement to stand by as people are cornered and slaughtered. International bodies have defaulted on the use of coercive force on behalf of justice as an equal regard for all, hence a basic defense of human dignity. Failing to make a serious effort to stop genocide and 'ethnic cleansing' is the most obvious case of dereliction in this respect. In such cases, force is justified in order to defend those who cannot defend themselves, to fight those engaged in unjust acts of harming, and to punish those who have engaged in unjust harm. Force that observes limits and is premised on a concern with human dignity is frequently called upon to fight force that operates without limits and makes a mockery of human dignity. [118]

Principles and 21st Century Need for Reviving Citizenship

As the United States enters the 21st century, there is a genuine need to revitalize how citizens view their role by undertaking the following reforms with an emphasis on nurturing a strong sense of citizenship responsibility among the young.[119]

First, citizens must understand and accept that American citizenship does not automatically extend to them individual freedom without obligations nor generous taxpayer-funded social entitlements. Citizenship also involves responsibility and sometimes sacrifices. Freedom without citizen responsibility has never existed and cannot exist. The privileges and benefits of American citizenship are largely taken for granted. What is often forgotten are the sacrifices and burdens endured by the Founders in creating and sustaining the untried and unique democratic system of governance that they established.

Second, U.S. citizens need to periodically reaffirm their understanding and commitment to principles of an ethical civil society needed to sustain our democracy. This will include and require a strengthening of families and communities and replacing the culture of materialism and self-absorption with one that includes caring for others and an acceptance of a responsibility for one's civic self-sufficiency, not dependency on the federal government.

Third, U.S. citizens must maintain their commitment to the principle of "E Pluribus Unum." America's strength has always been bolstered by people from differing countries, backgrounds, ethnicities, religions, cultures, and languages coming together to form a society based on a common set of principles based on equality of opportunity which are celebrated in a democracy. A successful democracy must be based on the principles of equality of opportunity. Government enforced group preferences or quotas create a false equality, which implies that without government intervention certain groups of citizens are inherently inferior and incapable with equal opportunities of achieving satisfying and rewarding lives. This trend is discussed in greater detail in the next chapter.

Fourth, citizens must increase their interest and involvement in the processes of their democratic government at all levels. Without such involvement, they cannot provide the essential checks and balances which are the responsibility of our citizens under the Constitution to become more informed and engaged on the important political and public policy issues and regular communication with their elected representatives. It also involves exercising their right to vote.

Fifth, citizens will need to make the performance of the nation's educational institutions a priority. To best play their role, citizens need to recognize and be prepared to arrive at informed decisions and respond more quickly than ever before in the age of technology. A strong education, including a sound understanding of the founding period in American history can provide U.S. citizens with valuable background information. In addition, for citizens to carry out the new global dimension of their responsibilities, they also must be better educated and informed on some of the vital international issues and developments of the day. "[The] amount of formal education is almost without exception the strongest factor in explaining what citizens do in politics and how they think about politics" Stanford University Professor of Political Science Norman Nie and D. Sunshine Hillygus explain.[120]

The Institute for American Values identified the institutional qualities necessary for democratic self-governance. Among those elements are the family, which the Institute described as "the cradle of citizenship" on account of its defining role in transmitting such virtues as honesty, trust, responsibility; the local community in which children grow up; religious institutions that provide the nation with its spiritual and philanthropic "backbone;" voluntary civic organizations in which citizens promote social good; primary and secondary education/higher education, which is crucial to providing citizens with the knowledge necessary for informed decision-making, and; the media.[121]

The Founders intended that the nation be a free society in which the citizens would undertake the responsibility to safeguard their own freedom as the best safeguard against tyranny. To succeed, citizens would need to rely on a culture of virtue (more about the nation's current culture is discussed in the following chapter) and healthy institutions through which they could exercise their civic roles and responsibilities. To date, that model was worked exceptionally well in propelling the United States to a position of great prosperity and world leadership. In the complex and dangerous world of the 21st century, that model along with its supporting culture and institutions will prove vital in ensuring that citizens can continue to play the role the Founders gave them more than 200 years ago. How well the citizens will play that role will ultimately define how successfully the nation can navigate its great challenges of the day.

21st Century "Global Citizen" and Its Impact on the U.S. Citizen

The preceding chapter described a great convergence of forces that has increasingly transformed the world since the end of the Cold War—changing demographics, emerging technology and information revolutions, and globalization. This convergence of forces has given rise to a 21st century phenomenon that can loosely be described as the "global citizen."

The rise of "global citizenship" has not displaced the concept of national citizenship and rendered its rights and responsibilities obsolete. Rather, it means that the responsibilities of national citizenship have evolved to the extent that such citizenship increasingly entails a clear global dimension that extends beyond the traditional confines of national interest under which nations carry out their interactions with the rest of the world. This new dimension is most apparent in countries that are highly interconnected to the rest of the world, such as the U.S., whose economies, national security, and political relationships increasingly impact and are in turn impacted by international events. As a result tensions between more local or immediate citizenship responsibilities and broader, longer-term global ones are being created. To be effective, citizens will need to understand the stakes and benefits involved in the sometimes competing responsibilities and have the capacity to formulate reasonable accommodations in the decision-making process.

This new dimension is shaped by such challenges as dealing with global economic inequality, shifting demographics and international terrorism and rogue states that possess weapons of mass destruction (Chapter 4 contains a more detailed discussion of these factors, particularly with respect to the new challenge posed by global terrorism). In such an environment Americans have a global leadership role that involves creating and maintaining global political stability and economic growth, defeating international terrorism and mitigating the threat posed by rogue states. In the face of these developments, the post-World War II international institutional arrangements, such as the U.N., NATO, the World Bank, IMF, and WTO, are increasingly antiquated and ineffective. American citizens will be vital to cultivating the evolution and formation of a new international institutional arrangement that has the flexibility and authority necessary to effectively address the great challenges of the new century. Their input will be essential in helping adapt existing pillars of the international institutional architecture to the emerging realities of the 21st century.

This is a highly demanding and arguably unprecedented role. Never before has the world been as interconnected as it is today. Never before has a powerful nation like the United States been impacted by distant events as it has today. Never before have radical non-state movements presented a direct threat to Americans living at home. Yet, this is the world of today. To be successful, America's citizens will need to be prepared and capable of handling the burden of this new role. What will be required in the U.S. is a strengthening of a society that recognizes the importance of personal responsibility and sometimes the need to make major sacrifices, emphasizes individual opportunity, differentiates between right and wrong and is compatible with democracy, personal freedom, and civil society. This will entail a fostering of a culture that is supportive of these tasks, an educational system that provides the skills and knowledge necessary to undertake these responsibilities, and access to timely and reliable information on which they could reach decisions and act. Formidable barriers that potentially hinder this role will need to be overcome. These efforts best can be understood and carried out in the context of the skills citizens will need to develop and best perform their global obligations. As discussed further in Chapter 3, many of these values and virtues have eroded in recent years. Such trends combined with cultural and moral relativism have undercut the bedrock of values that significantly defined U.S. culture during much of its historical experience. Symptoms of cultural erosion have manifested themselves in the form of a poisonous counterculture, suspicions among some that excellence is the product of unfair advantage, and the gradual erosion of ethics and the rule of law. When addressing the threats posed by international terrorism and rogue states, a sound understanding of history will be an essential foundation for global citizenship. An historical framework could shield citizens against dangerous and naïve ideas being advanced by some who ignore or dismiss earlier historical realities. The U.S. and its allies can avoid reliving some of humanity's worst catastrophes by understanding the lessons gleaned from the pre-World War II experience of rapid disarmament and appeasement, and the consequences of a weakness-driven approach to rising Fascism.

3

20th Century Corrosion of the U.S. Founding Culture

"If a nation expects to be ignorant and free, in a state of civilization, it expects what never was and never will be."

—*Thomas Jefferson in a letter to John Adams (28 October 1813)*[122]

A nation's culture is significantly comprised of all its historical and current values, traditions, and beliefs that defines and underpins its society and which make it distinct from other nations. Many of these values are often combined historical, social, political, or economic in nature. In the U.S. the overall philosophical underpinnings needed to support its free, democratic society are the important values set by the Founders and their Founding principles. These values include creating a government limited in its authority with a mission of securing personal freedoms for its citizens and the fostering of an empowered and responsible citizenry. "Culture, at its best, can be one of the most powerful forms of voluntary restraint in human behavior. It gives life structure and meaning. It sanctions a whole set of habits, behavioral restraints, expectations and traditions that pattern life and hold societies together at their core."[123] It is vitally important, therefore, for citizens to preserve these democratic values and principles so that the U.S. can continue to maintain the strong and independent culture and values contemplated by the Founders.

At the beginning of the 21st century when the United States is facing the great and dangerous challenges from the threats presented by Islamic jihad and global terrorism, the capability of preserving democratic values and principles must deeply exist and be readily available. At the same time, the cultural and religious virtues such as "right and wrong", those basic components in strong and success-ful democracies created which protect human rights and provide the citizens with the moral clarity and sense of purpose, are needed to sustain the long, difficult, and costly sacrifices required to prevail in the global war on terrorism and protect against the spread of nuclear weapons.

The culture of the 18ᵗʰ century which underlay the U.S. Founders ideas of democratic principles, virtues, and ideals has eroded significantly since the 1960s. The necessary, broad citizen consensus concerning rights and responsibilities has been largely weakened. The principles of limited government, personal freedoms and a morally empowered citizenry, have been corroded since the beginning of the 20ᵗʰ century, as U.S. citizens have been surrendering their power and free-doms to an expanding powerful central government. This phenomenon has been combined with an adopted a self-absorbed culture which has driven and shaped the values of moral relativism. The roots of such damaging upheavals lie in the autocratic ideology of the European Progressive Movement which spread into the U.S in the early 20th century and was based on the autocratic and seductive social utopian philosophies, which lead to Europe's decline and decay throughout the 20ᵗʰ century.

When a nation's social compact/culture is strong, and its society is based-on citizen freedoms and the rule of law, then political pressures arising out of changed circumstances can be democratically resolved by families in local com-munities working through private sector organizations e.g., civic institutions, obviating the need for an extensive and far-reaching central government. Alexis de Tocqueville in 1832 commented positively on America's newly evolved broad social compact that protected its citizens from an overly intrusive central govern-ment by evolving locally a form of de facto regulation of life through families, communities, and religious values, which largely removed any feeling of need to create large outside forms of government.[124]

To sustain their country's current democratic and free society, America's citi-zens in the 21ˢᵗ century must continue to create and preserve civic and social institutions to insure that they continue to be strong enough to provide the needed support for citizens to independently manage and shape their society such that its fundamental democratic values and principles of democracy can be pre-served and upheld.

20th Century Modernist Culture and Custodial Democracy

As larger socioeconomic changes stemming from the development and spread of technology and industrialization from the after-effects of World War I, and the onset of the Great Depression that occurred during the first half of the 20th century, new social and ideological challenges arose on how best to address inequality and poverty.

During the 1930s, U.S. President Franklin Roosevelt's "New Deal" created huge new and powerful federal regulatory agencies, which expanded significantly the size and centralized power of the U.S. federal government in a way judged by many to be unconstitutional. These agencies included a new Public Works Administration (PWA), Tennessee Valley Authority (TVA), the National Recovery Administration (NRA, regulating prices and wages), the Agricultural Adjustment Administration (to regulate the amount of crop production), and the Federal Deposit Insurance Corporation. Further expanding such a questionable role of the federal government, the Roosevelt Administration became responsible for the adoption of the National Labor Relations Act of 1935 legalizing labor collective bargaining. In addition it oversaw the passage of the Social Security Act of 1935 creating huge new tax payments to the federal government by both workers and employers to fund federal pay-as-you-go retirement programs. This era also saw the adoption of minimum wage laws. The overarching goal and focus of Roosevelt's socialistic New Deal was the federal government's autocratic creation and assumption of a large share of power, responsibility and oversight of matters, which heretofore had been granted under both state and U.S. constitutions to local citizens, families, communities, and the states.

A further massive expansion of the federal government's autocratic and socialist power occurred under the administration of Lyndon Johnson and the Democratic Party's Great Society programs and Civil Rights initiatives during the 1960s, which were also combined with additional social, cultural, and political movements led by the Democratic Party. Government mandated discriminatory preferences in the areas of affirmative action and social welfare, which soon led to a corrosive shift in cultural values, including moral relativism, multiculturalism, and political correctness, were the centerpieces undermining the U.S. Founders' vision of the independent civic role of the citizens set forth in the U.S. Constitution and the Bill of Rights. This huge 20th century socialistic expansion of the U.S. federal government generated sweeping conflicts in what had traditionally been largely the domain and responsibility of individuals, family, community, local and state governments. *National Review* editor John O'Sullivan summarized the impulse and mechanisms that drive such policymaking, "First, it discredits the dispersed moral sentiments of traditional society—such virtues as duty, fidelity, and chastity—that enable that society to work spontaneously without too close a bureaucratic supervision. Second, it seeks to deal with the moral problems thus aggravated by imposing its own moral values through law and regulation."[125] Among the central tenets of this "new morality" is the notion that all groups (as opposed to individuals) should be treated equally with equality being defined by equal outcomes[126] rather than the traditional American ideal of the citizen's rights to equal opportunity.

The 20ᵗʰ century evolutionary socialistic political schemes of equal outcomes and entitlements have led to the emergence of what social scientist Charles Murray terms a trend toward "custodial democracy i.e., the government's practice of subsidizing the underclass and thereby effectively insulating it from the larger society. In effect, custodial democracy takes as its premise that a substantial portion of the population cannot be expected to function as citizens." [127] Murray also warned at the beginning of the 21ˢᵗ century that American society should not be complacent to this emergent trend:

> At this moment, elated by falling crime rates and shrinking welfare rolls, we have not had to acknowledge how far we have already traveled along the road to custodial democracy…But suppose that our new *modus vivendi* keeps working. We just increase the number of homeless shelters, restore the welfare guarantee, build more prison cells, and life for the rest of us will go on, pleasantly…But no matter how well the *modus vivendi* works, we cannot forever avoid recognizing that something fundamental has changed about America's conception of itself…Custodial democracy draws from the much older tradition from which America dissented, that society must be divided into those who control and those who are controlled.[128]

The differences between American society envisioned by the Founders and that of a "custodial democracy" could not be starker. A custodial democracy entails a permanent dependent class expecting government mandates to assure equal outcomes in compensation, housing, and other "entitlements." The American Founders created a federal republic based on self-reliant individualism with the expectation that self-reliant citizens would be the most important safeguard of individual freedom. These governance principles were radically transformed in the 1960s into a "custodial democracy," with the federal government in assuming powers heretofore in areas left to civil society, substituting an assortment of large central government employment mandates, welfare payments, agricultural subsidies, and regulations. By seeking socialistic equality through such a mandated process in direct conflict with the U.S. Founders' governance framework of individual freedom and responsibility, the U.S. has incurred a great loss. It must seek to return as soon as possible to rely upon the citizens' talents, initiative, and education as the key to raising living standards when freed from failed 20th century socialistic government mandates and redistribution of wealth. By dividing and pitting people against one another through preferences, quotas, and even speech codes, "identity politics"—far from the claims of its advocates—has expanded the risks of social segregation, which is in direct conflict with the inclusive society established by the Founders.

Identity Politics: Government Mandated Discriminatory Preferences

Creating a new social norm in the 20th century was the idea of "Identity Politics". Identity politics allowed political groups to claim and assert "victims'" preferential rights through expanded and costly entitlements in the areas of employment, job advancement and increased compensation, additional financial opportunities, college admissions and granting government contracts on the basis of race, skin color, gender, ethnicity, and sexual orientation. Some now view these entitlements as unfair and antithetical to the preservation of citizens' rights and protections under the United States' constitutional democracy. American Enterprise Institute Adjunct Scholar John Fonte explains, "Civic patriotism or liberal democratic nationalism," on which a republic depends for sustenance, "is not based on 'blood and soil,' or race and ethnicity, or superiority and dominance over others. It is a love of country based on political allegiance, shared values, and a shared history and culture."[129]

"Identity Politics" was a politically exploitive outgrowth of the 1960s U.S. Civil Rights movement. When "accused of politicizing everything, identity politics responds that politics is already everywhere; that interests dress up as truth but are only interests; that power is already everywhere and the only question is who is going to have it," observes professor and author Todd Gitlin.[130] What is not mentioned nor generally recognized nor acknowledged, however, is that any attempt by the government to create equality where it naturally does not exist will inevitably require a strong, interventionist, centralized government mandate raising significant Constitutional issues of reverse discrimination and a major sacrifice of personal freedoms.

The political packaging of these programs under the mantle of "social justice" with its emphasis on egalitarianism and wealth redistribution has become an ideology of the post-modern period with little attention paid or care given to the discriminatory impacts on citizens and the nation whose individual rights and property have been significantly diminished and infringed upon—all under a cynical misnomer and unobtainable goal of creating "equality."

The U.S.'s constitutional governance process is based on America's founding principles of freedom and equal opportunity. It has proved to be disingenuous in attempting to create the capability for the U.S. government to assimilate its many cultures and values into a cohesive nation. "The American creed envisages a nation composed of individuals making their own choices and accountable to themselves, not a nation based on inviolable ethnic communities. The Constitution turns on individual rights, not on group rights."[131] It is this distinct characteristic that the late 20th century counter-culture attacked with particular vigor. Professor Arthur Schlesinger refers to it as a "cult of ethnicity" which emerged in modern culture.[132]

Balkanization rather than unity has become the objective of those who promote the cult of ethnicity. By highlighting such differences (whether ethnic, religious, racial, gender, and even sexual orientation) and by government mandates dividing Americans into antagonistic camps, the *e pluribus Unum* principle and foundation on which the American republic was established has been weakened seriously and its citizenry hugely divided.

Multiculturalism

Another facet of modernist culture is the philosophy of multiculturalism and its discouragement of assimilation in favor of a segregation of various ethnic groups retaining their former cultures, thereby seeking a fundamental rejection of the "Melting Pot" culture. Samuel Huntington described the U.S. Founding culture as follows:

> America's core culture has primarily been the culture of the seventeenth-and-eighteenth-century settlers who founded our nation. The central elements of that culture are the Christian religion; Protestant values, including individualism, the work ethic, and moralism; the English language; British traditions of law, justice, and limits on government power; and a legacy of European art, literature, and philosophy. Out of this culture the early settlers formulated the American Creed, with its principles of liberty, equality, human rights, representative government, and private property. Subsequent generations of immi-

grants were assimilated into the culture of the founding settlers and modified it, but did not change it fundamentally. It was, after all, Anglo-Protestant culture, values, institutions, and the opportunities they created that attracted more immigrants to America than to all the rest of the world.[133]

A large body of writing has examined the concept, purpose, and impact of "multiculturalism". Thomas Krannawitter, Vice President of the Claremont Institute, has written one of the better analytical pieces summarizing the issues, theories and intellectual flaws underlying the multiculturalism movement:

> [M]ulticulturalism does not easily square with the American political tradition. In fact, it may be said that America was founded in explicit opposition to the roots of multiculturalism. Rejecting the waves of modern philosophy crashing down on Europe at the time, the American Founders in 1776 achieved something never before attempted: they founded a nation upon a self-evident truth, a truth bound up in the universal 'laws of nature and of nature's God.'[134]

Krannawitter's concerns are genuine and significant. In a multiculturalist's world, where rights are assumed to be man-made creations rather than naturally-endowed, it becomes far easier for would-be authoritarians to rationalize the benefits from a drive to erode the freedoms derived from natural rights. In a world where relativism and not reason prevails, it becomes far more difficult for society to defend the virtues of freedom, democracy, and the rule of law. In that kind of world, the West and the United States are losing the intellectual foundation on which their societies were established and the unprecedented benefits that have been brought forth by Western civilization are now imperiled.

In the fall of 2003, William Bennett, of the Claremont Institute, provided the following additional analysis: "According to multiculturalism, no culture is better (or worse) than any other culture, because there is no objective standard by which all cultures are to be judged. What's right and wrong all depends on your culture. Multiculturalism drives modern liberal thought, and accounts for the liberal celebration of 'non-judgmentalism' and 'diversity.'"[135]

American Enterprise Institute Adjunct Scholar John Fonte contrasts the difference between a liberal democracy and a society that is premised in the progressive vision that took root in the U.S. in the 20th century:

> Liberal democracy and liberal-democratic nationalism are phenomena of the modern age, whereas the alternative progressive vision smacks of the pre-modern and post-modern. Instead of individual rights and national citizenship,

there is an emphasis on group rights and multiculturalism; instead of majority rule there is proportional representation for ascribed groups; instead of patriotic affection for one's own nation, multiple loyalties to subnational and supranational groups are emphasized.[136]

Led by the liberal left and the huge embrace by academe at all levels, the United States has been taking large strides toward the alternative progressive vision summarized by Fonte, by establishing group preferences and institutions of learning that emphasize multiculturalism and the deconstruction of U.S. history and western civilization.

Evolution of the U.S. Modernist Culture: Political and Cultural Changes in the 20ᵗʰ Century

To understand how U.S. values and standards were debased and weakened during the 20ᵗʰ century, we must first examine the history and roots of the U.S. utopian socialist movement.

Inspired, in part, by the social and political pressures generated by the Industrial Revolution in the late 19ᵗʰ century and thereafter by two horrible, costly World Wars, the public's view of the size and role of government changed significantly and the public increasingly yearned for public policy reforms that reflected its changed perspective. This trend began with the rise of a Progressive Movement that originated in Europe in the late 19ᵗʰ century. This movement called for radical political change, including redistribution of wealth by the government. Although the movement's concepts of "social justice" had not yet fully evolved, public pressures for political and social reform were rising. "As we saw, it was big business, incipient colonialism, corrupt politics, and the condition of the poor, the young, and the Blacks which disturbed men and women with a moral conscience," [137] Columbia University professor and writer Jacques Barzun observed. The Progressives in the U.S. argued that the founding principles set forth in the Constitution were obsolete in the 20ᵗʰ century and should be supplanted with new government-imposed values and laws, which were much more egalitarian and socialistic.

The global economic depression that followed World War I created additional pressures and challenges in the U.S. and Europe for the creation of a new utopian social and economic order. "Panics, unemployment, violence rose dramatically…there was widespread feeling that entrepreneurs were 'robber barons,'…."[138]

Two of the Progressive Movement's leading proponents, Herbert Croly and educator/philosopher John Dewey, argued for a new U.S. Constitution that would be significantly different from one based on individual freedom and limited government. They argued that a preoccupation with individual rights had led, by the early 20th century, to an unhealthy societal obsession with money leading to economic insecurity and inequality for most of the citizenry. In their view, the U.S. Constitution was simply outdated and the government needed radical change to bring about a larger, more "socialist" inspired and European-like central government to more equally redistribute wealth.

Croly and Dewey also argued that "harmful individualism" was increasing societal inequalities, and was "the direct and logical expression of the doctrine of nature and natural rights" which may have had "immediate pragmatic value" during the Founding period, but not any longer.[139] They also contended that American society should now be focused on the pursuit of "social justice." In their view, equality and liberty were conflicting philosophies of governance in which one was only possible at the expense of the other. Their philosophy therefore called for a shift in the federal government's mission from guardian of liberty to a grantor of privileges.[140]

During the first half of the 20th century, the federal government, with the assistance of the U.S. Supreme Court, began pushing beyond its original constitutional boundaries. By the 1890s, the U.S. federal government already had begun to restrict and regulate the financial activities of the nation's largest private firms through anti-trust legislation.[141] In 1913 President Theodore Roosevelt conceded there was a "necessity" to curtail private property rights,[142] and shortly, thereafter, because of the enormous pressure placed on the economy by the funding of WWI, the Sixteenth Amendment to the U.S. Constitution was ratified which stated that Congress "shall have power to lay and collect taxes on incomes, from whatever source derived…".[143] This gave the federal government virtually unlimited financial means and substantially increased its power and authority to seize and redistribute the nation's wealth. It was deemed necessary and justified by the travails of the Great Depression, which had created bank failures triggering a massive adverse impact on the nation's economy. The new Federal Income tax was termed "progressive" because it taxed higher incomes at much higher percentage rates. Here was the beginning of a sequence of events throughout the remainder of the 20th century that facilitated a socialistic shift toward larger and more activist government redistribution of wealth and other egalitarian lawmaking.

The 20th century leftist pressures for utopian social reform in the U.S. and the resulting new cultural and social ideologies that has come about, have roots that go back as far as the18th century in Europe.

> The roots of change rest with such thinkers as Jean Jacques Rousseau who believed that freedom increased as individuals surrendered more of themselves to the collective. And it moved forward in America through events such as the New Deal, which turned Thomas Jefferson's view of negative rights on its head, and created a system of 'positive rights,' in which individuals have a right to things that come at others' expense.[144]

A closer look at the philosophical lineage of the counter-culture is necessary for one to better understand its nature. A historical review of philosophy reveals a number of major themes that can be called precursors of present-day American culture. It also highlights some of the major tactics employed to spread the ideas and reveals a set of leading actors who, unwittingly or not, can be identified as the ideological founders of the current U.S. culture.

When examined separately, however, the theories of many of these "cultural pioneers," clearly are antithetical to the principles underlying the American Founding and the values based on democracy and freedom. The "counter-culture" is based on many of the egalitarian premises and the need to create a strong, centralized government such as those that arose and subsequently fell in many parts of Europe.

Jean-Jacques Rousseau (1712–1778) was arguably one of the first of the social-istic-autocratic counter-culture leaders. His impact on this period and the follow-ing one (not to mention Progressive thought in later periods) has been described as "probably greater than that of any single writer,"[145] and roughly 250 years after he fired the opening salvos against rationalism in his *Discourse*,[146] Rousseau's work remains a powerful influence on present-day Leftist Western thought.

One of Rousseau's significant influences on contemporary culture was his attack on reason. He would often argue that man is naturally virtuous and there-fore did not need science nor art to live morally. He further argued that the influ-ence of the arts and sciences were responsible for man losing his natural freedom, and worse still, not regretting his loss of freedom.[147] He also indicted the art of printing as one of the major sources of trouble that was plaguing society during his times.[148] Rousseau's attacks on reason are most notably visible at the opening of the 21st century in the hollowing out of the traditional liberal arts core curricu-lum in U.S. colleges and universities. American progressive academics have relied heavily on Rousseau's criticism of the arts and sciences to justify their heavily "deconstructed" literature and history to support their political multicultural ideology and attacks on Western civilization.

Rousseau also glorified the uncivilized "savage." He contended that the savage as a sort of natural man was stronger, more self-reliant, less given to illness, and more temperate than the civilized man and that because for the savage "any woman is good enough" there were no quarrels resulting from jealousy.[149] For Rousseau, the savage was the enlightened being and civilized man was, in many ways, the barbarian. This theme is especially apparent in the contemporary cultural relativist and multi-cultural perspectives where Western civilization and the United States are the modern equivalents of Rousseau's "civilized man."

In addition to encouraging conformity to a collective will, Rousseau also asserted that each individual could be the source of his or her own morality rather than the rules of etiquette which led to a standardization of man. "Thy principles are engraved in all hearts and to know thy laws requires but withdrawal into oneself," [150] he wrote in the *Discourse*. Today, this philosophy is a major force underlying the counter-culture's major tenet of radical individualism by which the counter-culture seeks to remove the limits society has placed on personal gratification be they by the institution of marriage or traditional mores. Moral relativism in which no moral preference is superior to another is also based on the belief that it is best for one to find one's own moral code.

Rousseau was also a staunch supporter of a collectivist society. He contended that all the evils of society ranging from envy to vengeance could be traced to the institution of private property.[151] Likewise, he held a similar view toward the limiting notion of individual self-interest and argued that every citizen must remain in a condition of equality, which would be lost whenever attention was focused on the individual.[152] These same themes pervaded communist and socialist societies that were created early in the 20th century—and later, mostly fell toward the end of the 20th century. They are also the unspoken themes that lie behind the more subtle but hazardous group rights theories requiring a powerful government to enforce them and regulatory takings of private property for redistribution that have become a dominant part of the American progressive movement's political agenda.

Rousseau favored an abdication of individual wills to a general will. Although such general will was meant to be a sort of lowest-common-denominator compact between individuals and their community where individuals would still be able to exercise a degree of freedom and preference, which was supposed to be achieved through free and unanimous choice[153], Rousseau, however, also articulated that in cases where individuals did not surrender their natural freedom to the whole community that the obedience of such individuals could be compelled.[154] "In order then that the social compact may not be an empty formula, it tacitly includes the undertaking, which alone can give force to the rest, that whoever refuses to obey the general will shall be compelled to do so by the whole body. This means nothing less than that he will be forced to be free," [155] Rousseau proclaimed in "The Social Contract" or "Principles of Political Right." In what would become a great oxymoron, the state could "force" men to become free! Since Rousseau believed that the general will was indivisible, he felt that there was no need for any separation of powers among the state's governing apparatus.[156] This philosophy was a central part of Roosevelt's "New Deal" reorganization of the federal government in the 1930s creating a new combination of legislative, executive, and judicial powers, contrary to the Constitutional law at the time, to be exercised by unelected federal administrative agencies. From the idea that freedom could be "forced" it was only a short step to the view that group rights laws and regulations also could be "forced" on individuals to advance radical egalitarianism.

Another important European political philosopher whose views influenced the Leftist American Progressive Movement, shaping of the counter cultural revolution is Karl Marx (1818–1883). Marx argued that reality is based on the material aspects of life not spiritual ones.[157] Combining British economics, German philosophy, and French political rhetoric, Marx contended there were a number of scientific rules that humans must follow in organizing society. First, they must all obtain the means of subsistence necessary to satisfy their basic needs; all products that satisfy those needs must be produced. Second, once production moves beyond the primitive stage man finds it useful to specialize which creates interdependence; at this point production becomes a social rather than individual activity and the basic relationship of society becomes one of socioeconomic classes and class conflict. Because the means of production are in a continual state of change, people's relationships with one another are constantly changing. Finally, he argued that all of society's institutions—its religious, social and political ones—are determined by social change stemming from changes in the production process.[158]

Karl Marx saw the capitalist society of his day as the next-to-last stage in the evolution of society and predicted that technological change would eventually polarize society so severely that the resulting larger and larger masses of the disenfranchised would eventually topple the order of his day. Then a conflict-free society would be achieved. Karl Marx, not content to derive satisfaction from his philosophical hypothesis, went beyond where the other philosophers had gone and advocated that the world be changed forcefully to bring his ideas to fruition. Karl Marx correctly recognizing the rise in influence of science described his "economic laws of society" as scientific in nature and termed his brand of socialism "scientific socialism." Therefore, unlike some of his contemporaries who were promoting their own versions of utopian societies, his kind was claimed to be based on hard fact not mere wishful thinking.[159]

Although Marxism has failed to deliver its purported ends, this has not shaken the Progressives' overall faith in the general concept of collectivism. Some have even adopted the practice of continually revising reality to fit the facts to Marx's theories.[160] Such revisionism is commonplace today, particularly in the nation's primary and secondary and higher education institutions where literary and historical texts are continually subjected to de-constructionism so as to create and reinforce the intended objective of de-emphasizing the Founding principles and ideals.

Another important Marxist philosopher was Antonio Gramsci (1891–1937). Gramsci introduced the idea of social transformation through "consciousness," the notion that values, morals, truths, and standards are not absolute but rather linked to given historical epochs, and the principle that the "group" should be the main concern of society. Gramsci did not focus on the economic distribution of wealth, but rather on the idea of ensuring "social justice" through government mandates for society.

An outcome of the pursuit of the Gramscian ideal of "Social Justice" is the contemporary egalitarianism that helped drive public policy changes that included the establishment of affirmative action quotas and preferences. "While economic Marxism appears to be dead, the Hegelian variety articulated by Gramsci and others has not only survived the fall of the Berlin Wall, but also gone on to challenge the American republic at the level of its most cherished ideas. For more than two centuries America has been an 'exceptional' nation, one whose restless entrepreneurial dynamism has been tempered by patriotism and a strong religious-cultural one. The ultimate triumph of Gramscianism would mean the end of this very 'exceptionalism'. The ideological, political, and historical stakes are enormous,"[161] the Hudson Institute's John Fonte explained. He also warned, "The slow but steady advance of Gramscian and Hegelian-Marxist ideas through the major institutions of American democracy…suggests that there are two different levels of political activity in twenty-first century America. On the surface, politicians seem increasingly inclined to converge on the center. Beneath, however, is a deeper conflict that is ideological in the most profound sense of the term and that will surely continue in decades to come."[162]

German philosopher Friedrich Nietzsche (1844–1900) is another European political philosopher whose ideas have influenced Liberal Left academics in the U.S. His observation that there are "no facts, only interpretations" that provided much of the rationale for justifying the use of moral and cultural relativism as a basis for attacking Western Civilization. Likewise, his view that moral constraints are harmful[163] has become a building block of the radical individualism that underlies today's permissive culture. The intertwined cultural and sexual revolutions of the 1960s gained no small measure of inspiration from Nietzsche's call for society to adopt a new set of values.

Of course, while Nietzsche seemed to favor a Darwinian order where the strong ultimately prevailed over the weak, the Liberal Left has added its own unique signature to this matter. While on the surface the Liberal Left's efforts to reduce the strength of non-preferred groups might seem a contradiction to what Nietzsche was seeking, they have created a ready-made explanation to demonstrate that there is no contradiction at all. In advocating radical egalitarianism, the "preferred" groups are favored because the dominant groups, in the minds of those seeking to impose equality from the top down, have gained their dominance not by legitimate means but by exploitation. After all, what other reason could there be for unequal outcomes in a world where everything is relative?

The father of psychoanalysis, Sigmund Freud (1856–1939), is also another European pioneer who blazed a trail shaping contemporary culture. Freud argued that current problems experienced by adults—neurotic anxiety, hysteria, and other psychological disorders—can often be traced back to childhood experiences, especially those pertaining to sexuality and sex-related conflicts that have been pushed into the mind's unconscious but which occasionally surface in disguised form.[164] This unconscious, he argued, is the major driving force of human behavior with even trivial words and actions having deeper meanings that pertain to unconscious drives, desires, and conflicts.[165]

In addition to the idea that the unconscious plays a role in human behavior, Freud theorized that the drive for pleasure in a child's life focuses on specific body parts and that the adult personality is shaped by the resolution of conflicts between these primarily sexual urges and societal standards. Failure to resolve these conflicts can lead to a life-long fixation where the particular conflict plays itself out in symbolic ways.[166] Under both of Freud's theories, the individual is viewed as a helpless prisoner of circumstances. In this sense, we are really slaves of ourselves and our circumstances. This theory is often relied upon by the Liberal Left to support their apologetic treatment of society's anti-social elements. They argue that these individuals deserve sympathy because they are the suffering victims of society and circumstances and, therefore, they should be dealt with leniently rather than held fully accountable for their actions.

The leaders in the sexual revolution such as Austrian-born psychiatrist Wilhelm Reich seized upon Freud's work to maintain that "the sexual question must be politicized" and that establishing "a satisfactory genital sex life" was the key to personal and societal freedom and happiness.[167] In this case, Freud's work had been stretched somewhat so as to fit the ends desired, not unlike the revisionism that was often being employed to explain away Marxism's accumulating failures.

Austrian philosopher Paul Wittgenstein (1889–1951) also can be considered a leader behind the emergence of the new culture. His insights pertaining to language and its influence have made language a useful tool for sociologists, anthropologists, and of course, the Liberal Left. Wittgenstein observed that language can do more than describe things. Words can give orders—words don't necessarily stand for any one thing; only when the range of possibilities has been exhausted can one describe a word's meaning. This theory rejects the idea that specific words stand for specific things and have fixed meanings. Rather it proclaims that words derive their meanings from the intentions of their users and, therefore, can mean different things to different people.[168] This thesis provided an additional frontier for the Liberal Left to use in constructing its support of the counter cultural revolution. First, it led to structuralism which asserted that language is nothing beyond structure that arose during the 1960s. It then led to the radical notion by Michael Foucault (1926–1984) that words are, in reality, an attempt by their user to exercise power over others which became the basis of de-constructionism. In theory, de-constructionism was supposed to be a means of understanding language. In fact, it has become a technique for attacking arguments against the new culture and its permissive values without having to respond to criticisms based on traditional intellectual, analytical, and scientific grounds. This technique has also proven effective in de-legitimizing those who seek to resist the new culture.

Contemporary writers who influenced the evolution of the counter culture include poet Allen Ginsberg and novelist William Burroughs, key members of the "Beat Society" which emerged during the 1950s, along with novelist Norman Mailer whose writings featured "a fascination with violence and an adolescent obsession with sex."[169] These writers played a key role in softening society for the launch of the cultural and sexual revolution that took place in the 1960s. "The Beats are crucial to an understanding of America's cultural revolution not least because in their lives, their proclamations, and (for lack of a more accurate term) their 'work' they anticipated so many of the pathologies of the Sixties and Seventies. Their programmatic anti-Americanism, their avid celebration of drug abuse, their squalid, promiscuous sex lives, their pseudo-spirituality, their attack on rationality and their degradation of intellectual standards, their aggressive narcissism and juvenile political posturing: in all this and more, the Beats were every bit as 'advanced' as any Sixties radical," [170] scholar Roger Kimball observes.

As a result of these "cultural pioneers" the basis for a new permissive culture was in place long before the collection of 59 student radicals, trade-union activists, and Socialist party organizers came together in Port Huron, Michigan to draft their political manifesto known as "The Port Huron Statement," usually identified as the first shot in the cultural revolution.

This document which was overwhelmingly ratified by the group on June 16, 1962 expressed pessimism with the *status quo* and proclaimed utopian ideas that had been expressed much earlier and arguably more eloquently in the past. This manifesto declared among other things: "We regard men as infinitely precious and possessed of unfulfilled capacities for reason, freedom, and love," and "The goal of man and society should be human independence:...finding a meaning of life that is personally authentic."[171] As was the case with Rousseau, human freedom was the stated object but the Nietzschean doctrine of what would become moral relativism was the true objective. But this was just the beginning. A radical transformation of society as complete as that advocated by any of the Liberal Left's "Founding Fathers" was the long-term purpose.

Some of the new principles advanced in the manifesto were "that work should involve incentives worthier than money or survival"[172] (a basic rejection of free market economics) and that system of social values in place at the time, man "is a thing to be manipulated, and that he is inherently incapable of directing his own affairs"[173] (shades of Rousseau's "Man is born free; and everywhere he is in chains"). "The American political system is not the democratic model of which its glorifiers speak. In actuality it frustrates democracy by confusing the individual citizen, paralyzing policy discussion, and consolidating the irresponsible power of military and business interests,"[174] the Statement observed in a trumpet blast against the system America's Founders had created. In a call for a more collective, activist, and redistributive state role, the Statement then complained that the "real, as opposed to mythical, range of government 'control' of the economy includes only: some limited 'regulatory' powers...a fiscal policy built upon defense expenditures...without a significant emphasis on peaceful 'public works'...very limited 'poverty-solving'" and "regional development programs...which have been only 'trickle down' welfare programs."[175]

This group's themes built on radical egalitarianism and individualism were clear and it was prepared to fight for those values. Society was not. In remarkably few years after the Port Huron convention, massive "Great Society" redistribution programs were in place and the cultural revolution was well underway.

How then did the '60s radicals succeed so quickly in largely constructing the new society they sought? In addition to public complacency, a number of techniques borrowed from the past proved highly effective.

First, the radicals recognized the magnitude of the benefits that could be obtained by strategically targeting society's key institutions. Once captured, these institutions could be used to achieve and sustain their cultural overhaul. Rousseau blamed the arts and sciences for corrupting man. The 20th century Liberal Left seized the institutions of higher learning to become beacons of their message. Higher Education soon became a fertile ground for their message and not by accident. "The academic life contains reinforcing counterparts to the way in which extracurricular life is organized. The academic world is founded on a teacher-student relation analogous to the parent-child relation which characterizes *in loco parentis*," the Port Huron Statement asserts that "the university could serve as a significant source of social criticism and an initiator of new modes and molders of attitudes" and advised "To turn these possibilities [the quest for their version of social justice] into realities will involve national efforts at university reform by an alliance of students and faculty. They must wrest control of the educational process..."[176]

LBJ's Great Society: Affirmative Action, Identity Politics, Diversity

President Lyndon Johnson's Great Society programs in the 1960's were rooted in the radical egalitarianism described above and sought to further expand the federal government's role and mission to foster societal equality through aggressive wealth redistribution, welfare and social entitlement programs, and a broad civil rights legal agenda of discriminatory preferences that heavily focused on equal outcomes rather than equal rights or equal opportunity. "We seek...not just equality as a right and as a theory," President Johnson told an audience at Howard University in Washington, D.C. in 1965, "but equality as a fact and equality as a result."[177] These theories were subsequently expanded into rigid Government-mandated quotas and group preferences under affirmative action programs referred to as "diversity" initiatives to provide citizens with the "right" to welfare and other entitlements.

By the 1970s, the federal government became increasingly powerful and invasive of citizens' rights, a consequence which the U.S. Founders feared when drafting the Constitution. Unfortunately, the U.S. when entering the 21st century had neither its citizens nor the courts functioning as the check or balance provided for in the U.S. Constitution to prevent such outcomes.

Instead, the Supreme Court had been interpreting the Constitution in a fashion that opened the way for the expansion of the federal government. The judicial branch's usurpation of power began in the late 19th century with the expansion of a legal concept known as "substantive due process." Judge Robert Bork explains that, "substantive due process, though it had originated in the judicial desire to protect slavery, had now been validated as constitutional doctrine [in the U.S. Supreme Court's 1877 *Davidson v. New Orleans* decision]...Since the clause [Due Process Clause] was designed only to require fair procedures in implementing laws, there is no original understanding that gives it any substantive content. Thus, a judge who insists upon giving the due process clause such content must make it up. That is why substantive due process, wherever it appears is never more than a pretense that the judge's views are in the Constitution. That has been true from *Dred Scott* to today."[178]

The U.S. Supreme Court's *Lochner v. New York* decision of 1905 added to the intellectual ammunition employed in the evolution of the powerful new concept of substantive due process. Bork further writes, "[A] different view of police power, to which Peckham [Justice Rufus Peckham] subscribed, came into being: that the power had inherent limits independent of any constitutional prohibition, and that judges could enforce those limits by invalidating legislation even where the Constitution was silent. That idea, of course, gave judges free rein to decide what were and were not proper legislative purposes."[179]

Bork reveals that in his 1905 *Lochner* opinion, "Justice Peckham, defending liberty from what he conceived to be 'a mere meddlesome interference,' asked rhetorically, '[A]re we all...at the mercy of legislative majorities?'" The correct answer, where the Constitution is silent, must be 'yes.' Being 'at the mercy of legislative majorities' is merely another way of describing the basic American plan: representative democracy. We may all deplore its results form time to time, but that does not empower judges to set them aside; the Constitution allows only voters to do that."[180] Thus, the seeds of judicial activism were planted in an attempt to confer a constitutional authority upon both the U.S. Supreme Court and the Congress which has never been lawfully conferred.

The New Deal Era of the 1930s saw the U.S. Supreme Court radically remade in a fashion that abandoned traditional conceptions of federalism and economic due process. Its 1934 *Nebbia v.* New York ruling permitted New York's Milk Control Board to establish minimum and maximum retail prices for the sale of milk. In *West Coast Hotel Co. v. Parrish*, the U.S. Supreme Court upheld a minimum wage law. *Olsen v. Nebraska* (1941) further allowed for market price regulation by upholding a state law setting maximum employment agency fees. In *Wickard v. Filburn* (1942), the Court set a significant precedent by holding that a farmer who grew wheat for his own farm's consumption could be penalized for exceeding the quota established by the Secretary of Agriculture aimed at maintaining the price of wheat.[181] According to Bork, "Due process protection of economic liberties has never returned."[182]

Affirmative Action

Affirmative action was instituted during the 1960s and expanded in the 1970s as a way to "compensate" for a history of institutional "racism" against Black Americans. It was believed by many that institutional racism was directly responsible for the disparity of opportunities and unfavorable outcomes faced by Black Americans. Had such racism not been present, it was presumed that Black Americans would be represented in universities and the workplace in a proportion equal to their share of the population.

However, this was not the case. Therefore, the proponents of affirmative action policies believed that without affirmative action Blacks as a group would not, on average, be admitted to colleges, hired for jobs, or accepted broadly in society. In their view, if the "American dream" were to apply to Blacks, Blacks would need a "helping hand" from the government to overcome the institutional barriers that deprived them of opportunities available to others. Its aim was to ensure that Blacks could be able, with a small measure of help, to have a chance to catch up with their White peers in such areas as hiring promotions, academic admissions, and business opportunities. With this assistance, it was argued that they would be able to fare as well as any citizen on measures of performance e.g., educational attainment and wages.

The same strategy was employed in an attempt to help women and other minorities combat other similar institutional and societal biases. Affirmative action expanded during the 1970s to provide preferences to a number of other "disenfranchised" groups. However, today these programs are increasingly viewed by their critics as unfair and "reverse discrimination."

"[A] new form of discrimination has become widespread in today's workplace," writes noted author Dinesh D'Souza. "Like discrimination of the old sort, it employs racial classification to prefer less qualified members of some groups over more qualified members of other groups. The new discrimination is legal as the old used to be. What differentiates the new discrimination is that it targets whites, specifically white males, and sometimes Asians. Another novel feature of this discrimination is that it is clad not in the robes of a racism that dares not speak its name, but in the full regalia of moral indignation and social justice. The new discrimination is justified as an indispensable instrument for fighting racism."[183]

Contrary to the aims of its advocates, there is evidence that affirmative action has actually victimized its purported beneficiaries by isolating them in many ways from the objectives that had been sought. John H. McWhorter, himself a Black American and Professor of Linguistics at the University of California-Berkeley, has cataloged the disappointing affirmative action outcome in his book *Losing the Race: Self-Sabotage in Black America* (The Free Press, 2000). McWhorter's research and personal experiences reveal several distressing results that call into question the purported benefits from the entire affirmative action experiment and build a strong case for its termination.

The first great "evil" of affirmative action Professor McWhorter identifies is its creation of an aura of "private doubt" in the justification of the preferential admission of African American students into universities.[184] The same is true for Blacks in the workforce and wherever else they can take preferential advantage of affirmative action programs. McWhorter writes,

> As an institutionalized leg up, affirmative action leaves black Americans with the most systematically diluted responsibility for their fate of any group in America. The white student who gets a letter announcing his admission to Duke can go out and celebrate a signal achievement, although the luck of the draw almost always plays some role in a white or Asian person's admission to a school. Can the black middle manager's daughter getting the same letter have the same sense of achievement if her SAT scores and grades would have barred any white or Asian from admission? The truth is no—she can only celebrate having been good enough among African-American students to be admitted.[185]

Although Blacks may feel no overt stigma, Professor McWhorter argues, affirmative action policies often remove them from the world of academic achievement and superior performance. He believes that if they were aware of this phenomenon, most would call for an end of such set-asides. Granting preferential admission at schools where they otherwise would not be academically qualified also has led to a sizable number failing to complete their university educations.

Rather than abolishing racism, first institutionally and then later in the hearts and minds of others, the mandating of the preferential inclusion of Blacks into higher education and in the hiring and promotion in the workplace, affirmative action has increasingly created a growing resentment for the reverse discrimination it has created. To perpetuate such unfairness indefinitely can only sustain and expand the racism that affirmative action seeks to eliminate.

Additionally, Black students often under perform because their teachers expect too little of them. Affirmative action reinforces this tragic outcome by excepting them from the pressures of competition it has created a self-fulfilling prophecy of underperformance.[186]

Balanced against these adverse effects, Professor McWhorter identifies a number of benefits that he believes would result if affirmative action preferences were eliminated. These include the ability to combat effectively the concept of "victimology." He concludes that "Comforting" approaches, such as affirmative action, heal wounds but do little to address the underlying problem of differing outcomes, the need to combat separatism, and the need to address why Blacks are given lower levels of performance expectation. Abolishing affirmative action, in Professor McWhorter's mind, would open the door for Blacks to achieve on the basis of their own real merit and wipe away the doubts that plague them as unqualified and the only ones who benefit from affirmative action.[187]

Additional evidence now has become available that affirmative action fails to address the fundamental challenges confronting minority students who wish to attend and complete college. The Manhattan Institute's Jay Greene and Greg Forster reveal, "We can beef up affirmative action all we like and it won't increase the flow of minority students into college, because the K-12 system just doesn't produce enough 'college-ready' high school graduates. The shocking reality is that fewer than one in five minority students are 'college ready.'"[188]

The June 2003 Supreme Court rulings on affirmative action in higher education admissions criteria offered a more restrained assessment while acknowledging that such programs have the potential to inflict reverse discrimination and harm. Writing for the Court in *Grutter v. Bollinger*, Supreme Court Justice Sandra Day O'Connor asserted that there was a "compelling state interest" for promoting diversity through "narrow tailoring" under which "a race-conscious admissions program not unduly harming members of any racial group" and that such action to promote diversity "remains subject to continuing oversight to assure that it will work the least harm possible to other innocent persons competing for the benefit."[189] She also declared, "We are mindful, however, that '[a] core purpose of the Fourteenth Amendment was to do away with all governmentally imposed discrimination based on race.'…Accordingly, race-conscious admissions policies must be limited in time."[190] She also suggested, "In the context of higher education, the durational requirement can be met by sunset provisions in race-conscious admissions policies and periodic reviews to determine whether racial preferences are still necessary to achieve student body diversity."[191]

Although the U.S. Supreme Court upheld the University of Michigan Law School's consideration of race as a factor in admissions decision-making in *Grutter v. Bollinger*, it rejected the University of Michigan's College of Literature, Science, and the Arts' use of affirmative action in *Gratz v. Bollinger*. In that decision, Chief Justice Rehnquist delivered the Supreme Court's opinion and asserted that the University of Michigan employed an overly broad approach toward promoting diversity that was inconsistent with the Constitution, as it failed to provide an "individualized review" of each applicant. "We conclude…that because the University's use of race in its current freshman admissions policy is not narrowly tailored to achieve respondents' asserted compelling interest in diversity, the admissions policy violates the Equal Protection Clause of the Fourteenth Amendment."[192] This set of decisions suggests that affirmative action will continue to exist for a limited time being, though its use will be constrained to narrow parameters, which could either mitigate or perpetuate the concerns about merit and fairness expressed by Professor MacWhorter.

Finally, in its *Gratz vs. Bollinger* decision, the U.S. Supreme Court affirmed that those who suffer unlawfully from the barriers imposed by such discriminatory preferences as those reviewed by the Supreme Court may seek damages. The Supreme Court held:

> Petitioners have standing to seek declaratory and injunctive relief…The 'injury in fact' necessary to establish standing in this type of case is the denial of equal treatment resulting from the imposition of the barrier, not the ultimate inability to obtain the benefit…In the face of such a barrier, to establish standing, a party need only demonstrate that it is able and ready to perform and that a discriminatory policy prevents it from doing so on an equal basis…Hamacher's personal stake, in the view of both his past injury and the potential injury he faced at the time of certification, demonstrates that he may maintain the action.[193]

With individuals having the ability to seek relief from the consequences of discriminatory admissions policies—even well-intentioned ones—it is possible that in the longer-range, such policies might eventually be discontinued as the Supreme Court places a renewed emphasis on the Constitutional principle of equal opportunity.

The Counter-Culture and Changes to the Value System

During the 1960's those leading what can be described as a counter-cultural revolution adopted a subtle but deliberate long-term strategy to transform the nation by altering its culture. Roger Kimball, managing editor of the *New Criterion* observed, "In a democratic society like ours, where free elections are guaranteed, political revolution is almost unthinkable in practical terms. Consequently, utopian efforts to transform society have been channeled into cultural and moral life."[194]

Those leading the counter-cultural revolution cloaked their ambitions under the banner of enhanced individual freedom. Their actual objective was to gain increased political and social power by removing the moral precepts and values on which the American civil society had been established from the citizens and the culture. In reality, rather than creating a more free society, society was to be divorced from "the very things that underwrite freedom, that give it content, that prevent it from collapsing into that merely rhetorical freedom that always turns out to be another name for servitude."[195]

Today, the counter-culture has a strong presence among universities and foundations.[196] Each of these institutions has had a profound impact on cultivating the minds and values of Americans. Numerous foundations, including the Ford, Rockefeller, and MacArthur Foundations, have now spent millions of dollars in advocating an ideology of "social justice" through group ("victim's") rights and group empowerment. Academe has become a breeding ground for "group rights" ideologies backed by "speech codes" and "political correctness" that stifles debate and intellectual creativity.

Citizens Losing a Sense of their Country's History and Culture

The ability of American citizens to gain an accurate sense of their own history and discern the lessons and experiences of the past and apply them to the present is integral to retaining a democratic soul. When the historical memory is lost, a nation loses one of its most important anchors. This loss of memory would only serve to aid those who continually seek to gain power, at the expense of diminished freedom and the authority of the citizens, over their government. Without a thorough understanding of the nation's history and traditions, the country's fundamental democratic legacy is not only at great risk, but also is viewed with less reverence by the citizens who fail to understand their role and responsibilities which accompany their democratic freedoms.

The importance of a sound knowledge of a nation's history by its citizens cannot be understated. In *Heaven on Earth: The Rise and Fall of Socialism*, American Enterprise Institute scholar Joshua Muravchik explains, "The idea of socialism did not march through history of its own accord. It was invented, developed, popularized, revised, exploited and in some cases abandoned by a chain of thinkers and activists. It was modified again and again, sometimes for ulterior motives but also because, for all its unmatched allure, it proved maddeningly difficult to implement."[197] More importantly, Muravchik reveals that the Marxists employed "history" as justification for their movement. He writes that Karl Marx and Friedrich Engels "shifted the basis of socialist hopes from individual experiments to broader historic trends, which fortified it against empirical failure."[198] Preceding the rise of Marxism, some of the radicals behind the French Revolution were able to effectively spread a zero-sum mentality that pitted various elements of French society against one another. "[A]n egalitarian society would also, the Equals believed, serve to eliminate want. In the image of the economic world projected in the writings of Babeuf and his fellows, nature provided a relatively fixed bounty. Therefore, a person could 'only succeed in having too much by arranging for others to have not enough,'" Muravchik explained.[199]

In an environment in which the incidence of historical illiteracy is sufficiently great, the examples of the French Revolution and also Marx and Engels demonstrate that demagogues can misuse history to lend artificial legitimacy to their causes even if such causes are at odds with human liberty and historical reality.

To undermine the value of citizens learning their nation's history and literature, new linguistic schemes and theories of structuralism and techniques for deconstructing words and ideas have been employed in academe. Such techniques are reflected in the decision by textbook publishers to create and enforce bias guidelines, strip such words as "Founding Fathers," "fisherman," and "mankind" from textbooks; require a roughly 50-50 balance between the sexes and the methodology employed by test publishers such as the Educational Testing Service (ETS) including the removal of questions and material from examinations on which the males and females score very differently.[200]

Diane Ravitch explains, "When we as a nation set out to provide universal access to education, our hope was that intelligence and reason would one day prevail and make a better world where issues would be resolved by thoughtful deliberation...Intelligence and reason cannot be developed absent the judgment that is formed by prolonged and thoughtful study of history, literature, and culture, not only that of our own nation, but of other civilizations as well..."self-censorship" by textbook and test publishers, is not what our children get today. Instead, they get faux literature, and they get history that lightly skims across the surface of events, with no time to become engaged in ideas or to delve beneath the surface. Not only does censorship diminish the intellectual vitality of the curriculum, it also erodes our commitment to a common culture."[201]

Those advancing the counter-cultural revolution have sought to reduce the study of American history with history course requirements dropping significantly in the closing years of the 20th century, an approach entirely consistent with the Marxist re-education efforts in the Soviet Union. "The elimination of a nation's true history, expertly practiced in the Soviet Union and the Third Reich, guarantees commissars an uncontested field as they bring up generations with blanks instead of history in their heads," notes Balint Vazsonyi.[202]

"The reason their efforts have been so feeble is that they lack...vision of a happy future that will unfold after their chosen dragon is slain. For their parents and grandparents, the name of that vision was 'socialism,' an ideal that lay at the center of much of the turmoil of the twentieth century."[203]

Through the weakening of its culture, the U.S. entering the 21st century has infected significantly its key social and political institutions. Failure to promptly address and overcome these cultural weaknesses and divisions exposes the United States to some of the vulnerabilities similar to those that ultimately confronted history's earlier great powers at the onset of their decline.

The Misuse of Universities

The counter-culture movement has already made American colleges and universities the breeding ground for fermenting and spreading its radical ideas. In their admissions policy, core curriculum, the hiring and granting of tenure to faculty, student financial aid, student life and codes of conduct, "diversity" is the all-too-common mantra.

The trustees, administrators, and faculty responsible for this perversion of the academic mission of higher education carefully mask their efforts to stifle free speech by wrapping those efforts under the banner of "preserving personal dignity." The true character of their pursuits, however, cannot be denied when the evidence is so strong and clear.

Author Jonathan Rauch observes, "[N]o social principle in the world is more foolish and dangerous than the rapidly rising notion that hurtful words and ideas are a form of violence or torture…That notion leads to the criminalization of criticism and the empowerment of authorities to regulate it. The new sensitivity is the old authoritarianism in disguise, and it is just as noxious."[204] Put bluntly, he continues, "It leads to the doctrine that people should be punished for holding false or dangerous beliefs. It leads…toward an inquisition."[205]

Therefore, "victims" of an oppressive Western society were identified. As victims, their champions argued that they were properly entitled to government-created and mandated preferences in employment, hiring and promotion, admission to educational institutions, benefits under government contracts all under the rubric of a system of "social justice."

"As more and more people realized that they could win concessions and moral victories by being offended, more and more offended people became activists," [206] notes Jonathan Rauch. Soon, the "victim's movement" took on a life of its own, building momentum, and leading to today's destructive "Identity Politics". By successfully pulling these disparate groups of "victims" together under the "social justice" umbrella, the left gained the critical mass needed to advance politically and culturally their ideological agenda. As a result, in the 20th century, the U.S. witnessed an extraordinary expansion of its federal government well beyond the Constitutional constraints envisioned by the Founders.

Higher education is of crucial importance to a nation's overall culture. With their immense enrollment, colleges and universities have become major training grounds and recruitment centers for political activists of the left. Moreover, federal expenditures in the form of student loans and financial assistance have helped underwrite the development and spread of leftist ideology, expose students to cultural and moral values that can be at odds with those of America's founding culture. This has given the political left access and control over many of the nation's most noteworthy cultural institutions, employing sizable numbers of leftwing intellectuals who use the university setting as a vehicle for advancing their philosophies, and once captured, they can utilize the hiring and tenure process to effectively exclude those whose ideologies differ from those of the political left.[207]

When entering the 21st century, many U.S. academic institutions are captive to the counter-culture and its influence. David Horowitz reveals, "Some years ago, a distinguished member of this radical generation, Richard Rorty, summarized its achievement in the following words: 'The power base of the left in America is now in the universities, since the trade unions have largely been killed off.'"[208]Horowitz observes, "Contemporary academics see themselves not primarily as educators, but as agents of an 'adversary culture,' at war with the world outside the university."[209]

Higher education became a fertile ground for carrying the message of the Liberal Left. "The university could serve as a significant source of social criticism and an initiator of new modes and molders of attitudes..."[210] "To turn these possibilities [the quest for their version of social justice] into realities will involve national efforts at university reform by an alliance of students and faculty. They must wrest control of the educational process..."[211]

Indoctrination by the Media

The media has had a large impact on our citizens' lives and values. Through its impact, it can either enhance or undermine the understanding and effectiveness of the citizens carrying out their role and responsibilities in a successfully-functioning democratic society.

"[T]elevision has become an unavoidable and unremitting factor in shaping what we are and what we will become...Yet it is intricately entwined in the braid of life, so much that it is easy to mistake it for an entirely passive servant," observes Syracuse University communications professor George Comstock.[212]

The ideological imbalance of much of the U.S. mass media has had an adverse impact on both citizens and the popular culture. An ineffective or biased media can lead policymakers and their constituents to make incorrectly founded decisions, especially when decision-making by elected officials is heavily poll-driven. Media inaccuracy and negativity can lead to citizen apathy, cynicism as well as loss of confidence in their political leaders. This is especially dangerous and confusing when U.S. foreign policy is faced with difficult and costly alternatives and policies such as the ongoing global war on terrorism.

Lifestyle, celebrity, entertainment and celebrity crime/scandal increasingly dominated the news to the point that by the late 1990s there evolved a dramatic retreat from reporting on public policy issues and foreign affairs. As a result, features on celebrities and people-oriented news had largely replaced traditional news reporting.[213] Straight news accounts fell from 52 percent of stories in 1977 to 32 percent in 1997.[214] These trends were not confined to television, alone and also swept through the print media further transforming the nature of news and quality of reporting. Between 1977 and 1997, the proportion of news coverage dedicated to government and political affairs fell from 40.2 percent of stories to

15.9 percent on ABC World News, from 38.9 percent to 18.7 percent on CBS Evening News, and from 32.7 percent to 18.5 percent on NBC Nightly News.[215]

During the same time, foreign affairs/international events coverage fell from 23 percent of items reported to 19.2 percent on ABC, from 18.9 percent to 14.4 percent on CBS, and from 19.6 percent to 12.4 percent on NBC. Meanwhile, the soft news content (lifestyle stories, reports on entertainment and celebrities, and those concerning celebrity crimes) rose sharply. On ABC World News such stories increased from 4.2 to 10.8 percent of all reports. On CBS Evening News the increase brought soft news from 3.0 percent of all stories to 9.6 percent. Similarly, on NBC Nightly News, the soft news content rose from 6.1 percent to 13.5 percent of stories.[216]

In terms of major newspapers and magazines, between 1977 and 1997 the percentage of front-page stories devoted to government/political affairs in the *Los Angeles Times* fell from 38.7 percent to 31.2 percent. In *Newsweek*, these stories declined from 23.1 percent to 9.6 percent and in *Time*, these stories all but disappeared (falling sharply from 15.4 percent to 3.8 percent). The same held true concerning foreign affairs/international events coverage. In the *Los Angeles Times*, these stories dropped from 26.1 percent to 17.5 percent of front-page stories. In *Newsweek* and *Time*, they fell from 9.6 percent to 5.8 percent of stories and 21.2 percent to 5.8 percent of stories respectively. [217]

During this same 20-year period, the proportion of front-page stories attributed to soft news rose sharply. In the *Los Angeles Times*, soft-news-related front-page stories spiked upward from 2.6 percent to 9.2 percent of all stories. Soft news cover stories in *Time* doubled from 15.4 percent to 34.7 percent of cover stories. In *Newsweek*, however, they actually declined from 32.7 percent to 26.9 percent of stories.[218]

However, in *The New York Times*, front-page stories devoted to government/political affairs or foreign affairs and international events slid only slightly from 55.0 percent of stories in 1977 to 52.6 percent in 1997. Soft news stories rose from 1.2 percent to 3.0 percent of all front-page pieces. [219]

Following the terrorist attacks on the U.S. of September 11, 2001, however, the media expanded dramatically its coverage. A study conducted by the Project for Excellence in Journalism—an initiative launched by journalists to raise their professional standards—revealed that factual reporting had increased while only 25 percent of coverage dealt with opinion, analysis or speculation. A few months later, however, previous patterns of media coverage began to reassert themselves with the above areas rising to 36 percent of the items covered.[220]

The issue of ideological bias in the media has gained notice for more than a decade. In a February 13, 1996 op-ed piece published by *The Wall Street Journal*, veteran CBS journalist and winner of seven Emmy Awards Bernard Goldberg revealed, "The old argument that the networks and other 'media elites' have a liberal bias is so blatantly true that it's hardly worth discussing anymore. No, we don't sit around in dark corners and plan strategies on how we're going to slant the news. We don't have to. It comes naturally to most reporters."[221] Why does this bias come "naturally" to most reporters? One need only refer back to the success of the counterculture movement in establishing a powerful influence in the nation's colleges and universities in which reporters and those in other professions are trained.

In a democratic republic such as the United States, no choice is more fundamental than that of citizens' regularly choosing the nation's leadership. Toward that end, the media's shortcomings are matters for serious concern. The media serving the U.S. has a prominent and responsible role to play in providing citizens with the information necessary for them to make an educated judgment and political choice.

Washington Post journalists Leonard Downie, Jr. and Robert Kaiser highlight the importance of quality journalism. They explain:

> Good journalism holds communities together in times of crisis, providing the information and the images that constitute shared experience. When disaster strikes, the news media give readers and viewers something to hold on to—facts, but also explanation and discussion that can help people deal with the unexpected. So on September 11, 2001, and for some time after, Americans remained glued to their televisions, turned in record numbers to online news sites and bought millions of extra copies of their newspapers to help absorb and cope with the horrors of shocking terrorist attacks on the United States. In the weeks that followed, good reporting allowed Americans to participate vicariously in the investigations of the terrorists and the government's planning for retaliation. Journalists could educate Americans about Islamic extremists, the history of Afghanistan, the difficulty of defending the United States against resourceful and suicidal terrorists, and much more. Journalism defined the events of September 11 and their aftermath. In those circumstances the importance of journalism was obvious, and much discussed.

> Whether widely noticed or not, good journalism makes a difference somewhere every day. Communities are improved by aggressive, thorough coverage of important, if everyday, subjects like education, transportation, housing, work and recreation, government services and public safety. Exposure of incompetence and corruption in government can change misbegotten policies, save taxpayers money and end the careers of misbehaving public officials. Rev-

elations of unethical business practices can save consumers money or their health. Exploration of the growing reach of computer databases can protect privacy. Disclosure of environmental, health, food and product dangers can save lives. Examination of the sways society cares for the poor, homeless, imprisoned, abused, mentally ill and retarded can give voice to the voiceless. News matters.[222]

For example, the underlying message to those who lack the information and perspective to understand the stakes involved in Iraq's transformation to become a democracy is that Iraq is a hopeless quagmire from which American disengagement is arguably the only feasible option. In reality, a premature American disengagement could have led to the collapse of Iraq's nascent effort to build a democratic state, and alternatively to its transformation into a permanent base of Islamist terrorism similar to the pre-9/11 role of Afghanistan, combined with a destructive civil war among Iraq's ethnic groups potentially drawing Turkey and Iran into the conflict presented an alternative scenario to be avoided at all costs.

The Rise of the Internet

One of the most profound developments in the dissemination of news and entertainment is the rapid spread of the Internet. With its global reach, the Internet has made it possible for visitors to receive and transmit content (text, images, audio, and video) in near real-time across the globe.

Today, a majority of Americans have Internet access at home or at work. According to the 2004–05 edition of the *Statistical Abstract of the United States*, 165.9 million adult Americans now have Internet access.[223] That's almost 80 percent of U.S. adults.[224] More than three-quarters of them used the Internet in the last 30 days.[225] Internet penetration has exploded over the most recent 5 years for which statistics are available. In 1998, 62 percent of households with computers had Internet access.[226] In 2003, the figure had soared to 88 percent of such households.[227]

Internet access among computer owners varies directly both with respect to education and income. 68 percent of computer owners with only an elementary school education had Internet access, while 84 percent of high school graduates and 94 percent of college graduates who owned computers had such access.[228] In terms of computer owners based on income, approximately 75 percent of those with incomes of under $15,000 per year had Internet access, while more than 90 percent of those with annual incomes of $50,000 or more had Internet access.[229]

Such statistics suggest possible discontinuities in access to the growing share of information now available over the Internet. As a result, the premium on a quality education has likely been made even more important in the Internet age.

Currently, the rise of the Internet is transforming the news market. By September 2005, daily newspaper circulation had fallen to 45.2 million copies.[230] Many readers had migrated to newspaper websites with such readers now accounting for about one-third of all Internet users.[231]

The Internet has become particularly prominent in the lives of younger Americans. In fact, teenagers are playing a leadership role in the creation of web content, such teens are now referred to as "screenagers."[232] On November 3, 2005, *The New York Times* reported, "using the cheap digital tools that now help chronicle the comings and goings of everyday life—cellphone cameras, iPods, laptops and user-friendly web editing software—teenagers…are pushing content onto the Internet as naturally as they view it…According to the Pew survey, 57 percent of all teenagers between 12 and 17 who are active online—about 12 million—create digital content, from building web pages to sharing original artwork, photos and stories to remixing content found elsewhere on the web. Some 20 percent publish their own web logs."[233]

All said, the Internet's explosive growth has raised a number of issues that will ultimately need to be resolved if it is to fulfill its potential in assisting citizens in becoming informed and engaged:

- Identification of credible content

- How to gain understanding from enhanced communications with people overseas but not erode the common basis of American culture

- How to prioritize among a growing number of websites

- How to use the Internet to complement additional sources of information and knowledge

- Learning how to avoid the spread of propaganda yet ensure maximum freedom of speech/political participation.

Mass Media and Entertainment

Given the pervasiveness of TV, the mass entertainment industry also has an important influence on the nation's culture and values. It has been noted that 98 percent of all U.S. households have at least one television set,[234] 84 percent have at least one VCR,[235] the number of videos rented daily is 6 million[236] (while in contrast 3 million library items are checked out daily).[237] 66 percent of Americans watch TV while eating dinner.[238]

Television's influence is especially all-encompassing among children, even very young ones. American one-year-olds watch, on average, 6 hours of TV per week.[239] That figure increases to almost 20 hours per week for those between the ages of 2–11[240], and just over 20 hours for those in the 12–17 age range.[241] In fact, the average American youth watches 1,154 hours of TV each year[242] but only attends school for 900 hours.[243] American children also watch an estimated 360,000 TV commercials prior to graduating from high school.[244]

At a time when the authority of religion and the family in shaping cultural norms and values has eroded, the power and impact of the entertainment industry in this area has grown in at least relative terms. Contemporary American mass entertainment has employed its creative faculties to depict an increasingly inaccurate and unattractive picture of the founding period in U.S. history, the behavior of its males, and multicultural deficiencies of its social and political institutions. U. S. values also have been encroached to a deeply troubling extent by the permissiveness and moral relativism that has been injected by the media and liberal left educators into U.S. culture over the last half of the 20ᵗʰ century.

So sweeping has been mass entertainment's transformation into a soap-box attack against American traditional values, that syndicated columnist Don Feder, in *The Boston Herald* observed in March 1999 that, "Communism's impact on movies a half-century ago is insignificant compared to the hegemony of Hollywood's current political commissars. The party line…is anti-American, anti-business, feminist, and hostile to organized religion."[245]

Of course, the Hollywood establishment denies that it goes out of its way to portray American society and values in a skewed, exaggerated, if not unfavorable manner. "To test this argument, a small number of teens who lived in the presumably violent city of Los Angeles, were asked how many murders they had seen in real life. They all said 'none.' They were then asked how many murders they had seen in movies and on television, and the estimate was somewhere in the many thousands…movies and television do not actually reflect the real world for most people, but rather that the entertainment moguls choose to emphasize and exaggerate some of the more outlandish aspects of our society…"[246]

Sexually explicit material, the use of foul language, and portrayals of graphic violence are also commonplace. A study conducted for the Henry J. Kaiser Foundation in Menlo Park, California, which reviewed 1,351 programs on 10 network and cable channels randomly selected in 1997 and 1998; found that more than half of all U.S. television shows included some form of sexual content.[247]

An analysis of TV programming on six networks (NBC, CBS, ABC, Fox, WB, and UPN) by the Parents Television Council found sexual content, foul language and violence not only widespread, but also continuing to increase. During the 1998 sweeps, for every hour of programming, there were 3.5 sexual references, 1.6 incidences of foul language, and 1.2 incidences of violence.[248]

Since 1975 three-quarters of television episodes have depicted the U.S. political or legal system as corrupt. The only times government institutions are portrayed as serving the public, are when "mavericks" or "whistleblowers" fight the system to make it work.[249] Businessmen are generally portrayed more negatively than those in other occupations (except public officials), they commit crimes three times more often than characters in other occupations. In addition, they are shown as being motivated by greed five times as often as those in other occupations, and using their often ill-gotten money for self-satisfaction three times more often than other characters.[250]

Males are often portrayed as "rude, crude, sex-crazed, sexist, childish and blindly egotistical."[251] New York Times reporter Anita Gates writes, "anyone who watches television regularly could get the impression that one of the two sexes on this planet is not only dimwitted and uncouth but darned proud of it."[252]

There continues to be growing evidence that mass entertainment media has had a significant impact on the cultural perceptions, values and norms of the U.S. public. Some studies indicate how much TV has influenced children's behavior and values. One survey found two-thirds of children surveyed think their peers are influenced by what they see on TV and almost two-thirds believe that shows such as The Simpsons and Married with Children encourage children to disrespect their parents.[253] "The consensus among social scientists is that very definitely there's a causal connection between exposure to violence in the media and violent behavior,"[254] The American Psychological Association warns that children "may be more likely to behave in aggressive or harmful ways toward others" as a result of seeing violence on television.[255]

ABC President Bob Iger confirmed at the 1998 National Association of Broadcasters Convention that "Television does exert an enormous influence over our culture and values"[256] 80 percent of Hollywood executives believe there is some link between TV violence and real-life violence.[257] Mass entertainment's impact on the broader culture has been demonstrated after approximately 30 years of research on television programming to have been "Beyond simply reflecting our changing sexual mores, television has endorsed the changes, and may have accelerated their acceptance…"[258] Film critic Michael Medved writes, "According to all available research on the subject, the most significant aspects of that influence are gradual and cumulative, not immediate, and they occur only after extended exposure."[259]

The toll inflicted by mass entertainment through its expanding presentation of sex and violence can be particularly severe on children who are in their formative years. Drs. L. Rowell Huesman and Leonard Eron, psychologists at the University of Illinois, have found a statistically significant relationship linking children who watched large amounts of TV violence at age 8 and the probability that they would engage in violence or child/spousal abuse at the age of 30. [260] The American Medical Association, American Psychological Association, the American Academy of Child and Adolescent Psychiatry and the National Institute of Mental Health have all reached similar conclusions with respect to the tie between future violence/spousal abuse and exposure to violence through mass entertainment.

A study by the International Adult Literacy Survey, the collaboration among seven governments and three intergovernmental organizations revealed that those most likely to watch TV for significant periods of time generally have reduced literacy levels. More than 10 percent of those at the lowest level of literacy watch more than five hours of TV each day while over 20 percent of those at the highest level watch less than an hour of TV a day.[261]

The Impact of Modern Culture on Family and Marriage

The U. S. Founders envisioned that the habits, customs, and traditions incorporated in a morally healthy culture would make it possible for citizens to carry out their role and responsibilities necessary to achieve successful democratic governance. Citizens would be guardians of both their rights and freedoms, but also of the institutions through which they would carry out their democratic roles and responsibilities. Modern culture, however, has nurtured a permissive environment that has seriously undercut the institution of marriage, which is vital and necessary to create and sustain the quality of a civil society essential to a successful democracy.

Marriage and strong family bonds are crucial to the development of good democratic citizens. It is predominantly through family that the necessary societal values and virtues are transmitted from one generation to the next. The decline in the number of successful marriages throughout the 20th century has weakened

U.S. civil society by promoting social inequality.[262] Increased social inequality, in turn, adds pressure on the social compact and thereby further undermines the effectiveness of democracy.

Marriage builds the personal bonds of trust and caring for one another that is integral to nurturing and sustaining strong families and communities. It is civil society that makes it possible for citizens and communities to care for each other and solve their society's problems without the intervention of government with the attendant diminishment of their personal freedoms.

Throughout most of written history, the "family" has been universally found and understood to be the basic unit of successful society. Not surprisingly, the traditional notion of family and marriage based on centuries of observation and experience was bound into the teachings of the world's major religions. Practices inconsistent or harmful to this vital institution were forbidden. Once created through marriage, the family was considered inviolable and permanent. Marriage was considered a lifetime obligation not only by the major religions, but also by the broader standards of civil society.

During the 20th century, however, the once near-universal consensus on the significance of the family and the obligations of its members was significantly undermined and eroded. With the retreat of religion, the moral relativism of modernity and the weakening of the institution of family, numerous alternative lifestyles and values gained mainstream legitimacy. The result has been a downward trend in the percentage of married couples in the U.S. since the 1960's. 68 percent of U.S. adults were married and living with their spouses in 1970[263]. By 2000, the figure stood at 60 percent after having undergone a slight recovery in the immediately preceding years.[264] In 1960, there were 3.9 marriages for every divorce, by 1970 there were 3.0 marriages for every divorce. By 1976 there were just 2.0 marriages for each divorce. Although this ratio in recent years has remained relatively constant[265] this is because fewer people are marrying.[266]

The erosion of the American family has adverse implications for the future and currently is contributing to some of the problems associated with the decline in the quality of U.S. education. Columnist Nick Jans observed in *USA Today* in 2003 that:

> America is in big trouble. Schools, after all, mirror society; the shortcomings of the former are inextricably tied to the latter's failings...The fault lies squarely in the failures of the home, and in the disintegration of the traditional family. For many reasons—dual incomes, divorce, separation and more—quality face time between parent and child has shriveled. Schools struggle to take its place.[267]

A landmark study by Judith Wallerstein found that ten years after their parents' divorce, 60 percent of young adults were en route to failing to attain the level of education achieved by their fathers.[268] Research by Nicholas Eberstadt of the Harvard Center for Population and Development Studies found that marriage is a much more powerful predictor of infant mortality than poverty, or age or education. A mother's risk of infant mortality more than doubled in cases where the mother is unmarried.[269] Research also has found a strong relationship between crime and the absence of fathers in children's lives.[270] Equally troubling is the report at the 1999 American Psychiatric Association Annual Meeting, by Dwain Fehon, PsyD. that the "children who had high exposure to community violence more often reported abuse and neglect in their early childhood" and that these children experienced increased symptoms of Post-Traumatic Stress Disorder (PTSD), substance abuse, depression and hopelessness.[271]

Marriage is also the key to helping perpetuate future intimate relationships. NYU's Judith Siegel explains, "The marital relationship observed by the child acts like a blueprint upon which all future intimate relationships will be built. For these reasons, it is important for parents to step back and examine the lesson plan they have created for their own children. Parents should ask themselves what their children might be noticing and question whether they are helping them create the best possible future."[272] The role of the parent is particularly important when it is considered that children often first learn from observation. [273]

The ability of the family to transmit virtues and values from generation to generation is particularly crucial to civil society and the future welfare of the nation. As Edward Shils explains, "a nation is never an affair of a single generation. It is not only that the process of formation of a national collective self-consciousness can only be gradual; but quite apart from this necessary precondition of formation, a nation always has a traditional legitimation. The connection with the past is effected through descent but what is transmitted is…the relationship which ancestors had in and to the territory."[274] He then adds, "A nation is by its nature a trans-generational entity. It would be a contradiction in terms to conceive of a nation as a phenomenon of a single generation." [275]

The weakening of marriage and the family has adversely impacted the children of broken families ranging from poverty, to future dysfunctional living arrangements, to a lack of education. Children living with a single mother are six times more likely to live in poverty than children whose parents are married. More than 70 percent of families in the lowest income quintile are headed by single parents. Cohabitation doubles the rate of divorce, and divorce reduces the income of families with children by 40 percent. Married couples in their mid-fifties accumulate four times the wealth of divorced individuals (especially important today with the projected financial crisis of the Social Security system created by the dramatic shift in intergenerational demographics).[276]

At the same time, divorce also breeds mistrust. This is most troubling as a basic level of trust is essential to a successful functioning civil society. A study of university students whose parents were divorced has revealed that 82 percent of these students did not trust their current partner. This phenomenon has been seen in other such studies.[277] Research has also demonstrated that the more contentious the divorce, the more severe are the adverse consequences that plague the children of divorce.[278] In fact, children who are exposed to marital hostility exhibit extreme behavior at a rate that is an astounding 600 percent greater than the average rate of the general public.[279]

Nearly half of American families experience poverty subsequent to a divorce.[280] Families with children having a combined pre-divorce income of $43,600 experienced an immediate drop in post-divorce income to $25,300.[281] This 40 percent cut in family income creates major problems for a parent in covering the expenses of rearing a child. Research has found that for every 10 percent increase in the probability of divorce, a man's "marriage wage premium" drops 8 percent.[282] In short, divorced men have the probability of earning less than their married-male counterparts. 75 percent of all women who apply for welfare assistance are estimated to do so because of broken marriages or cohabitation.[283] Such circumstances can lead to numerous harmful social pathologies in even some of the most basic areas. Himmelfarb notes, "[W]e have become demoralized…[W]e have lost our ability as a society to tell the difference between right and wrong. Even people who live decently no longer have the confidence to make the case for virtue."[284] This is a terrible loss that strikes at the heart of the nation's democratic system and puts all of its benefits at risk.

There is also strong evidence that family dysfunctionality translates into future family dysfunctionality across generations. "[T]he consequences of divorce flow from generation to generation, since the children of divorce are more likely to experience the same problems and pass them on to their own children," observes Fagan.[285]

It also has been found that the risk of divorce doubles for couples who live together prior to marriage and quadruples when one has lived with someone other than the current spouse.[286] Additional risks of divorce exists for those who have had a prior divorce, marriage into a step family, married while under the age of 20, or getting married as a teenager while pregnant.[287]

Finally, the financial stresses involved with the breakdown of a marriage and divorce can lead to disastrous long-term financial consequences. Studies by authors Linda J. Waite and Maggie Gallagher have shown, "On the verge of retirement, the typical married couple had accumulated about $410,000 (or $205,000 each), compared to about $167,000 for the never-married, just under $154,000 for the divorced, about $151,000 for the widowed, and just under $96,000 for the separated."[288] An additional study that examined median net worth of younger households found similar results. In that study, married families had accumulated the most wealth while both single mothers and cohabiting couples were at the bottom.[289] These savings advantages are due to "economies" that exist in married families as the incomes for married men are higher, though not too different from those of single men.[290]

Marriage has other important benefits not available to those who are not married. Married couples generally still view their marriage relationship as "permanent" even in the face of our society's high divorce rates and rising incidence of alternative living arrangements. This expectation causes married partners to lead their lives differently and more constructively than if they were in a temporary relationship.[291] Such positive behavior is often referred to as "specialization" by economists and has several benefits. Like any partnership, the combined talent pool of the family is deeper than if the individuals were living apart. Also, the partners acquire learning experiences in various tasks resulting from the shared burden in a permanent relationship and often get good performing several of those tasks.[292] Marriages also create "economies of scale" in which couples only need one set of furniture (singles have two sets), one home, and can pool their labor e.g. cooking or paying the bills for two.[293] Marriage also improves the lives of the partners because the permanence helps make each partner critically important and special to the other. This benefit can lead to more emotionally fulfilling relationships.[294] Married partners also learn to trust one another much more so than non-married individuals as they jointly own goods[295] (this joint ownership also gives each a stake in preserving or enhancing the value of those goods which would not exist without the bond of ownership).

Finally, marriage has results in reduced mortality rates. Unmarried persons have mortality rates that are 50 percent higher among women and 250 percent higher among men when compared to married persons.[296] Research has also found that marriage has the effect of "reducing" a cancer patient's age by up to ten years when it comes to the body's ability to heal or fight the disease.[297] Married men are also more likely to voluntarily lead their lives in a healthier fashion than their unmarried peers. For example, married men drink about half as much as unmarried men and are smoking at lower rates as well.[298] Overall, marriage is also particularly effective in reducing the incidence of death related to personal behavior e.g. suicide, alcoholism-related diseases, etc.[299]

New research published by the Institute for American Values in 2005 highlighted the above benefits of marriage and drawbacks of divorce. Among the twenty six conclusions reached by researchers were the following:

- Marriage increases the likelihood that fathers and mothers will have good relationships with their children.

- Marriage has important biosocial consequences for adults and children.

- Divorce and unmarried childbearing increase poverty for both children and mothers.

- Married couples seem to build more wealth on average than singles or cohabiting couples.

- Parental divorce (or failure to marry) appears to increase children's risk of school failure.

- Parental divorce reduces the likelihood that children will graduate from college and achieve high-status jobs.

- Children who live with their own two married parents enjoy better physical health, on average, than do children in other family forms.

- Marriage seems to be associated with better health among minorities and the poor.

- Marriage appears to reduce the risk that adults will be either perpetrators or victims of crime.[300]

The Weakening of the Important Role of Religious Institutions by Secularism, the Corrosion of Moral Values and Moral Relativism

Research has also demonstrated that religion can help foster a morally healthy and virtuous civil society. It strengthens families and marriages, fosters greater overall emotional happiness, and reduces the incidence of social pathologies such as teen pregnancy, suicide, and drug abuse. Religious and youth related activity create a vitally important and necessary social capital in a culture which government can never provide. In fact, government welfare and social programs often remove the opportunity for families and friends to provide support and assistance in time of need thereby depleting social capital and eroding citizen freedoms. Notwithstanding this significant contribution, the U.S. has allowed the cultural revolution of the 1960's to erode the authority and ability of religious institutions to help citizens acquire the moral standards, discipline and virtue needed in a successfully functioning civil society. Religion is expected to be a critical safeguard for the nation's democratic system of governance, by ensuring that citizens would recognize that their rights came from the Creator and that the government's authority was based on a limited grant of authority from the citizens in a prescribed system of checks and balances. The attack on religion's moral authority has stemmed out of the elements of the Enlightenment, modern science, Marxist precepts, and the Progressive Movement's utopian "social justice", all which have portrayed religion as inhibiting "freedoms."

Darwinism eroded the belief that man was bound to a Creator by a compact that included moral virtue and thereby has set the stage for the moral relativism movement where religion's voice was just one of many. In a "relative" world, who was to say which voice was the more important? Thus, the role of religion, which for many centuries had been the underpinning of moral values and virtue, has become diminished and increasingly vulnerable.

Prosperity from the Industrial Revolution in the early 20ᵗʰ century also contributed to undermining the moral authority of religion. Material wealth helped to remove the hardships that once defined life. A growing range of comforts produced an attitude for "living for the moment," which uprooted the beliefs that self-discipline and adherence to religious values would earn one an eternal life of happiness and reward. As a result, the religious moral restraints and incentives that once governed human behavior gradually eroded thereby directing them away from the virtues conducive to higher levels of civil behavior.

If the decline in religion is accelerated or even deepens, it will have broad negative ramifications for America's democratic society which depends significantly on a virtuous culture for sustenance. In a successful democracy, it is the people who are free and empowered through their representatives to make, uphold, and support the laws on which society depends. No system that depends on creating and sustaining such a unique blend of freedom, responsibility, and justice can survive without a civil society and a morally virtuous public.

Rabbi Harold Kushner asserts that there is a definite link between religion, morality, and the rule of law.

"I remember what Ivan Karamazov says in the Dostoevsky novel *The Brothers Karamazov*: 'If there is no God, everything is permitted.' By affirming the hypothesis that there is a God, I affirm that certain things are right and certain things are wrong. Take away the hypothesis that there is a God who not only exists but who cares about what kind of people we are, and except for the fact that I might get arrested, why shouldn't I do wrong? Why shouldn't I kill and steal and commit adultery? There would be no reason not to. Then the weak could fall victim to the strong and there would be nobody to stop it."[301]

Professor Seyyed Hossein Nasr, a professor of Islamic Studies at George Washington University argues that the West's infatuation with secularization is resulting in its destroying itself. "The phenomenon of post-modernism in the West questions not only religion in the West, but modernity itself…with unbelievable social dislocations, which are getting more and more severe every year, we in America are destroying the very environment which feeds us."[302]

Secularism is religion's rival for the control of the public sphere. It is antithetical to democracy and its fundamental premise of a society built on the rule of law. Secularism "is a system of thought that limits itself to human existence here and now in exclusion of man's relation to God here and hereafter. In short, it is the practical exclusion of God from human thinking."[303]

Pope John Paul II taught us that, "this secularism cannot but undermine the sense of sin. At the very most, sin will be reduced to what offends man. But it is precisely here that we are faced with a bitter experience…that man cannot build a world without God but this world will end by turning against him."[304] Moreover, he argues that religious freedom could help the U.S. advance toward the ideals of its founders. "Do not be afraid to search for God," he advises. Then it will truly be the land of the free and the home of the brave."[305]

In framing the Declaration of Independence, the Founders drew authority for their cause from the "Creator," acknowledged His pivotal role in the outcome of their effort, and sought His assistance.

The opening words state in clear and unambiguous words that, "When in the Course of human events, it becomes necessary for one people to dissolve the political bands which have connected them with another, and to assume among the powers of the earth, the separate and equal station to which the Laws of Nature and of Nature's God entitle them…"[306]

The American Revolution was based and carried out in the belief that it was the Creator's purpose and design. The very next paragraph, and arguably the most powerful declaration in support of individual freedom ever expressed, asserts, "We hold these Truths to be self-evident, that all Men are created equal, that they are endowed by their Creator with the unalienable Rights, that among these are Life, Liberty, and the Pursuit of Happiness..."[307] First, the Founders asserted that man's basic rights stemmed from a Creator and supported their claim by postulating that the truth concerning these rights and their God-given nature is not novel or known to just a few but self-evident.

The signers of the Declaration, knowing that they were risking their lives, property, and sacred honor, appealed to God to bless their cause and publicly acknowledged that the success of their effort depended on a "firm Reliance on the Protection of divine Providence..."[308] Even before the onset of the American Revolution, the First Continental Congress began its September 7, 1774 opening session with a call to God for help. "Plead my cause, O Lord, with them that strive with me, fight against them that fight against me. Take hold of buckler and shield, and rise up for my help...Say to my soul, 'I am your salvation.' Let those be ashamed and dishonored who seek my life; let those be turned back and humiliated who devise evil against me," read the Episcopal clergyman who read the first official prayer from the 35th Psalm.[309] Then, as the Revolution was intensifying, the Continental Congress proposed a day of fasting with the intent of seeking God's assistance. "Resolved, That it be recommended to all the United States, as soon as possible, to appoint a day of solemn fasting and humiliation; to implore of Almighty God the forgiveness of the many sins prevailing among all ranks, and to beg the countenance and assistance of his Providence in the prosecution of the present just and necessary war," read the Fast Day Proclamation of December 11, 1776.[310]

Not only did the Founders appeal to God for his continued help, they saw in the success of their revolution, the hand of God. In fact, it was hard not to acknowledge that there must have been some form of divine intervention. At the start of the American Revolution, Great Britain was the world's foremost superpower, the colonies were badly disorganized and lacking of both money and munitions, and a large portion of the population remained loyal to British rule. Few could reasonably have expected that the colonies would have had the audacity and courage to seek to fight for their independence, much less succeed in defying the enormous and even impossible odds against them. Even the weather, as if by Divine Providence, seemed to work in favor of the American Army. At a time when Washington's Army appeared hopelessly trapped on Long Island, a dense but benevolent fog rolled in for almost 12 hours allowing them to evacuate safely[311] Mere chance could not possibly have provided such luck. It had to be something more, the Founders believed. "It is impossible for the man of pious reflection not to perceive in it a finger of the Almighty hand which has been so frequently and signally extended to our relief in the critical states of the revolution."[312]

Not surprisingly, in recognition of religion's importance, George Washington prohibited blasphemy by his troops during the American Revolution. He and those who pledged to each other their "lives," "fortunes," and "sacred honor" saw the American Revolution as a sort of crusade whose outcome rested on God's protection.[313] As they felt that victory depended on God's favor, the Founders, including George Washington, didn't want his troops doing anything that might debase them in the eyes of their fellow citizens and more importantly incur and put them in disfavor with divine Providence.

The Founders' conviction that God had intervened actively and frequently in aiding them during the American Revolution also confirmed in their minds the truth in the Old Testament revelation of a personally interested and engaged Creator, one that has intervened time and again to help His people, even when they had frequently strayed from His ways and defied His will. The "God who gave us life," Thomas Jefferson stated, "gave us liberty at the same time."[314]

As a result, once the American Revolution was won, and when the Founders, in organizing the governance of the new nation, entrusted the freedoms and powers to individual citizens, they also assumed that religion would be the bedrock on which the new nation's morality under their Creator would rest. Morality, they knew, was crucial to the success of their noble but unprecedented experiment in democracy. Religion "is a wellspring of the civic virtues that democracy requires in order to flourish," [315] writes scholar William Bennett.

Almost a decade later when they sought adoption of the U.S. Constitution, the Founders maintained their appeal to God. "[L]et our gratitude mingle an ejaculation to Heaven for the propitious concord [the proposed Constitution of the United States] which has distinguished the consultations for our political happiness," Madison and Hamilton wrote in Federalist No. 20.[316]

Nearly a century later after the bloody battle of Gettysburg in 1863, President Abraham Lincoln acknowledged the still inseparable relationship between the United States and God. In his Gettysburg Address, he honored the dead, recognized God, and pledged that the American experiment would go on. "It is rather for us to be here dedicated to the great task remaining before us—that from these honored dead we take increased devotion to that cause for which they gave the last full measure of devotion—that we here highly resolve that these dead shall not have died in vain—that this nation, under God, shall have a new birth of freedom—and that government of the people, by the people, for the people, shall not perish from the earth."[317]

Finally, religion also plays an important community role. Indeed, it is a pillar on which the notion of community depends. Harvard University professor of public policy, Robert D. Putnam writes, "Regular worshipers and people who say that religion is very important to them are much more likely than other people to visit friends, to entertain at home, to attend club meetings, and to belong to sports groups; professional and academic societies; school service groups; youth groups; service clubs; hobby or garden clubs; literary, art, discussion, and study groups; school fraternities and sororities; farm organizations; political clubs; nationality groups; and other miscellaneous groups. In one survey of twenty-two different types of voluntary associations, from hobby groups to professional associations to veterans groups to self-help groups to sports clubs to service clubs, it was membership in religious groups that was most closely associated with other forms of civic involvement, like voting, jury service, community projects, talking with neighbors, and giving to charity."[318] Again, we see the interrelated nature of the fabric of American life. More importantly, we see that religion is a key to producing informed, vigilant, and engaged citizens on which the nation's democracy depends if it is to remain effective.

Conclusion

Although this chapter is lengthy and fairly detailed in its analysis of the evolution of what became modern American culture and values, it provides necessary context and background information for citizens who are concerned about their country's fate. Citizens need to understand that the broader national culture can change, as the evolution of modernist culture demonstrates, and that the consequences of such potential changes merit attention particularly at this juncture in time when the United States faces the uncertainty and enormous challenges of adapting to the 21ˢᵗ century's emerging realities and the dangers of the ongoing war on terrorism.

As the United States finds itself in a time and place in which it is confronted by both institutional and national security challenges, it could well also face new challenges to its culture. Countries and their institutions are, in general, most vulnerable to these pressures during trying times. In fact, the whole process that led to the evolution of modernist American culture gained impetus at a time when the U.S. was faced both with the task of having to adapt to the ramifications of an Industrial Revolution that was sweeping the nation and soon thereafter occurring the hardship of the Great Depression.

At the opening of the 21st century, the prospects of such cultural change are arguably greater than in the past. With technology and travel eroding the barriers of distance and time, increasingly frequent and intense cross-cultural contact is all but certain. Such contact is not necessarily a bad thing. At its best, it could well help enrich American culture.

At the same time, it could also bring about a competition of alternative values. Some of such alternative values might be at times antithetical to the nation's founding principles and incompatible with the long-term interests of its democratic governance and institutions.

History demonstrates that there is no such thing as a fixed or permanent culture. Even long-standing cultures tend to change slowly over time. As a result, the future state of the nation's culture should not be taken for granted.

How the U.S. culture evolves in the 21st century, even if its changes appear almost subliminal in the context of everyday events and concerns, it matters greatly. In a successful democratic society, a nation's culture forms the proverbial glue that ties together its institutions and citizens. It is the invisible and informal substance that defines who we are and whom we will become as a people and country.

Our culture can nurture and reinforce America's free society and democratic institutions. At the same time, however, it can also erode its freedoms and democratic institutions.

The cultural changes that occurred in the United States, beginning late in the 19th century and thereafter accelerating during the 20th century, were comprised of both homegrown and imported elements. Homegrown innovations included the rise of destabilizing academic tools such as linguistic de-constructionism and other philosophical and political underpinnings ranging from those of Rousseau to Marx.

This new culture was founded, in part, on principles such as moral and cultural relativism, political correctness, and equal outcomes. Its policy approaches involved identity politics, multiculturalism, and preferences. Rather than seeking to enhance the nation's unity among its diverse population, its emphasis too often was on divisiveness, pitting one group against another.

By the late 20th century, not only had the U.S. Government expanded to a role far larger and intrusive than that envisioned by the nation's founders, some of the nation's key value-transmitting institutions such as education were increasingly disseminating values of a counterculture that differed markedly from those that prevailed for much of the American experience.

While many of the policies and the values on which they rested were advanced in order to address genuine social problems and injustices (ranging from the social transformation brought about by the nation's industrialization, the need for civil rights, etc.) and to appeal to the public's sense of fairness (initially premised on the idea of equal opportunity but transformed by the counterculture into a pursuit of equal results), the actual values and policies were at times ineffective and even counterproductive. For example, the vast welfare system that ballooned during the New Deal and Great Society years imposed an enormous new cost- and regulatory-structure on American taxpayers that largely endures to this day. Some have even argued that is has brought about the real threat of a new arrangement that can be described as "custodial democracy" as noted earlier. At the same time, if one examines poverty statistics, the decrease in poverty actually slowed in the years following the institution of the Great Society. During the rise of the counterculture, the United States also witnessed explosive growth in policymaking without appropriate checks and balances through judicial activism and the promulgation of regulations. Such policymaking runs counter to the integrity of representative government as it allows for the de facto establishment of laws outside of the legislative process for which final accountability of lawmakers rests with the voters. Consequently, it is important that citizens understand among the following:

- The nation's culture can and does change.

- New cultural values may arise from within the United States or be imported from abroad.

- These new values may or may not be consistent with the fundamentals and needs of free and democratic society.

- Citizens need to examine such values or emergent values against the democratic and institutional context on which the United States was established.

- Citizens need to recognize that the culture helps determine the most fundamental relationships among members of society, both within the public sphere of civil society and in private family life.

- In the current era of globalism and challenge presented by international terrorism, the culture will likely see pressures for change that could bring either benefits and/or drawbacks.

This chapter provides an extensive framework that sets forth the evolution of America's culture to its present state. It also identifies some encouraging trends that have manifested themselves in more recent years. This analysis also forms a body of knowledge that can help encourage citizens to remain engaged and informed on matters of public policy and national culture with the understanding that not only are both interrelated and complementary, but also that their relationship is a crucial one during the current period of challenge that is facing the United States.

4

The State of American Public Education

Today, public primary and secondary education is big business. More than 40 million students are enrolled in America's public schools.[319] Simultaneously, annual public school expenditures approach $290 billion or roughly $5,900 per student.[320] While there are many good public schools, there are at least as many mediocre ones, especially in the inner cities.

> The substitute listened patiently as his third-graders attempted to read. One by one, they faltered. Not one could string more than a few words together. It was a most dismal but not unexpected performance. This particular class was rated near the bottom in its school, located in a heavily Hispanic neighborhood in New York City. Suddenly, one of the girls breezed flawlessly through her selection. The substitute was stunned. After class, he asked the girl what she was doing in a class for bad readers. Surely, something was wrong. The little girl responded that she had been placed in the class because the authorities believed she was "a bad reader who had fantasies of being a better reader than she was." The girl was frustrated but could do little. The substitute then had her read from her brother's sixth grade text. Again, she succeeded. He then brought her case to the principal. The principal was astonished at the substitute's "nerve." How dare a lowly substitute question her decision? He would be better leaving such matters as this to the "experts." Besides, the principal argued, the girl had probably memorized what she had read beforehand, of course, even if she had, with all due respect for the "experts' expertise," this would hardly have been the work of a dim student. The substitute persisted. Reluctantly, the principal agreed to test the girl. The girl succeeded and was moved to a class appropriate for a pupil of her abilities. Some twenty years later, the girl, Milagros Maldonado, was honored as one of Manhattan's teachers of the year, and the substitute, John Taylor Gatto, was named New York State Teacher of the Year in 1991.[321]

Tragically, the Milagros Maldonado story plays itself out repeatedly. For many, there is no happy ending. However, this is just the tip of the iceberg. America's poorly performing public schools, many of which are concentrated in urban areas[322], continue to put the lives of millions of children[323] and ultimately the nation's future at risk.

Worst of all, the plight of America's public schools is not news. Rather, it is an old story that just won't go away. Fifteen years after The National Commission on Excellence in Education warned, "educational foundations of our society are presently being eroded by a rising tide of mediocrity that threatens our very future as a Nation and a people" If "an unfriendly foreign power had attempted to impose on America the mediocre educational performance that exists today, we might well have viewed it as an act of war."[324] Surprisingly little has changed. Although efforts for reforms have been initiated in many instances, much of the ground lost since 1960, during the country's slide toward mediocrity, has still not been recovered. Urban schools remain as bad as ever.

The deficiencies in America's underperforming public schools, along with other factors, take a tremendous toll on the children unlucky enough to become ensnared in their classrooms. Many lose the desire to learn, their orientation in the much larger world around them, and their sense of the past which defines them and helps point the way to the future.

John Taylor Gatto explains, "The children I teach are indifferent to the adult world..." they "have almost no curiosity..." and they "have a poor sense of the future, of how tomorrow is inextricably linked to today."[325] He continues, "The children I teach are ahistorical; they have no sense of how the past has predestinated their own present, limiting their choices, shaping their values and lives."[326]

In other words, a sizable portion of America's children, who comprise the nation's future, are either culturally illiterate or in danger of becoming culturally illiterate. Cultural literacy is far broader and more important than the ability to read. "To be culturally literate is to possess the basic information needed to thrive in the modern world," writes Professor E. D. Hirsch, Jr. of the University of Virginia adding, "The breadth of that information is great, extending over the major domains of human activity from sports to science."[327] At least equally important, cultural literacy is also the gateway to opportunity. "Cultural literacy constitutes the only sure avenue of opportunity for disadvantaged children, the only reliable way of combating the social determinism that now condemns them to remain in the same social and educational condition as their parents. That children from poor and [culturally] illiterate homes tend to remain poor and [culturally] illiterate is an unacceptable failure of our schools..." Hirsch declares.[328]

Ailing Public Education

Despite The National Commission on Excellence in Education's clarion call for fundamental reform, many of America's public primary and secondary schools are not providing their students quality educations. There is ample evidence that they are not providing them with the information and skills necessary to prepare them for their responsibilities as citizens, for higher education, and for their careers.

In spite of the increasing flurry of recent political and public attention education has garnered[329] and such input-oriented reforms as reduced pupil-teacher ratios[330], the problems plaguing the nation's public schools remain serious and largely unsolved.

One of the most important and reliable barometers signaling the health of the nation's public school system is the performance of American children on standardized tests.[331] Signs of growing difficulties first manifested themselves in the early 1960s as SAT (the Scholastic Aptitude Test, now known as the Scholastic Assessment Test) scores began to fall and public concern slowly gathered. For nearly two decades the scores fell steadily and significantly before stabilizing then rising somewhat. By 1980, the combined verbal and math SAT score fell to 890 from 978 in 1963, a decline of almost 9 percent.[332] Since then math score has recovered, but the verbal score remains well below its former level. By 1994, the mean math score was still 5 percent below its 1962 level, while the verbal score was almost 12 percent lower.[333] When the fact that SAT grading procedures were changed during this period is taken into consideration, the decline in scores grows even larger.[334]

As SAT scores fell, critics attempted to explain away the change as a statistical anomaly due, not to declining educational quality, but to the fact that larger numbers of students were taking the exam. In the past, they argued, only the elite took the exam. Now, the average student was increasingly taking the exam. A closer look at the statistics shatters this myth.

Although the number of test-takers increased by more than 50,000 between 1962 and 1983, the number of students scoring above 700 (the academic superachievers) on the verbal section of the exam fell sharply during this 20-year period.[335] "Rot at the top" had set in, reported Charles Sykes who has written numerous books dealing with educational issues.[336]

"Before the College Board disclosed the full statistics in 1984, anti-alarmists could argue that the fall in average verbal scores could be explained by the rise in the number of disadvantaged students taking the SATs," Hirsch argues. "That argument can no longer be made....To be precise, out of a constant pool of about a million test-takers each year, 56 percent more students scored above 600 in 1972 than did so in 1984....the percentage drop was even greater for those scoring above 650—73 percent."[337]

Furthermore, a blue-ribbon panel established by The College Board headed by Willard Wirtz found that increased test-takers had contributed to the decline in SAT scores until roughly 1970. After 1970, the population taking the SAT had stabilized, yet the decline in SAT scores accelerated.[338]

Of course, SAT scores were not the only standardized exam scores that fell. Scores on other standardized exams dropped as well. The National Assessment of Educational Progress (NAEP) which measures the academic performance of the nation's 9-, 13-, and 17-year-olds reported that science scores, though improving recently remained lower in 1996 than in 1969. Despite moderate gains in math scores since the early 1980s, math scores are about the same or somewhat higher than they were in 1973. Reading scores are generally higher than those registered in 1971, and writing scores are roughly the same as they were in 1984.[339]

Since 1990, however, with the exception of science where academic performance has continued to improve strongly and math where there have been slight gains, academic performance in reading and particularly writing has been declining.[340]

Despite an emerging consensus that the quality of education has improved somewhat in recent years, a closer look at the statistics presents a potentially disturbing situation that merits greater investigation than is possible in this book. Early schooling (through the age of 13 or eighth grade) may have improved since 1990 while later schooling (after the age of 13 or eighth grade) may have deteriorated significantly in important areas.[341] This trend, if further substantiated, would not bode well for American primary and secondary education, particularly as it appears to be evolving at a time when the public's attention has increasingly been focused on education.

When it comes to international comparisons, American students do far worse than their foreign counterparts. The results of the Third International Math and Science Study, which tested students in 41 countries at ages 9 and 13 and in their last year of high school during the 1994–95 school year, placed Americans 28th in math and 18th in science. U.S. students averaged 143 points below first-place Singapore in math and 73 points below first-place Singapore in science. Overall, U.S. students scored 13 points below the world average in math and just 18 points above the world average in science.[342]

Put another way, just 5 percent of American eighth graders would have placed in the top 10 percent of test-takers in math and 13 percent in science. In contrast, 45 percent of Singapore's students would have placed in the top 10 percent in math and 31 percent would have placed in the top 10 percent in science.[343] This means that, at the very least, America's pool of elite students is shallower than that of Singapore and perhaps that of numerous other nations as well.

Standardized test scores and international comparisons are not the only indicator of weak performance. Increased remediation in higher education is another distinct sign that things are not well in American primary and secondary education.

Presently, nearly one-third of all new freshmen entering the nation's campuses, including more than half of those enrolling in the California state system, need remedial courses to overcome their lack of preparation for university-level work.[344] Moreover, the number of freshmen enrolling in remedial courses is either holding steady or increasing on most campuses.[345] Not coincidently, American universities and colleges have been driving the rigor out of their curricula, eliminating core requirements, and rapidly expanding a cafeteria menu of relatively mushy electives.[346] Even then, the United States suffers from one of the highest university dropout rates in the industrialized world.[347]

When it comes to serving minorities, the performance of America's elementary and secondary schools has been mixed. When it comes to the Black dropout rate, the nation's schools have all but eliminated the huge disparity between Blacks and Whites.[348] Today, 10 percent of Blacks fail to earn a high school diploma as opposed to 9.7 percent of Whites.[349] However, very little progress has been made when it comes to cutting the Hispanic dropout rate. Currently 24.7 percent of Hispanics fail to complete their high school education.[350] This situation is mirrored in differences between racial and ethnic groups on assessment exams. Generally, the Black-White gap has narrowed, however, the Hispanic-White gap has narrowed little and even widened in some cases in recent years.[351] This lack of progress is very worrisome given the expected rapid growth of the Hispanic population.

One of the major consequences of the shortcomings of the American primary and secondary education system is that employers are having difficulty finding workers who have the skills and attitudes that they require.[352] Some of this difficulty is due to the tight labor market, particularly with regard to highly-skilled, technologically-sophisticated positions. However, the Hudson Institute's Richard Judy and Carol D'Amico point out, some of the skilled labor shortage is due to the "increasingly desperate need to overhaul the country's public-education systems."[353]

A survey of Fortune 500 CEOs found that students coming into the current workforce were "dramatically lacking in higher-level thinking skills, the ability to diagnose and solve problems, and the fundamentals of math, reading and writing." In addition, the CEOs said that a majority of new workers lacked initiative, the ability to work effectively in groups, and were unable to apply what knowledge they had to solving new and unfamiliar problems.[354] In a recent survey of 450 New York City business leaders, only 10 percent of respondents said that a high school diploma demonstrated that a given student mastered basic schools and two-thirds said that the problems plaguing the city's schools were widespread.[355] Of course, this finding is not confined to the New York City area. A poll conducted by Public Agenda found eight in ten employers said recent graduates lacked basic grammar and spelling skills.[356] A follow up poll by Public Agenda found that 32% of employers who hire new public high school graduates think the graduates have the skills they need. Moreover, the percentage of students they ranked as having fair or poor skills increased in every area except computer skills.[357]

The business leaders surveyed were not talking exclusively about graduates with advanced skills. "It is almost impossible to hire competent clerical and/or entry-level help for administrative work from the New York City schools," the chief financial officer of an advertising agency wrote. "Our recent successful hires were from Illinois, Toronto, Ireland, etc."[358]

Today, American companies spend more than $30 billion annually teaching their new employees the basic skills that is more properly the responsibility of the primary and secondary education system.[359]

Public sentiment, while less harsh than that of the employers, also corroborates a need to improve elementary and secondary education with near unanimous agreement that the need for urban education reform was urgent. When asked in a 1998 Phi Delta Kappa/Gallup Poll how they would grade the public schools in their community, 46 percent of respondents gave them an A or B and 45 percent gave them a C or less. However, when asked how they would grade public schools in the nation, just 18 percent gave them an A or B and 69 percent graded them C or lower.[360] Given that people generally have confidence in their own abilities to make choices, it is not surprising that they viewed their communities' schools as being far better than those nationwide.[361] Even then, a large number lacked confidence in the public schools in their communities. In fact, in a separate CNN/Gallup poll, 53 percent of Americans said that they were dissatisfied with their local schools.[362]

When asked to evaluate the effectiveness of public schools, a growing plurality said that they were getting worse. Even among public school parents, the most optimistic group for essentially the same reason as those who have believe their communities' schools are better than the nation's, confidence was eroding.[363]

When it comes to improving inner-city schools, 86 percent of respondents believe the need is very important and 96 percent believe the need is either very important or fairly important. Nine years ago in 1989, 74 percent felt the need was very important and 93 percent felt it was either fairly important or very important.[364]

Naturally, opinion surveys reflect what individuals and parents say. What they do is even more important. Again, current trends reflect a growing assessment that public education is in serious trouble. Between 1965 and 1980, prior to the ongoing Era of Reform, public school enrollment increased by 9.1 percent and private school enrollment fell by 3.4 percent. Since 1980, however private school enrollment been increasing at a slightly faster rate than public school enrollment. From 1980 to 1995, public school enrollment rose 10.8 percent, while private school enrollment increased grew 11.3 percent. Even more impressive than the accelerating growth of private school enrollment is the explosion in home schooling where parents are choosing to educate their children at home. In 1985, roughly 50,000 students were home schooled. In 1995, that figure had grown to between 500,000 and 750,000 according to Patricia Lines of the U.S. Department of Education.[365] Some estimate that the home schooling number is substantially higher, perhaps 1.2 million.[366] In any case, home schooling has grown rapidly in recent years.

Today, some twenty years into the Era of School Reform[367] the state of American public education is not good. Proficiency scores, particularly international comparisons, are troubling. There are emerging signs that recent gains may be fizzling out. Educational progress for minorities, particularly Hispanics remains poor. Business leaders lack confidence in the public education system. Parents are not strongly confident in public schools. Many are increasingly seeking alternatives for their children.

Deficiencies uncovered by one indicator or another might point to a confined, relatively easy-to-address problem. Together, the strong consensus of all these indicators of educational performance point to widespread difficulties that remain unresolved even as the public and political leaders increasingly focus on education issues. Well into the Era of School Reform, the nation's children still cannot count on "an educational system which will provide opportunities to excel."[368]

What is the Problem?

The nation's public school system as a whole, despite pockets of excellence scattered around the country, is achieving poor results because it has failed to carry out its basic mission to provide its students with the information and skills necessary to prepare them for their responsibilities as citizens, for higher education, and for their careers. Instead, America's public schools have become increasingly fad-driven with little coherent sense of purpose, much less a commitment to performance.

"Whether the issue is reading or mathematics, outcome-based education or open classrooms, public schooling in this country lurches from one trend to its opposite with alarming speed and little forethought," many educators now argue, reports Ethan Bronner of *The New York Times*.[369] Worse still, many of the trends being embraced then discarded are not new ideas. Rather, they are previously failed ideas from the past that have been simply repackaged and stamped "new and improved."[370] With such an approach, the outcome of most educational reform proposals should not be in doubt. They have failed before and they will fail again. "The main experience of education historically is that of failed efforts," says Professor Gerald Graff of the University of Chicago's School of Education.[371]

How then do the educators justify their repackaged, doomed-to-fail reforms? They argue that the reforms failed, not because they were inherently flawed or just plain bad ideas, but because they were never "properly" tried.[372] Thereafter, the once-failed reforms are resurrected and tried again (though not properly), and again the result is no different from what it was when the particular reforms were first attempted.

Even though school reforms have mostly been failures, one would hope that there would be near universal agreement on what is the purpose of public education and the role public schools must play. Not so. "Almost everyone's first impulse is to think that the purpose of schools is to provide children with academic training, with essential information about society and the world, with an understanding of citizenship in a democracy…," John Chubb and Terry Moe of the Brookings Institution observe. "On reflection, however, it should be apparent that schools have no immutable or transcendent purpose. What they are supposed to be doing depends on who controls them and what those controllers want them to do."[373] In other words, they do pretty much what they please.

This is not to say that there is no consensus on anything among the educators who comprise the public school system as well as among those in the Schools of Education who train them. One of the hottest rages now sweeping the education landscape is the notion of "student-centered" classrooms. There, traditional teaching is considered too authoritarian, a fixed curriculum is considered stifling, and learning depends on what students want to learn with teachers acting as mere "facilitators."[374] In the late 1990s, American public education is bubbling with cooperative learning, alternative assessment techniques (tests show bad performance therefore they are bad measures), cultivation of positive self-esteem and good feelings[375] a far cry from the hard-core academic work that was once the bedrock of American public education. For many, this change might be shocking, but it should not be. In today's politically correct, hypersensitive culture, there is little place for hard work and rigorous standards.

Not unexpectedly, the results of the new "enlightened" approach to primary and secondary education are not encouraging. Given that schools can now do pretty much what they please, the explanation for their continuing difficulties is that schools are asked to do too much.[376] For once, there is some truth to this account. "Today, schools have many more purposes than they had decades ago," report Chubb and Moe who note that some observers, primarily those who studied effective schools, have found "the proliferation of school objectives is a serious problem. It has robbed schools of any clear sense of purpose and caused schools to lower their academic expectations for most students."[377] "By abandoning their basic mission, public schools have been trying to do everything for everybody in order to satisfy increasing demands the public and political leaders have been placing on them. "In some of our national moods we would like the schools to teach everything, but they cannot," Hirsch states, adding, "There is a pressing need for clarity about our educational priorities."[378]

Restoring the Purpose of Primary and Secondary Education

The fundamental purpose of primary and secondary education must be to provide students with (1) a common literacy crucial to their becoming well-informed, engaged citizens, (2) a basic framework of analytical skills and knowledge needed for productive work, higher education, and continual learning, and (3) opportunities that will nurture their development into distinct persons.

Expressed another way, the singular purpose of primary and secondary education is to advance student learning says urban educator Anthony Alvarado.[379]

More than anything else, the well-being of the American Republic depends on a literate and informed citizenry.[380] "If a nation expects to be ignorant and free, in a state of civilization, it expects what never was and never will be," Thomas Jefferson warned.[381]

A literate and informed citizenry requires, in part, a common knowledge base and common values that make possible universal public discourse. "People cannot effectively meet in the classroom or in the marketplace unless they can communicate with and learn from each other," Hirsch declares. "A shared public culture that enables public communicability is essential to an effective community at every age and stage of life."[382] For our country to function, citizens must be able to reach some common understandings on complex issues, often on short notice and on the basis of conflicting or incomplete evidence," The National Commission on Excellence in Education stated in its landmark report, A Nation At Risk.[383] Teaching cultural literacy, as this education in a shared body of knowledge is called, is considered a priority by today's parents. In a study funded, in part, by the National Education Association (NEA), 85 percent of parents said that it is necessary that "kids, whatever their racial or ethnic background, learn that we are all part of one nation."[384]

The notion of shared values was particularly important to the nation's Founders. Virtually all of the Founding Fathers who commented on the purpose of education wanted schools to teach "fundamental values and provide moral instruction."[385] What they had in mind was not so much religious instruction but education in the values integral to the functioning of a democratic form of government.[386] Such a republic requires "an understanding of the rule of law; an appreciation of liberty and the constitutional principles that preserve it; and respect for the life, liberty, property, and opinions of others," notes author David Harmer.[387] "Democratic government makes the idea of political rights penetrate right down to the least of citizens," observed Alexis de Tocqueville.[388]

Primary and secondary education must also provide students with the requisite skills and knowledge needed for productive work, higher education, and continual learning if they are to succeed and the nation is to prosper.

"The best jobs created in the Innovation Age will be filled by Americans (and workers in other advanced countries) to the extent that workers possess the skills required to compete for them and carry them out...If jobs go unfilled in the U.S. because we haven't sufficient skilled workers to fill them, they will quickly migrate elsewhere in our increasingly global economy," predict Richard Judy and

Carol D'Amico of the Hudson Institute.[389] In the survey of Fortune 500 CEOs, "All respondents emphatically included teaching of analytical, logical, higher-order, conceptual, and problem-solving skills, which in their collective judgment, are vital if this country is to remain globally competitive."[390]

With technological change and globalization transforming the world, higher education is becoming of paramount importance.[391] Therefore, it is especially important that primary and secondary educational institutions ensure that their graduates possess the requisite skills and abilities to fully benefit from a university education.

The current dynamic global business environment increasingly necessitates that learning become continual. Learning must now take place at home, in school, and in the workplace. "Because the entire economy, not just its low-cost production sectors, will face competition from lower-paid but highly skilled foreign workers, virtually everyone will need the kind of education that allows them to continuously learn new skills and develop new lines of work," report Paul Hill and Lawrence Pierce of the University of Washington and James Guthrie of Vanderbilt University.[392] The new jobs [in a knowledge-based economy] require a good deal of formal education and the ability to acquire and to apply theoretical and analytical knowledge...Above all they require a habit of continuous learning," Peter Drucker adds.[393]

Finally, with innovation and creativity becoming ever more critical to individual and business success, primary and secondary education must also help students develop into their own unique selves. "Whatever an education is, it should make you a unique individual, not a conformist; it should furnish you with an original spirit with which to tackle the big challenges; it should help you find the values which will be your road map through life...," argues John Taylor Gatto.[394] It must help ensure the American man or woman remain a person of, what De Tocqueville described more than a century ago, "burning desires, enterprising, adventurous, and above all, an innovator."[395] These traits are what have made discovery, invention, and entrepreneurship so decisive in the American experience.

Dumbing Down America

Notwithstanding the significant challenges it faces, America's public education system is a major contributor to the dumbing down of the nation. These are not isolated problems confined to urban educational wastelands.[396] They represent an institutional problem[397] that has proven largely resistant to the reforms of the last twenty years.

The biggest problems include a lack of commitment to academic achievement and excellence, grade inflation and social promotion. Also occurring is a continuous assault on standardized tests and other objective measures of achievement by the education establishment, together with an ongoing deterioration in the quality of teachers and their education training. Finally, there has been a misplaced emphasis on special programs for various constituencies, except of course the gifted. Individually, each of these situations presents a serious challenge to the education system. Together they interact with one another and they are even more damaging.

The Retreat from Academic Excellence

One of the most profound and troubling differences between modern public education and that of the past is the considerably diminished importance modern primary and secondary education places on hard work and academic achievement. "There was, once, a clear value expressed implicitly and explicitly throughout our schools: 'work plus discipline equals reward,' which was a long way of saying 'merit,'" Ben Wattenberg of the American Enterprise Institute says.[398] But this all changed as society adopted a new view that "poor student performance wasn't even the fault of the students; it was America's fault. And so, students were entitled to reward without hard work," Wattenberg continues.[399] Thus, on average, primary and secondary schools grew less demanding. Instead, they began offering wider ranges of courses and an expanding menu of electives.[400] "American children are not getting the science and mathematics education they deserve," warn William H. Schmidt, national research coordinator, and other scholars associated with the National Research Center for Third International Math and Science Study (TIMSS) at Michigan State University.[401]

In fact, one reason American 12th graders have fared so poorly on international comparisons with their peers abroad is that two-thirds of American 12th graders, according to Jeannie Oakes, an education professor at the University of California in Los Angeles, "Have never been in a classroom where these subjects are taught."[402] This lack of exposure to rigorous math is especially prevalent in inner city schools where a disproportionate number of minority students are educated. The College Board which administers the SAT exam says that a big reason for the large gap in the math scores of Black and White and Hispanic and White students is that minority students are not as likely to take demanding math courses as their White counterparts.[403] The international gap and domestic racial gap in academic achievement should not be surprising. "Research has shown...that course work is a key to student achievement," reports Chubb and Moe. "Students who take more academic courses and more courses that are academically rigorous tend to achieve more than students who do not."[404]

Even when American students have access to higher-caliber math, the quality of the lessons they receive is doubtful. When researchers at the University of California studied eighth-grade math lessons for the TIMSS, they ranked 23 percent of the lessons in Germany and 30 percent in Japan as high quality. In contrast, none of the U.S. lessons were rated as high quality and 87 percent were described as low quality.[405] Consequently, on the Second International Association for the Evaluation of Educational Achievement (IEA) study, U.S. high school students who were enrolled in calculus classes, generally the nation's top math students, could only muster average levels of achievement attained by their international peers.[406]

The retreat from academic excellence extends beyond course work. It has culminated in some schools stamping out anything that might bring recognition to student achievement. In *Dumbing Down Our Kids*, Charles Sykes catalogs a number of noteworthy recent examples. In one case, seven high schools in Fairfax County, Virginia have abolished class rankings. In another, Los Angeles schools implemented a revised grading scheme that eliminated the grade of "outstanding." The Illinois Junior Academy of Science, a private group dominated by state teachers, banned the Avery Coonley School from competing in the statewide science fair after the school won its fourth consecutive team prize.[407] The list goes on. The message is clear: achievement must not be rewarded. Indeed, Sykes recounts, Charles Willie, a professor of education at Harvard, asserts that the goal of education should not be "excellence" but "adequacy" and that non-traditional types of intelligence, such as "singing" and "dancing" should be treated as being of equal worth to "communication and calculation."[408]

The American retreat from academic excellence comes at a time when world standards are rising.[409] "The standard of literacy [cultural literacy which is broader than reading] required by modern society has been rising throughout the developed world, but American literacy rates have not risen to meet this standard," observes Hirsch. "What seemed an acceptable level in the 1950s is no longer acceptable...when only highly literate societies can prosper economically."[410]

Raising the Grades/Promoting Everyone

As standardized test scores fell or held steady over the last decade, one would reasonably expect that student report cards would mirror this trend. The opposite is true.

Although grade inflation is usually associated with higher education, recent evidence suggests grade inflation also exists at the primary and secondary education level as well. Some believe it may even have reached epidemic proportions. "I think grade inflation is rampant and has effected every single school. It's everywhere," G. David Hardman, Jr., director of admissions of the upper school at the St. Albans School for Boys remarked.[411] "Grade inflation has reached the point where even outstanding students accepted at the best law schools are often deficient in writing skills and need remedial courses," adds Boston University chancellor John Silber.[412]

The College Board reported that over the last 10 years, the number of test-takers with A averages grew from 28 percent of the total to 38 percent of the total. At the same time, the SAT scores of those students fell 12 points on the verbal section of the exam and 3 points on the math portion.[413] "Though higher numbers of people taking the SAT report getting A's, A-plus and A-minus grades, their actual performance on the test has declined over time," Jeffrey Penn, a spokesman for the College Board observed. "We see that as evidence of grade inflation."[414] Concerned about the possible existence of grade inflation, the College Board has commissioned a further study on the matter.[415] That grade inflation has either broken out or is rampant is no accident. In part, it relates to the need of schools to cultivate favorable public opinion when asking the public to support increases in education funding.[416] "There is some indication that the grades parents assign [their children's schools] are somewhat affected by the success their children have had in school," reads the findings of the 30th Annual Phi Delta Kappa/Gallup Poll of the Public's Attitudes Toward The Public Schools.[417] Nearly one-third more parents of high achievers assign high grades to their children's schools than those of average or below-average achievers.

Social promotion which involves moving students to the next grade level regardless of whether or not they merit it is another practice that typifies today's public schools. It is the first cousin of grade inflation, and may in fact be bolstered by grade inflation.

"Students are routinely passed [advanced to the next year or grade level] who do not have grade level competences...," Chester Finn told the U.S. Senate in February 1998.[418] The numbers are staggering. Since 1983, more than 10 million students have reached 12th grade without having learned to read at a basic level, 20 million have reached 12th grade without basic math skills, and 25 million have reached their senior year with an inadequate understanding of U.S. history.[419] A recent study revealed that more than half of City University students and almost half of State University of New York students would fail the U.S. Citizenship Test.[420] While it would be easy for some critics to brush off these dismal results, a study called "Losing America's Memory: Historical Illiteracy in the 21st Century," conducted by the American Council of Trustees contained news that is nothing short of scandalous. Fully 81% of seniors at the top 55 American colleges and universities received either a D or an F on history questions drawn from a basic high school curriculum.[421]

Acknowledging that New York City schools had been promoting students who did not deserve it, Schools Chancellor Rudy Crew pledged to hold back fourth and seventh graders unable to meet minimum standards for their grade level, starting in spring 2000, while admitting that nearly 50,000 current students would be affected should the policy be implemented immediately. Already the Chicago public school system and Colorado schools have adopted similar requirements.[422]

The practice of social promotion has major adverse implications for its intended beneficiaries and for society overall. "Social promotion kills an educational system," declared Paul Vallas, CEO of Chicago's public schools. "You have to lower your standards. You have to dummy down the curriculum. The children who are behind never get caught up. The children at grade level get taught to inferior standards."[423]

Lacking the requisite skills, they find it more difficult to succeed in college. This is documented by the growth in remedial education, the high college dropout rate, and finally poor performance in the workplace.

Even students themselves, the supposed beneficiaries of grade inflation and social promotion, overwhelmingly support and articulate the need for higher standards. In a public opinion survey of teenagers taken by Public Agenda in 1997, 74% of teenagers said that schools should only promote students to the next grade when they have learned what is expected of them, 75% said that they would work harder if more were demanded of them, and 76% said that students should not be permitted to graduate from high school unless they demonstrated a sufficient mastery of the English Language.[424]

Tarring the Messenger

Like the uninvited guest that wrecks the party, standardized tests have come under intense attack over the past two decades. They have been dismissed as flawed, biased, and irrelevant by their critics.[425]

"Articulate critics have charged that such tests measure only a narrow spectrum of abilities; that the tests by their very nature discourage creative and imaginative thinking; that the results of the tests have far too significant an effect on the life chances of young people; that the emphasis in a multiple-choice test is wrongly on 'the right answer' and on simplicity instead of thoughtful judgments; that the tests favor the advantaged over the disadvantaged while claiming to be neutral; and that the tests are inherently biased against those who are unfamiliar with the language and concepts of the majority culture. In short, say the critics, the tests corrupt education, subjugate millions of students to their mechanistic requirements, and limit access to educational opportunity, "writes Diane Ravitch.[426] Some civil rights leaders blame cultural bias in standardized tests for the large differences in Black-White scores, although in a recent survey of African-American parents, the majority rejected the bias argument.[427]

Criticisms aside, standardized tests, because they are objective measures, are an important diagnostic tool for measuring academic progress. Such objectivity is not possible with nonstandardized tests or other alternative measures of assessment.[428]

Standardized exams since they are objective, help identify student strengths and weaknesses and provide an estimation of a given student's academic ability. "My own view is that the tests have become increasingly controversial because they have become increasingly indispensable," Diane Ravitch observes.[429] "Without effective monitoring, neither good teaching nor good educational administration is possible," Hirsch notes.[430]

Teaching Mediocrity

As go the teachers, so go the schools. At least that is what, the National Commission on Teaching and America's Future found in a recent study which established that "teacher expertise is the single most important determinant of student achievement."[431] This report was not the first to link teaching to student achievement. "The differences in the teaching staffs of high and low performance schools appear to have much more to do with the quality of teacher service than with its quantity," wrote Chubb and Moe[432]

Good teachers also serve as bulwarks against ill-conceived fads that undermine the educational process.[433] Today, teaching quality appears to be a weak link in the public school system.

Presently, the nation's public schools employ almost 2 million teachers.[434] To put this figure in perspective, this army of educators significantly exceeds the number of active-duty personnel enlisted in the U.S. Military.[435] However, for all its size, the firepower of the nation's army of teachers is dangerously lacking.[436] This army could be further depleted by the fact that one-third of today's teachers are expected to retire over the next ten years.[437]

True, 95 percent of public school teachers hold university degrees,[438] but, as Diane Ravitch observes, "...huge numbers of teachers are teaching subjects in which they have neither a college major nor a minor."[439] These teachers are termed "out of field" teachers by the U.S. Department of Education. Ravitch adds that almost 40 percent of science teachers, 34 percent of math teachers, 25 percent of English teachers, 55 percent of history teachers, and roughly half of all inner-city teachers are "out of field."[440] This is an especially serious problem, as students generally learn more from teachers who have had more coursework in the subjects they teach.[441]

The matter of teacher quality is not the only thing undermining the teaching profession and school performance. Classroom environment also impacts academic achievement. Research has demonstrated that effective classrooms maximize learning time, experience fewer disruptions, spend less time on administrative tasks, and inspire students to remain focused on academics inside and outside the classroom.[442]

At present, the most commonplace form of teaching is "direct instruction" which can be traced to the turn of the 20th Century.[443] Such teaching can be effective, especially when combined with regular homework, presentation of new material in small steps, routine tests, and instructional reinforcement.[444] Nevertheless, this traditional teaching is often criticized for seeking "to impose the same content on every student, without taking into account the child's individual strengths, weaknesses, and interests..."[445] As these criticisms resound, alternative methods are catching on. In one notable experiment with new teaching, in 1987, the State of California replaced traditional phonics instruction (learning to read by sounding out the components of each word) with a literature-based method that avoided students' having to learn the mechanics of reading first. The results were dismal.[446]

Regardless of teaching method, few teachers, according to W. James Popham, establish clearly stated instructional objectives and then seek to achieve those objectives.[447] In fact, things have eroded to the point where former New York State Teacher of the Year John Taylor Gatto tells a story to describe the "seven lessons" that "are universally taught from Harlem to Hollywood Hills."[448] In this tale, the first lesson is confusion; everything that is taught is taken out of context, incoherent, or contradictory.[449] This situation closely resembles the plight of the nation's public schools in which they have lost sight of their basic mission and lurched from fad to fad.

The Decline in Public Education

Over the past several decades, the state of American public education has become the focus of increasing public and political concern. During that time, student performance on standardized tests fell, American students often wound up wearing the dunce cap in international comparisons, companies increasingly complained that their new employees lacked basic skills, and the nation's inner city schools had become intellectual wastelands. A "rising tide of mediocrity" was threatening the nation's future.[450]

The alarm bells were sounded and the reformers rushed to the rescue. Despite waves of reform, America's retreat from academic excellence continued, grade inflation reared its ugly head, and teachers grew less competent. An early recovery on standardized test scores that commenced in the 1980s began to evaporate by the 1990s.

On the surface, the reformers' inability to turnaround the underperforming public school system is a big mystery. Upon closer inspection, however, one can see that the climate for success remains unfavorable. Rather, it heralds more difficulty ahead.

American public education has eroded for five important reasons. First, it remains a virtual monopoly insulated from competitive pressures to improve performance. Second, reformers continue to focus most of their time and resources on input-oriented measures rather than establishing clear performance measures that can provide a basis for outcomes measurement. Third, schools of education are failing to develop outstanding or even competent teachers and inadequate programs exist for retraining teachers in mid-career. Fourth, powerful teacher unions coupled with a weak and ineffectual bureaucratic governance system have created a culture where there is no incentive to improve and little, if any, penalty for poor or failing performance.

More than 85 percent of all primary and secondary school students attend public schools[451], today many of which are experiencing difficulties. For most, particularly low-income families whose children are often relegated to crumbling urban schools, there is no other alternative. Indeed, it was this lack of alternatives for inner-city children that led Arthur Levine, president of Teachers College, Columbia University, to write of failing urban schools, "These schools damage children; they rob them of their futures. No parent should be forced to send a child to such a school. No student should be compelled to attend one....after much soul-searching, I have reluctantly concluded that a limited school voucher program is now essential for the poorest Americans attending the worst public schools."[452]

Without meaningful competition, few positive changes are likely. "The public school system has a virtual monopoly shielding it from pressures for reform while consuming more than $280 billion a year[453] in taxpayer money that is used to fund the nation's schools. This monopoly is a major reason behind the well-documented underperformance of the country's public school system.

By their nature, monopolies serve consumers poorly and are generally unlawful. In the case of schools, the affected consumers are children, their parents, and society overall. The consumers of the public school have no other alternative available and generally support higher levels of school funding rather than cuts in an attempt to increase school performance. As a result, the public school system has fewer built-in incentives for improvement and little penalty for poor performance. "The parent who would prefer to see money used for better teachers and texts rather than coaches and corridors has no way of expressing this preference except by persuading a majority to change the mixture for all," writes Milton Friedman.[454] When consumers cannot effectively exercise their will, they lose their importance to the monopoly. Not surprisingly, Joseph Sobran writes, "Education...has ceased to be concerned with the individual. It has become a form of mass production."[455] Harmer notes, "Since the government schools [public schools] have a captive market, they don't need to improve to keep their customers; most customers have nowhere else to go. Occasionally a great success story emerges...and most government schools keep right on doing what they were already doing. Success is barely observed; when in a free market it would be assiduously imitated."[456]

Insulated from competition, monopolies more often than not grow ever more bureaucratic. The public school system is no exception.[457] This has important consequences. As a rule, expanded bureaucracy is usually associated with worsened performance.[458] With regard to schools, worsened performance means lowered academic achievement.[459] "The government school system's insulation from competition foster an ambivalent attitude toward academic excellence," conclùdes David Harmer. "Excellence rarely if ever arises from ease; but the system's aversion to the challenge of the market is reflected in its reluctance to challenge its students."[460]

Finally, their size and captive market make monopolies fertile ground in which powerful, entrenched labor unions with enormous leverage and their socialist culture can take root. Not unexpectedly, today, the public schools' teachers are powerfully organized and their major trade association, the National Education Association (NEA) is one of the largest contributors to the Democratic Party.[461] Until their monopoly power becomes subject to competitive pressures, there exists an insurmountable obstacle for meaningful educational reform.

"If only stingy taxpayers would spare a little more money, schools could be excellent," goes the conventional thinking among educators. "Then schools would have more computers, more equipment, more teachers, and everything would be better." Although this argument might sound compelling, real world experience has demonstrated repeatedly again that the postulate "More Resources = Better Performance" just isn't true.

"Over the last two decades, as school performance has deteriorated and stagnated, per pupil spending on schools has increased nearly 100 percent after inflation, class sizes have shrunk more than 20 percent," observe Moe and Chubb.[462] "[I]f there's anything we have learned from thirty years of experience, it is that quantity-oriented programs do not boost educational achievement," Chester Finn, Jr. testified to the U.S. Senate.[463] Yet, the education debate invariably focuses on inputs. Thus, at the end of the day, school-spending increases, school performance in many areas continues to decline and at best, just muddles along. The taxpayer is left holding an increasingly larger bill.

A recent study by the Organization for Economic Cooperation and Development (OECD) shows that average U.S. school expenditures are the third highest of 22 OECD countries, yet U.S. students between the fourth and eighth grades made the least progress of the 17 OECD nations in math and the second least in science. These discouraging results come even as U.S. primary schools spend 75 percent more per student than the international average.[464] University of Rochester economist Eric Hanushek examined 400 separate studies of the effects of resources on student achievement and found that while a few studies showed that increased spending enhanced achievement, a few also showed that more spending hurt achievement, and most showed that it had no impact whatsoever.[465]

Apparently, spending is not the same thing as educating. How the money is spent matters more than how much is spent. Craig D. Jerald, one of the directors on a study pertaining to urban school performance, recounts, "Some districts, such as Washington, D.C. have spent heavily on administration rather than instruction, viewing the school system as a place to provide jobs for adults rather than educate young people."[466] The Washington, D.C. story is not an isolated example of misplaced priorities and wasteful spending. It is a microcosm for what takes place all across the country.

In its Education Savings and School Excellence Act of 1998, the Congress found, "While it is unknown exactly what percentage of Federal education dollars reaches the classroom, a recent audit of New York City public schools found that only 43 percent of their local education budget reaches the classroom. Further, it is thought that only 85 percent of funds administered by the Department of Education for elementary and secondary education reach the school district level; and even if 65 percent of Federal education funds reach the classroom, it still means that billions of dollars are not directly spent on children in the classroom."[467] Moreover, one of the other findings revealed that only 52 percent of the staff employed in public elementary and secondary school systems were teachers.[468] Even more disturbing, when increased federal funding was provided which resulted in New York City hiring an additional 800 teachers, only one out of two of these teachers had the proper certification.[469] This lack of certification greatly limited their classroom role. Worse still, there is no evidence that this experience was unique to the New York City schools.

Maybe more dollars do not necessarily make a difference, but more teachers and smaller class sizes do. Guess again. The old "Quantity is not Quality" maxim again comes into play. Since 1970, the pupil-teacher ratio has been falling steadily.[470] Since 1982, the number of public school teachers has increased 16 percent.[471] School performance, as was substantiated earlier, has not improved meaningfully. "No matter what the source of evidence, the answer about effectiveness is the same: Broad policies of class-size reduction are very expensive and have little effect on student achievement," Hanushek discloses from his survey of 277 studies on student-teacher ratios and their effect on student achievement.[472]

At the same time schools were adding teachers to their classrooms, they were busily acquiring computers and obtaining Internet access. During the 1984–85 school year there were 63.5 students per computer in the public schools. By the 1996–97 school year, that ratio had shrunk almost 90 percent to 7.3 students per computer.[473] In 1994, 35 percent of public schools had Internet access. Two years later, that figure had risen more than 85 percent to 65 percent of public schools.[474] To date, the classroom impact of adding computers is the same as that for the other boosts in inputs: largely nonexistent.

"[I]f computers make a difference, it has yet to show up in achievement," says Samuel Sava, executive director of the National Association of Elementary School Principals. He adds, "Teachers in five of the seven countries [whose 4th graders outperformed American students on the math portion of the TIMSS] reported that they 'never or almost never' have students use computers in class. The American teachers said that 37 percent of their students had used computers in at least some math lessons, triple the international average."[475]

Today, while the U.S. ranks near the top in all the educational resources, it ranks near the bottom in performance. "Most people would call this miserably low productivity, but that is a concept practically unknown in education-policy circles," declare Chester Finn, Jr. and Herbert Walberg.[476]

Perhaps if the nation's public schools were not a virtual monopoly insulated from the competitive forces of the marketplace, they would discover the concept of productivity which would lead them to a far better solution than their mantra "More Resources = Better Performance."

Although teacher quality is an important determinant of academic achievement, current admissions policies and the curricula of the nation's schools of education are creating a shortage of quality teachers. Many have confused the growing shortage in quality teachers with a broader shortage of teachers overall.[477] As with school resources, the problem lies not with quantity but with quality.

"Every year in this decade, colleges and universities have been awarding more than 100,000 bachelor's degrees in education, and the numbers continue to grow," remarks National Center for Education Information in Washington president Emily Feistritzer. But the quality of these new teachers is suspect or worse.[478] "As seasoned teachers retire they are being replaced by those who were educated in dysfunctional urban systems and teachers' colleges with no standards to speak of," writes columnist Brent Staples.[479] Something is amiss at the training grounds for the nation's future teachers.

A look at the country's schools of education uncovers two serious problems. First, the nation's education schools are accepting students who rank far below the caliber of those admitted into other programs of higher education. Second, their curriculum fails to provide the education and training required for future teachers to learn and the skills and expertise they need to become effective in their field.

Students admitted into the nation's colleges of education rank below the national average. In 1997, the average combined score for all students who took the SAT exam was 1,106. For those entering schools of education, the average was 964.[480]

The sub-par quality of those entering various schools of education is not a new phenomenon. It has been documented for many years. "Over time, I saw a steady decline in the quality of these future teachers," reported Sheila Schwartz who recently retired from the faculty of State University of New York (SUNY) at New Paltz, where she taught English education. "Many had writing skills that ranged from depressing to horrifying, especially when we remember that these same people eventually went on to teach writing to high school students."[481]

Schwartz is not the only one who has recognized the link between teacher skills and student achievement. "They [candidates for education degrees] are afraid of math; they are afraid of arithmetic; I'm not saying anything about geometry," says Tatyana Flesher, a math professor at Medgar Evers College in Brooklyn. "If they carry this attitude to the classroom, you will maybe have kids who don't know geometry."[482] Nationally syndicated columnist and author Thomas Sowell gets to the heart of the matter declaring, "...what is even more important than what these applicants lack intellectually is how dangerous such people are in our classrooms." International assessments of country-by-country comparative educational achievement also confirm the U.S. decline in teacher quality.

Some schools have been reluctant to raise their admission standards because of the experience of Boston University. As it raised the average SAT score for freshmen entering its education school to 1,227 Boston University wound up reducing its freshmen class by 75 percent and lost $35 million in tuition in the process.[483] This problem could, however, be mitigated by a phasing in of the increase in standards with advance notice to secondary schools of the new educational background required. The difficulties facing America's teacher colleges are not limited to their admission of ill-prepared applicants. Another major problem lies in how prospective teachers are prepared for their careers.

A rapid erosion of rigor from the curricula, not to mention the increasing mission of socialization, at American institutions of higher education[484] is also pervasive in the country's education schools. "We seem to have reached the point described in Kurt Vonnegut's futuristic short story, 'Harrison Bergeron," in which everyone must be drafted down to the lowest common denominator because, in a democracy, we don't want any hurt feelings," Schwartz observes.[485] This attitude is highly contagious and has already spread like wildfire through a large portion of America's schools.[486] "Schools are about many things, teacher educators say (depending on the decade), self-actualization, following one's joy, social adjustment, or multicultural sensitivity, but the one thing they are not about is knowledge," writes Heather MacDonald.[487]

Another thing many are not about is sufficient real-world training. *The Washington Times'* Education writer Carol Innerst reported, "...for years, legions of prospective teachers never set foot in a K-12 classroom until their senior year, when they were assigned to a local school for an obligatory semester or less of student teaching."[488] "In one class after another I was presented with fancy theories abut how best to teach students, from professors who hadn't been in a classroom in twenty years," one recent Master's graduate from Columbia University's Teachers College stated.[489]

Finally, teacher education schools have done little to address the problem of "out-of-field" teachers raised by Diane Ravitch. Legions of prospective teachers have been "free to take snap courses to fulfill their degree requirements. Many avoided solid courses in math, English, science and history, precisely the subjects they would have to teach in public school," Innerst says.[490] "That ideals of accommodating and integration still remain viable for mission-oriented enterprises is demonstrated by professional training schools that are in a healthy state, such as those for engineering, law, and medicine...Contrast that condition of cooperation with the glum and resentful isolation of education schools," writes Hirsch, Jr.[491]

Already states are taking action to head off the growing crisis afflicting America's education schools. Pennsylvania has enacted reforms that require prospective teachers to maintain a B average in liberal arts courses and in the subject area in which they wish to teach prior to their being admitted into schools of education. Texas now requires that 70 percent of a school's graduates, including 70 percent of each of its ethnic groups, pass the state's certification exam. New York now requires that 80 percent of those attending its schools of education pass a required certification exam.[492]

In Texas, New York, and the other 48 states, state education programs would have their work cut out for them. For example, in Texas, 40 percent of the state's teacher colleges would fail and could risk losing their accreditation in three years if they do not improve.[493] Also, in New York, in which as 28 percent of students pass their proficiency exams, more than one-quarter of its schools of education, including 40 percent of those in the CUNY system which supplies most of New York City's public school teachers, would fail.[494]

If America's primary and secondary schools are, in the words of the report released by the OECD, "by far the weakest link in the chain of human capital-building institutions,"[495] then teacher education might well be the weakest link in the nation's knowledge-building institutions. Considering the importance of good teachers and the present situation troubling America's primary and secondary education system, the need for improving teacher education is urgent. Virtually every school of education should take heed. As Silber acknowledged, "America became a literate country before there were any schools of education. We would be justified in demanding that schools of education either raise their standards or shut their doors."[496]

One of the largest and most influential roles played in the primary and secondary education arena is that of the public school teachers' unions. Together, the membership of the two largest unions, the National Education Association (NEA) and the American Federation of Teachers (AFT), exceeds 3 million persons.[497] Moreover, unlike in the private sector where the share of union membership has fallen, membership in the teachers' unions has increased briskly. Between 1961 and 1995, the NEA saw its membership nearly triple and membership in the AFT increased more than thirteen-fold.[498] On the financial front, the NEA's budget amounted to $230 million for the fiscal year ended August 31, 1997 and the AFT's budget came to approximately $65 million.[499]

Expanding membership in teacher unions has serious implications for the nation's public schools. Like any labor union, the NEA and AFT seek to control the labor market in which their members operate. The unions do so by requiring that all teachers hired by the public schools fall under the terms of a union contract, restricting access to teacher employment except under terms that are agreed upon by the union; working to ensure that teacher unions play an important role in selecting school management, barring lock outs, and, if necessary, either by threatening to strike or by striking.[500] These requirements make the teacher unions, particularly the NEA with its huge membership, especially potent.

> Unions also make demands about the structure of teachers' jobs, right down to the number of minutes of preparation time, assignments to lunch or hall duty, tutoring students, participating in extracurricular activities, and anything else teachers might be asked to do (or want to avoid doing)...And more generally still, unions make demands about the structure of the school as a whole, intended to carve out larger spheres of influence for teachers in the making of school policy, and intended...to ensure that teachers are protected from discretionary acts of authority by the principal.[501]

The resulting rigidity makes it difficult for schools to deal with ineffective staff and enact reforms that could increase their overall effectiveness and productivity.

Recognizing the NEA's influence, Sykes writes, "The National Education Association occupies what may well be a unique place in society...A measure of its unchallenged power within the educational establishment is that the NEA can be both critic and defender of the system at the same time. A prime architect of and apologist for the status quo, the NEA often claims a leading role in educational 'reform' efforts."[502] Indeed, this power was on display when the New York State Board of Regents voted to ban lifetime licensing but passed the slimmest standards for renewal and shelved performance evaluations from the process.[503]

The influence of the teacher unions extends beyond the schools. They are formidable political players, too. Chubb and Moe argue, "Organized teachers could offer money, manpower, publicity, and votes to politicians eager for electoral support; and, especially in state and local elections, where turnout is typically very low, these proved to be attractive inducements..."[504] During the 1970s, the NEA was a prime force behind the creation of a federal Department of Education. On the eve of President Jimmy Carter's signing the legislation creating the new department, leading NEA officials celebrated the occasion offering a toast that read: "Here's to the only union that owns its own Cabinet Department."[505]

When it comes to politics, education is not the only thing on the NEA's and AFT's agenda. Both the NEA and AFT have ideological social agendas that encompass a wide range of political issues, and generally the ones that have helped precipitate the cultural decay that has taken place since the 1960s. For example, the NEA's objectives include on-site childcare services, sex education programs (covering family planning, sexual orientation, sexually transmitted diseases, etc.), universal health care for children, single-payer health care for the nation, comprehensive programs of AIDS education in school curricula, and government funding of the arts.[506] The AFT's objectives are similar to the NEA's, however, the AFT does not publish the most extreme parts of its social agenda so as to avoid criticism.[507]

Teacher unions even attempt to govern the actions of their members in their private lives and extra-curricular activities. In one remarkable example, in New Jersey, a high school english teacher, John Anagbo, was reprimanded by his union for attending the school's senior prom during contract negotiations. "[Y]ou betrayed 649 colleagues," the union angrily told Anagbo threatening, "So do not be surprised...that your colleagues have lost respect for you."[508]

Finally, the National Congress of Parents and Teachers (the PTA) has come under the influence of the NEA. When asked in 1992 by Myron Lieberman of the Social Philosophy and Policy Center at Bowling Green State University, the PTA's legislative representative in Washington, D.C. could find no point of disagreement with the NEA.[509] Consequently, the NEA has effectively neutralized the principal public policy voice of primary and secondary education's consumers.

The teacher unions' monopoly within the public school monopoly has contributed to increased bureaucracy, inferior performance, and administrative rigidity, while weakening parental and community influence over school governance. Until these circumstances are fundamentally changed, a continuation of the declining academic achievement that typifies many of the nation's public schools.

The Role of Governance

School governance is an important ingredient for the ultimate success or failure of public elementary and primary schools and the public education system as a whole. Some even argue that the school "principal is the key variable in a school."[510]

Research shows that although school requirements may be a good indicator of what a school is seeking to accomplish, "the best measures of a school's true goals are the priorities articulated, or not articulated, by the principal, and the objectives perceived and internalized by the teachers," report Chubb and Moe.[511] In fact, their research reveals that effective schools have principals whose motivation to control the affairs of their schools, dedication to teaching, and vision are above average.[512]

In the realm of public education, the governance situation is set up for anything but success. More often than not, it is designed for failure. Worse still, public school governance is inherently flawed at a time when teacher unions are powerful enough to wreak significant damage on the public school system.[513]

The biggest problem plaguing public school governance is a suffocating centralization that permeates the system. Compounding the matter is the growing centralization of education finance and control at the state level which undermines the accountability of local school boards and administrators. "Higher state shares make school boards and administrators less accountable to local citizens because they need not justify expenditures as carefully," writes Herbert Walberg, who observes "Larger state shares also entail increased regulation, reporting, bureaucracy, and distraction from learning....Affixing responsibility for results seems impossible."[514]

Authors Paul T. Hill, Lawrence C. Pierce, and James W. Guthrie are even harsher in their evaluation of the current governance arrangement in public education. They state that the present situation has among the following adverse impacts on schools. Schools are now more or less operated directly by political decision-making bodies, schools are dominated by a concern for jobs and other issues, schools now practice "defensive" education in which they seek to avoid charges of discrimination and negligence, principals and teachers have become preoccupied with compliance and the avoidance of controversy.[515]

At the same time, school boards often usurp or undermine the power of school principals. Although, on the surface it might seem like a good idea for school boards to wield strong authority, in practice school board micromanagement generally weakens school performance. Scholars Chubb and Moe have found that ineffective schools much more than effective schools have above-average levels of school board influence, and such school boards have above-average influence concerning the curriculum, hiring of teachers, dismissal/transferring of teachers, and setting disciplinary policy.[516] This general rule is not particularly unique to public school governance. The same experience can be found throughout Corporate America. Boards of Directors that tend to micromanage are usually have an adverse impact on the performance of their organizations.

Fundamental school reform and substantially improved school performance will rest with the creation of a governance system that is sensitive to the needs of the schools' customers, namely parents and students. To achieve this, today's highly centralized system of governance will have to be significantly decentralized with principals regaining their responsibility to lead their individual schools.

Also, of interest, is an article that appeared on February 9, 2006 in *The New York Times* in which the author identifies a number of areas of standardized testing to be expanded into universities and colleges to allow easier comparisons on education quality and to prove that students are learning. Additional testing initiatives will obtain data to assess students' writing, problem solving and analytical/critical thinking. One-third of the annual investment in higher education comes from the federal government which appears to be planning new regulatory oversight on private colleges and universities.

Effective School Reform Cannot Wait

Education has moved to the forefront of the national debate not just because it concerns the future economic well-being of America's children in a sophisticated global economy, but because it also has a pervasive impact on all corners of society. It is at the core of who we are as Americans and how we lead our lives.

Education is the critical underpinning of self-government. "Citizens must…be literate, able not only to master the rudiments of reading, writing, and computing, but able to use these tools as ways of understanding the world and making their voices heard in it," writes Ohio University education professor George Wood.[517] Hirsch adds, "The need in a democracy to teach children a shared body of knowledge was explained many years ago by Thomas Jefferson when he described his bill 'to diffuse knowledge more generally through the mass of the people.' A common grade-school education would create a literate and independent citizenry as well as a nesting ground for future leaders. It would be a place where every talent would be given an equal chance to excel, where 'every fiber would be eradicated of ancient and future aristocracy; and a foundation laid for a government truly republican.'"[518]

As important as an informed citizenry is to democratic self-government, at least equally important are the values and knowledge society passes from one generation to the next. These values and knowledge form the bedrock of democratic society by which an informed citizenry and the institutions in which they participate transform information into effective policies that guide their actions.

Aside from the family, education is the key means by which societies perpetuate themselves. It is the critical vehicle by which they can continue to improve; economically, politically, and socially.

"No public policy issue is more important to any nation than education," David Boaz of the Cato Institute declares. "Education is the process by which a society transmits its accumulated knowledge and values to future generations. Education makes economic growth possible, in the first instance by ensuring that each new adult does not have to reinvent the wheel, literally. By passing on what it has already learned, the present generation enables the next generation of philosophers, scientists, engineers, and entrepreneurs to stand on the shoulders of giants and see even further."[519] In this sense, education is the engine that drives progress.

If the recent impeachment proceedings are any indication, this bedrock is breaking down. An informed and responsible citizenry would understand their constitutional role and insist that their representatives in Congress carefully enforce the applicable law and facts. Repeated opinion polls, however, have from the outset revealed approximately two-thirds of the public from the beginning prejudged the matter and leaped to the conclusion that the President should not be removed from office. They opposed the matter ever reaching the impeachment stage and strongly opposed calling any witnesses. The result was the opening of a major divide with the other segment of the public that is unlikely to be closed anytime soon. This will make it extremely difficult to govern in a democracy where broadly shared values are necessary in order to maintain a civil society guaranteeing broad-based individual freedoms.

Nevertheless, even as the public seems unable to grasp the importance of the impeachment process to the preservation of the rule of law upon which their nation rests, many do acknowledge that they often take U.S. freedoms for granted and that they believe that the nation is losing the values and beliefs that make it unique.[520] The paradoxes and conflicts are troubling and confusing. Many pundits have theorized that the explanation for this phenomena has been inter-generational and cultural spawned by the culture wars of the past 30 years. The moral relativism and deconstructionism and attacks on Western values and institutions taught in the schools during this period, many believe was a strong contributing factor. This deserves careful attention.

There are, however, some bright spots. School reform initiatives have gradually evolved into drives for expanded accountability. Thirty-six states now issue various kinds of annual report cards on their schools.[521] School choice efforts are gaining momentum.[522] In the school choice movement, state-funded charter schools increased dramatically in number and provided the first glimpses of the enormous benefits that could be possible with full-fledged school choice be it through vouchers, tax credits, charter schools, or privately-funded scholarships.

At the same time, the "quality" of state academic standards have been improving somewhat. "More states have become more serious about their responsibility to identify the essential knowledge and skills that today's students must master in order to be contributing citizens and workers…," note Chester Finn, Jr. and Michael Petrilli in a special Fordham Foundation report on state standards.[523] Overall, they find three encouraging trends concerning standard-based school reform: First, state standards are becoming more specific and measurable; second, content is becoming more important, and; third, states are becoming less reliant on the so-called educational "experts" when it comes to developing and implementing standards.[524]

Nevertheless, they find that only five states combine strong standards with strong accountability while thirty states combine poor standards with weak accountability, indicating that there still is much room for improvement.[525] Overall, this special report provides a highly detailed look at the state of standard-based reform (by subject matter and by state) while mentioning that standard-based reform and market-based reform (through school choice, private initiatives, etc.) complement one another.

However, with most of the input-based reforms fizzling, and the nation beginning to lose a sense of its basic identity at a time when the world economy is becoming ever more demanding, the need for effective reforms is particularly urgent. Building on the early successes realized by the school choice and outcomes accountability movements should be aggressively pursued. Realistically, however, the progress needed can never be achieved until the public school and union monopolies are exposed to competitive pressures to improve their performance.

Restoring Excellence[526]

The nation's educators and political leaders must learn and act on the lessons from the past, namely that more resources are no guarantee of creating well-educated students. Rather their emphasis must be placed on clearly defined and measurable educational achievement standards. Most importantly, they will have to accept the need and benefits from competition and begin acting as entrepreneurs competing for demanding customers who could easily take their patronage elsewhere. This will not be easy. The need is so great, however, and the stakes so high, that the public must insist on nothing less.

Three dominant lessons from past reform efforts should be kept in mind. First, governors, more than any other political leader, have the standing and influence to lead and implement the reform initiatives. Second, the longer a prospective reform is permitted to languish in the political process, the more likely it will be watered-down or eventually killed. Third, a state's intellectual capital does matter in ensuring that good ideas get pushed forward while bad ones are curbed.[527]

Universities and colleges can facilitate the recovery process by setting higher admission standards and refusing to admit students failing to pass entrance examinations. This policy would end any notion that all is well in the nation's primary and secondary schools and place the responsibility and accountability where it belongs. Pressure for reforms would quickly follow.

Teacher Colleges Must:

> 1. Raise admission standards. Given the vital importance of the teaching profession, standards for admission should be among the highest of any of the professional schools. This policy should enable education schools to reduce significantly remedial education costs and focus their resources directly on their basic missions. Changes in the career compensation structure for teachers as well as the public school culture are important and urgent for higher quality students to be attracted to education schools.

2. Restructure and strengthen their curricula and establish course requirements to ensure graduates have substantive experience in the areas they plan to teach and the educational background to score well on the certification exams. Curricula dealing with pedagogy and teaching methods should utilize best practices rather than unproven and sometimes unproven trendy fads. It is clear that the present system is broken and a zero-based approach to developing a new curriculum should be adopted.

3. Model themselves after medical schools by requiring that all teacher candidates gain hands-on experience through a one- or two-year paid residency in one of the nation's schools. Competition for the teaching residencies should be stiff.

4. Schools receiving financial assistance from federal or state governments should be required to announce publicly the range and distribution of scores and overall average scores of the graduation certification test. State education officials should participate in the development of the tests to ensure their rigor and that appropriate requirements for passage are set.

School Principals and Administrators Should:

1. Eliminate social promotion and grade inflation. Make summer school mandatory for poorly performing students.[528]

2. Ensure that all teachers have a competency in the subject matter that they teach. Establish requirements and provide incentives for teachers to pursue mid-career training and instruction. They should place special emphasis on ensuring that quality teachers have regular and meaningful opportunities to renew themselves intellectually.[529]

3. Set standards that exceed state requirements and actively seek to bring about accountability.[530] Some argue that school superintendents should remove themselves completely from the operations aspects of their schools, leaving this task to professional managers, and instead devote themselves entirely to awarding and revoking school charters and reporting to the public on the performance of the schools falling under their jurisdiction.[531]

4. Solicit more parental involvement and feedback. Regularly communicate with parents on all school-related matters that could affect their children.

5. Base teacher compensation on market-related factors (e.g. supply/demand considerations where higher compensation can be offered to overcome shortages of teachers with specialized skills) and classroom and school performance (e.g. bonuses for highly effective teachers). At least 10 states plan to test performance-based compensation and the Denver schools teachers union has approved a two-year pilot program to test performance-based compensation.[532] These changes should make it easier for individual school districts to attempt similar programs. These and other performance-related compensation criteria should be a high negotiating priority for inclusion in union contracts.

6. Create learning partnerships with local colleges and universities where talented high school students can take courses that are otherwise not available. For example, high school students proficient in calculus could enroll in a beginning engineering course or those who have distinguished themselves in the sciences could attend pre-med classes.

7. Regularly work with college and university administrators to ensure that curricula are consistent with the preparation of students to meet employment qualification standards that increasingly are becoming more stringent.

8. Work with state and local government officials to minimize administrative bureaucracy and paperwork demands on teachers, thereby freeing their time to improve their teaching effectiveness.

9. Help finance specialized professional education for outstanding teachers that goes beyond any state or local requirements.

10. Employ graduation examinations in all major subject areas. Administer these same exams at the beginning of 7th grade (for the junior high school graduation exams) and 9th grade (for the high school graduation exams) for purposes of assessing educational value-added. To facilitate the effort, all high schools could administer the Scholastic Testing Service's High School Placement Test to all students before and after they complete their high school educations.

11. Publicly disclose the results of graduation exams.

12. Outsource non-essential functions that outsiders could perform more effectively and efficiently than school personnel.

Teachers Can Enhance Educational Performance By:

1. Take a personal interest in the well-being of their students that extends beyond the classroom.

2. Find interesting ways to tie the teaching of curricula to student interests.

3. Communicate with parents concerning classroom activities and student performance. Solicit parental involvement in classroom activities.

4. Establish schedules that go beyond traditional school days.

There is powerful new evidence that parental involvement may be a vital ingredient in enhancing academic performance by their children. A study of Pentagon-run schools found that despite a demographic base that is poorer and more racially diverse than the national average, their students consistently excel on the National Assessment of Educational Progress (NAEP) exams and send 80% of their graduates to college. The big difference in these schools concerns the ability of the Military to order parents to become involved in the educational affairs of their children.[533]

Of course, parents should want to participate and assist in the education of their children without being compelled to do so. Parents can further educational excellence by becoming involved in the education of their children and in the local affairs of their children's schools by:

1.   Meet regularly with their children's teachers.

2.   Attend school events i.e. concerts, sporting events, etc.

3.   Volunteer in classrooms, for fundraisers, and for other functions.

4.   Attend school board meetings and voting in school board elections.[534]

5.   Create a supportive environment at home that encourages students to work hard and set high goals.

State Governments Can Assist The Effort By[535]:

1. Adopt legislation that expands the authorization of charter schools which can operate free from the administrative bureaucracies of state education administrators and compulsory unionization of teachers and staff. This legislation should ensure that local school boards do not have veto power in the establishment of charter schools. Continue to the extent practical to increase the number of charter schools to enhance competition and promote accountability. Renewal of their charters should be contingent on their fulfilling the mission for which they were established.

2. Adopt legislation that fosters other forms of school choice. Such legislation should award parents vouchers[536], refundable tuition tax credits, or tuition grants similar to the way higher education financial aid is administered. State governments should create "educational enterprise zones"[537] creating full-fledged school choice in areas where local schools are worst. These enterprise zones could be useful laboratories for studying the real-life effects of school choice. Competition from school choice is essential for the nation's public schools to begin the adoption of long overdue reforms identified earlier. 3. In the absence of adopting voucher or tax credit legislation, state and local government should at least give parents of home-schooled and private school children the chance to opt out of paying their share of taxes attributable to public school financing.

4. Establish clear, specific, demanding, and measurable objectives for their public schools, but grant the schools sufficient autonomy to develop their own strategy and practices for meeting those objectives, including the use of graduation exams.[538] Revoke accreditation for public schools consistently failing to meet those objectives. In addition, the states will have to be prepared to hold fast to these objectives even as the public, shocked by the dismal results of their schools, seeks to weaken or do away with tougher standards.[539] Early

efforts by states to take over failing school districts have not yet achieved satisfactory results.[540]

Unfortunately, in a troubling development, some of the states that had
been putting in place tougher standards coupled with rigorous testing are now
retreating from their ambitious plans to improve their primary and secondary
education system. "The state that is believed to have retrenched the furthest is
Wisconsin which acceded to parent demands last summer [Summer 1999]
that it withdraw a test that every student would have had to pass to graduate
from high school," reports *The New York Times'* Jacques Steinberg.[541]

Of course, dismal student performance or fears of such a performance on
exams similar to those that were withdrawn in Wisconsin have less to do with
unreasonably difficult standards than a lack of accountability. For example, in
New York State where even a sizable percentage of suburban schoolchildren
failed a new eighth-grade math test, the problem was that the standards had
never been tested before and "since no one was watching…teachers felt free to
ignore the state curriculum."[542]

5. Disclose the names of underperforming schools and excellent schools. Publicly shame poorly performing schools.[543] Publicly recognize outstanding
ones. Tie funding and continued operation to school performance.

6. Require that teachers continually upgrade their knowledge and skills by
participating in regular continuing professional education programs similar to
those required of other professionals. Make renewal of teacher certification
contingent on this professional education requirement.

7. Adopt legislation that removes the requirement that schools of education be
the sole providers of future teachers. Rather, those with an established mastery
in the subject areas they wish to teach should be encouraged to teach. Schools
could have their own instructional training programs for these prospective
teachers or rely on outside training programs much like many employers do
for their new employees.

"The fact that it makes sense to instruct novice teachers in applied teaching
knowledge does not justify the simplistic use of teacher training as a rigid legal
control over employment eligibility," explains Leo Klagholz in supporting
alternatives to education degree requirements. "[F]ew private schools and virtually no colleges or universities limit their hiring of new faculty members to
those who have completed teacher education. (Even collegiate schools of education do not do so)…Yet they succeed."[544]

8. Adopt right-to-work legislation that protects teachers from mandatory
unionization.

9. Establish open-enrollment laws where students can attend any school
within their district or even outside their district that has vacancies or a charter.[545]

10. Establish goals that within 10 years or less at least 10%–15% of current
primary and secondary school students will be enrolled in alternatives to traditional public schools so as to impose competitive pressures on traditional public schools to improve themselves.[546] This target could entail between 25,000

and 37,000 charter schools or an average of roughly 1.7–2.5 per school district, though the number would likely be substantially fewer.[547] In fact, some now advocate that state governors should "charterize" all urban schools in order to free them from bureaucracy and hold them accountable to demanding standards.[548]

The Federal Government, if it chooses to remain in the primary and secondary education arena, can assist school reform by replacing its current Title I and other programs with simple, unrestricted block grants awarded to the states and localities. Then, state and local officials who are more familiar with the unique problems and challenges facing their particular primary and secondary education schools would be able to address those challenges with results that the present one-size-fits-all, countless-strings-attached federal system never could hope to achieve.

Conclusion

At the close of the 20th Century, America's public schools remain weak. Academic achievement remains generally poor and, despite some recent improvements, there are some subtle signs that further deterioration might be occurring.

Underperforming schools pose a grave threat to the American way of life. They undermine the nation's future economic well-being and they impede the ability of its citizens to carry out the essential responsibilities of a democratic civil society.

Fortunately, not all news concerning America's primary and secondary education system has been bad. During the current decade, the rise of charter schools provided a compelling hint of the benefits of introducing competition into the school system. Reformers can build on these early successes by increasing school choice and by adopting many of the innovations found in charter schools. Even public schools are beginning, in some sense, to slowly move toward a more market-oriented outlook. "In a real sense, public school systems are becoming markets in which secondary schools compete for students," writes Daniel Duke of the Thomas Jefferson Center for Educational Design. "In the past, such competition was limited primarily to private and parochial schools."[549]

These changes are good for starters and do offer a tantalizing promise of better days for our nation's beleaguered primary and secondary education system. However, more remains to be done. Teacher colleges, public school teachers, parents, businesses, and state and local political leaders can take constructive steps to revitalize primary and secondary education.

Finally, if the charter school experience is representative of what is possible, a primary and secondary education turnaround is possible and can be accomplished before the current troubled system inflicts irreparable harm on the nation's economic, political, and social institutions.

5

Is 21st Century America Prepared to Win the Long-Term Global War Against Terrorism?

Early in the 21ˢᵗ century, the United States and its allies find themselves in the midst of a critical race against time to prevent state sponsors of terrorism and terrorist organizations from obtaining and using weapons of mass destruction. If terrorists succeed in detonating a nuclear device in a major city, the world would likely be profoundly changed. Stephen Krasner of the Center on Democracy, Development, and the Rule of Law warns, "The political fallout of such catastrophes would be dramatic for modern liberal societies, and not just those that are attacked. The United States, France, Britain, Japan, and Italy would not turn into police states, though their citizens would not only acquiesce but demand that their governments roll back some civil liberties. At the international level, conventional rules of sovereignty would be abandoned overnight. The major powers would implement new principles and rules. Their interests would demand it and their muscle would likely make success possible. The result would be a more stable and secure environment, although one not as attractive as the current system."[550]

The international climate following such a strike would be far more unstable and insecure than it is at present. Krasner notes that preemptive military strikes/wars would become the norm and that not all such wars would be truly based on an imminent threat.[551] He also speculates that the world's major powers would occupy geographic areas that might otherwise provide sanctuary for terrorists, revive the concept of trusteeships, and largely render the UN and its principles irrelevant.[552]

The current situation and the gravity of the long-term threat, if the issues concerning international terrorism and proliferation of weapons of mass destruction remain unresolved, fit well with the cycles of history discussed in Chapter 1. As international terrorism has grown into the preeminent external threat facing the U.S. and its allies, it is useful to provide a fairly detailed discussion of the issue.

Terrorism Becomes a Global Force

In Chapter 1, we learned that history's dynamism produces regular waves of challenge—some internal, some external—rising time and again. Authors William Strauss and Neil Howe refer to such cycles as having four phases or "turnings," where the "fourth turning" is a decisive period of secular upheaval in which the old civic order is replaced with a new one.[553] The terrorist attacks of September 11, 2001 (often referred to as "9/11") could well have marked the beginning of a new "fourth turning" for the United States. What is not in doubt is that those attacks changed the governing focus that assumed a relatively stable post-Cold War world. Historian Paul Johnson explains, "For America, September 11 was a new Great Awakening. It realized, for the first time, that it was itself a globalized entity. It no longer had frontiers. Its boundaries were the world, for from whatever part of the world harbored its enemies, it could be attacked and, if such enemies possessed weapons of mass destruction, mortally attacked."[554]

In this new environment, the future tests and risks that that lie ahead for the U.S. may well be more dangerous and costly than any previous perils. The risk of terrorists gaining access to and deliverability of weapons of mass destruction (nuclear, chemical, or biological weapons) combined with their willingness to attack innocent civilians in suicidal fashion creates a prospect for horrific destruction not before seen.

Many of today's international terrorists are suicidal and undeterred by the risk of death—in fact, some look forward to death as an act of martyrdom with heavenly reward. With a suicidal outlook and a willingness to kill thousands, as evidenced on 9/11, the real likelihood exists that some of these international terrorists would employ such weapons to inflict mass destruction on civilian populations if they should gain access to them. Consequently, the United States and its allies are now faced with a grim race against time to eradicate such threats from the terrorists who are the "new totalitarians" of the 21st century[555] and whose designs are at least as deadly as those of the 20th century.[556]

The deadly ambitions of the terrorists cannot be downplayed. Al Qaeda terrorist spokesman Sulaiman Abu Ghaith once boasted, "[W]e have the right to kill 4 million Americans, including 1 million children, displace double that figure and injure and cripple hundreds of thousands" adding, "We have the right to fight them by chemical and biological weapons…"[557] Even after having been weakened from the ongoing war on terrorism, Al Qaeda's ambitions remain expansive.

In addition to its magnitude, the threat posed by Islamist terrorism is likely to last for years, if not decades. "We are patient," Abu Salma Al-Hijazi, an Al Qaeda commander close to Osama Bin Laden warned, "Our patience will only end with the collapse of America and its agents...There is no doubt that the demise of America and its collapse will lead to the collapse of these fragile regimes that depend on it...We will not stop until we establish the Islamic Caliphate and until Allah's law is implemented in His land"[558]

The threat posed by Al Qaeda and its terrorist allies is the culmination of three major trends that have shaped terrorism beginning in the 1970s. First, several terrorist organizations have expanded their reach and presence to the extent that they have become global entities. Hezbollah and Al Qaeda are two such groups. Second, terrorists have increasingly recruited skilled personnel including engineers, computer programmers, scientists, and others to build their organizations' capabilities.[559] Third, the worst terrorist attacks have grown steadily deadlier. In the 1970s, the worst attacks claimed scores of lives. By the 1980s, terrorists had carried out attacks that killed more than 100 persons. 9/11 raised the threshold to thousands. In comparison, prior to 9/11 approximately 1,000 Americans in total had been killed by terrorists either in the U.S. or abroad since 1968.[560]

A September 1999 landmark report prepared by Rex A. Hudson under an interagency agreement by the Federal Research Division of the Library of Congress, *The Sociology and Psychology of Terrorism: Who Becomes a Terrorist and Why?* described the evolution of post-World War II terrorism. It explained, "Trends in terrorism over the past three decades...have contradicted the conventional thinking that terrorists are averse to using WMD [weapons of mass destruction]...In the 1990s, groups motivated by religious imperatives, such as Aum Shinrikyo, Hizballah [Hezbollah], and al-Qaida [Al Qaeda], have grown and proliferated. These groups have a different attitude toward violence—one that is extra normative and seeks to maximize violence against the perceived enemy, essentially anyone who is not a fundamentalist Muslim or an Aum Shinrikyo member. With its sarin attack on the Tokyo subway system on March 20, 1995, the doomsday cult Aum Shinrikyo turned the prediction of terrorists using WMD into reality."[561] Attacks by terrorists on various U.S. facilities that employ hazardous materials in their operation, such as petroleum refineries, could also be employed to surmount the need by terrorists to directly obtain weapons of mass destruction.[562] Terrorists may well use cyber-attacks aimed at "disabling or taking command of the floodgates in a dam, for example, or of substations handling 300,000 volts of electric power…to destroy real-world lives and property."[563]

In addition, a number of terrorist groups have begun to build alliances. For example, members of Hamas (Palestinian terrorist organization), Hezbollah (Lebanese-based terrorist group) and Al Qaeda met in March 2002 to discuss coordinating their activities.[564] The Hezbollah-Al Qaeda relationship may be even longer-standing.[565] Indeed, this relationship could be responsible for the deaths of more than half of all Americans murdered by terrorists since 1980.[566]

For now, cooperation is largely focused on logistics and training.[567] All three groups have their own respective "competitive advantages" from which the others could benefit. Al Qaeda offers vast international reach with a presence in more than 60 countries, along with computer and engineering experts. Hezbollah specializes in car and truck-bomb attacks. Hamas offers walk-in suicide bombers who employ belt-bombs to detonate civilian establishments. Some terrorism experts believe that the suicide bombing tactic could eventually be "exported" to the United States.[568]

The marriage of terrorist organizations and rogue states would present a possible worst-case challenge. In testimony before the U.S. Senate on May 21, 2002, Secretary of Defense Donald Rumsfeld warned, "I think realistically we have to face up to the fact that we live in a world where our margin for error has become quite small. In just facing the facts, we have to recognize that terrorist networks have relationships with terrorist states that have weapons of mass destruction, and that they inevitably are going to get their hands on them, and they would not hesitate one minute in using them."[569]

Weapons of Mass Destruction

Considering the dimension of weapons of mass destruction, the "war on terrorism" cannot be confined exclusively to combating terrorist organizations. It must also focus on addressing the dangers posed by the proliferation of weapons of mass destruction and the threat posed by a handful of rogue states such as North Korea and formerly Iraq.

What was widely believed by the world's intelligence community to be a significant threat stemming from weapons of mass destruction led President Bush to make the case for the recent war that removed Iraq's Saddam Hussein from power. Iraq's role as a state sponsor of terrorism, past development of weapons of mass destruction, previous use of such weapons, and its failure to heed the terms of repeated UN Security Council resolutions were all cited by President Bush.[570]

Even though actual WMD were not found in Iraq following the war, the former regime of Saddam Hussein likely retained its WMD ambitions and know-how. "He sought to balance the need to cooperate with UN inspections—to gain support for lifting sanctions—with his intention to preserve Iraq's intellectual capital for WMD," the September 30, 2004 *Comprehensive Report of the Special Advisor to the DCI on Iraq's WMD* revealed.[571] The report also added, "Saddam wanted to recreate Iraq's WMD capability—which was essentially destroyed in 1991—after sanctions were removed and Iraq's economy stabilized, but probably with a different mix of capabilities to that which previously existed. Saddam aspired to develop a nuclear capability—in an incremental fashion, irrespective of international pressure and the resulting economic risks—but he intended to focus on ballistic missile and tactical chemical warfare (CW) capabilities."[572]

Nevertheless, at the time the war was launched in March 2003, this latter information was not known. Instead, the world community believed that Iraq continued to possess actual WMD even though some of their views on how to address the threat differed markedly. Also troubling was the fact that Iraq maintained relationships with various terrorist organizations and provided bases to several terrorist groups including the Mujahedin-e-Khalq (MEK), the Kurdistan Workers' Party (PKK), the Palestine Liberation Front (PLF), and the Abu Nidal organization (ANO).

Against this backdrop, President Bush along with British Prime Minister Blair concluded that the risk of inaction was unacceptably high. To put the dangers of inaction into historical perspective, one need only look back to the decade-and-a-half prior to World War II. In his watershed book *Diplomacy*, Henry Kissinger provides a lesson concerning Great Britain and France's appeasement of Germany for the sake of peace. That endeavor turned out horribly. Kissinger wrote:

> The situation was as if made to order for Hitler's talent in waging psychological warfare. Throughout the summer [1938], he worked to magnify hysteria about an imminent war without, in fact, making any specific threat. Finally, after Hitler had engaged in a vicious personal attack on the Czech leadership at the annual Nazi Party rally in Nuremberg in early September 1938, Chamberlain's nerves snapped. Though no formal demands had been made and no real diplomatic exchanges had taken place, Chamberlain decided to end the tension on September 15 by visiting Hitler. Hitler showed his disdain by choosing Berchtesgaden as the meeting place—the location in Germany farthest from London and the least accessible...
>
> After enduring several hours of Hitler's ranting about the alleged mistreatment of the Sudeten Germans, Chamberlain agreed to dismember Czechoslo-

vakia...It was symptomatic of Hitler's negotiating style that he termed this subsequent locale a 'concession.'...In the interval, Chamberlain 'persuaded' the Czechoslovak government to accept his proposal...

The four leaders [Hitler, Chamberlain, Mussolini and Daladier] met on September 29 in Munich, the birthplace of the Nazi Party, the sort of symbolism victors reserve for themselves. Little time was spent on negotiations: Chamberlain and Daladier made a halfhearted attempt to return to their original proposal; Mussolini produced a paper containing Hitler's Bad Godesberg proposal; Hitler defined the issues in the form of a sarcastic ultimatum...In other words, the sole purpose of the conference was to accept Hitler's Bad Godesberg program peacefully before he went to war to impose it...

Munich has entered our vocabulary as a specific aberration—the penalty of yielding to blackmail. Munich, however, was not a single act but the culmination of an attitude which began in the 1920s and accelerated with each new concession...Finally, as so often happens, decisions cumulatively developed their own momentum.[573]

While the debate over the nature of Iraq's threat prior to the war may go on, what is clear is that the kind of debacle that led to World War II had been avoided in the Middle East. This precedent is not unimportant if it deters would-be rogue regimes from taking steps that would dramatically threaten international peace and security.

Citizen Perseverance during the 20th Century's Cold War against Communism

The Cold War probably offers the best model for the ongoing war on terrorism. Like the war on terrorism, the Cold War was a giant ideological struggle between democratic values and individual freedoms and Marxist utopian totalitarianism. Today, the United States and its allies are confronted by extremist quasi-religious totalitarianism.

During the Cold War with the Soviet Union, the U.S. and the West sought to address the military challenges head-on rather than through diplomatic appeasement. Arms control agreements were negotiated to minimize the risks of mutual destruction. In addition, the Soviets and their communist allies were not rewarded with concessions. Instead, the U.S. and its allies maintained a strong NATO alliance, which based intermediate range nuclear missiles in various parts of Europe. Throughout the more than four decade struggle, U.S. and allied resolve seldom wavered and never fractured.

Typical of the resolve against appeasement was President Reagan's March 8, 1983 address. In that speech, President Reagan strongly rejected any idea of appeasement or equivocation with the Communists even when many were arguing that the U.S. should take a more accommodative approach, and embrace the concept of a "nuclear freeze." In response the President shifted to focus to the character of the Soviet leadership in the following manner:

> [B]ecause these 'quiet men' do not 'raise their voices,' because they sometimes speak in soothing tones of brotherhood and peace, because, like other dictators before them, they're always making 'their final territorial demand,' some would have us accept them at their word and accommodate ourselves to their aggressive impulses. But if history teaches anything, it teaches that simple-minded appeasement or wishful thinking about our adversaries is folly. It means the betrayal of our past, the squandering of our freedom...I urge you to beware the temptation of pride—the temptation of blithely declaring yourselves above it all and label both sides equally at fault, to ignore the facts of history and the aggressive impulses of an evil empire, to simply call the arms race a giant misunderstanding and thereby remove yourself from the struggle between right and wrong and good and evil.[574]

Although some believed in the "good will" of the Soviet Union and that it would reciprocate with concessions of its own in return for American concessions, the Soviet leaders at the time actually believed that the U.S. was a nation in decline. This view was expressed by Soviet leader Nikita Kruschev in his widely publicized 1959 "Kitchen Debate" with Vice-President Richard Nixon. Kruschev rejected the perception of American greatness, predicting "Well then we will say America has been in existence for 150 years and this is the level she has reached. We have existed not quite 42 years and in another seven years we will be on the same level as America. When we catch you up, in passing you by, we will wave to you. Then if you wish we can stop and say: Please follow up."[575]

Kruschev's crystal ball was badly flawed. The Russian economy was incapable of keeping up with the growth generated by the West's system of democratic capitalism. In the 1980s the confidence and strength projected to the citizens of the Soviet Union and its Satellites by President Ronald Reagan and British Prime Minister Margaret Thatcher was too great a force for the world's Communist leaders to contain. Soon their peoples would be tearing down the Berlin Wall and demanding their personal freedoms.

The U.S. and its allies' 21st Century global "war on terrorism" is an ideological battle akin to the 20th Century's Cold War. In this ideological war, Islamist fundamentalists are using religion combined with an attack on western culture to further their totalitarian ambitions. This is a difficult war to wage. By its very nature, religious extremism is a kind of faith and can more readily be manipulated to circumvent the usual inquiry and proof generally required for the wide acceptance of secular ideologies. Although these 21st century Islamic fundamentalists have rejected key tenets of the Qu'ran that prohibit the killing of innocents (Hirabah) and suicide, they have been able to garner significant public sympathy within the Islamic world by cloaking their cause under the mantle of defending Islam and labeling the West as the "Great Satan" responsible for the poverty and cultural decay throughout the Islamic world.

Historical Background of the 21st Century War on Terrorism

The global "war on terrorism" is complex and multifaceted. It includes the increasing tensions between traditional Islam and the fundamentalist Islamic sects, as well as the fiercely contested Israeli-Palestinian dispute and the broader Islam vs. Judaism conflict. Also, included are elements of the historic rivalry between Christianity and Islam that are not dissimilar to the dynamics of the "Clash of Civilizations" that Samuel Huntington has described in his 1993 seminal thesis on future global conflicts.

Unfortunately the history of world religions, their inherent competition and conflict and their impacting for centuries on the development of Western civilization are only fragmentally presented, if at all, in U. S. secondary schools or in higher education.

Briefly, Islam is the youngest of the major monotheistic religions. With some 1.2 billion followers, it is the second largest world religion. At the same time, it is the world's fastest growing religion. It stretches across the Middle East through northern Africa and into Southeast Asia. In addition, there are Muslim minority communities scattered throughout the world.[576] Islam has two major traditions, the Sunni tradition and the Shi'ite (Shi'a) tradition. Approximately 90 percent of Muslims belong to the Sunni tradition, which contains four jurisprudential schools and a number of independent sects. The jurisprudential schools differ somewhat in their doctrines ranging from orthodox to scholarly.[577]

Princeton University Professor Emeritus of Semitic Literature Philip Hitti's Introduction to *Early Islam* provides invaluable historical context of Islam's origins, growth, and spread:

> Islam is a way of life that has religious aspects, political aspects and cultural aspects, and each of the three overlaps and interacts...Of all religions, Islam is nearest in kin to Judaism and Christianity. In fact the alienation between the Islamic and the Christian worlds is more one of politics and economics than of ideology...Islam the state was a political entity that based its laws on the canon law of the Koran and on the modifications of that law worked out by Muhammad's successors at various times and in various places. Initially, the state of Islam grew at the expense of the Byzantine and Persian empires, the two greatest forces in the Middle East during Islam's period of expansion, and this is still the heartland of Islam. At its height, however, the Muslim empire extended from Spain to India, exceeding in size and population even the Roman Empire in its prime...Islam the culture, unlike the religion and government of Islam, is not essentially an Arabian invention. [It] is a compound of other cultures—ancient Semitic, Classical Greek, and medieval Indo-Persian. It was formulated for Islam largely by the peoples it conquered, the neo-Muslims. For a period of about 400 years, from midway through the Eighth Century to the 12th Century, the achievements of this synthesized culture were perhaps unsurpassed. In fact much of the science and literature of the European Renaissance was inspired by Islamic models.[578]

Political and Religious Divisions within Islam

Islam is not homogenous. Rather, it contains two major branches and variation within those branches.

The Al Qaeda organization grew out of an Islamic religious movement known as the Salafiyya movement. Salafists believe that the version of Islam practiced by most Muslims has been corrupted and must be purified. The Salafiyya movement consists of numerous smaller movements, many of which are not as extreme as Osama Bin Laden and his Al Qaeda terrorist group.[579] "In almost every Sunni Muslim country the Salafiyya has spawned Islamist political movements working to compel the state to apply the shari'a—that is, Islamic law. Extremist Salafis believe that strict application of the shari'a is necessary to ensure that Muslims walk on the path of the Prophet. The more extremist the party, the more insistent and violent the demand that the state must apply the shari'a exclusively," writes Princeton University Professor of Near Eastern Studies Michael Scott Doran.[580]

One of the most extreme independent sects within the Salafiyya movement is the Wahhabi Sect, which arose in Saudi Arabia in the 18th century. Wahhabis, who comprise the dominant religious following in Saudi Arabia, "believe that all objects of worship other than Allah are false, and anyone who worships in this way deserves to be put to death. To introduce the name of a prophet, saint or angel into a prayer or to seek intercession from anyone but Allah constitutes a form of polytheism. Attendance at public prayer is compulsory, and the shaving of the beard and smoking are forbidden."[581]

"Extremist Salafis...regard modern Western civilization as a font of evil, spreading idolatry around the globe in the form of secularism. Since the United States is the strongest Western nation, the main purveyor of pop culture, and the power most involved in the political and economic affairs of the Islamic world, it receives particularly harsh criticism," Professor Doran explains.[582]

However, this animosity is not reserved exclusively for Western civilization. Even other Muslims are targets of the extremists' hostility. Salafis "consider themselves an island of true believers surrounded by a sea of iniquity and think the future of religion itself, and therefore the world, depends on them and their battle against idol worship."[583]

This hostility toward mainstream Muslims worldwide creates an opportunity and a need for Western nations to join with traditional Islam in working to overcome the Islamic extremists who commit violence in the name of Islam even as their acts violate fundamental teachings of the Qu'ran. Islamic scholar, Dr. Muqtedar Khan of Adrian College explained, "No matter how much we condemn it, and point to the Quran and the Sunnah to argue that Islam forbids the killing of innocent people, the fact remains that the perpetrators of this crime against humanity have indicated that their actions are sanctioned by Islamic values...While encouraging Muslims to struggle against injustice [Al Quran 4:135], Allah also imposes strict rules of engagement. He says in unequivocal terms that to kill an innocent being is like killing entire humanity [Al Quran 5:32]."[584]

The major challenge of the "war on terrorism" is not whether the U.S. and other western countries alone can meet the challenges of defending their freedoms and the democratic values of Western Civilization, but also whether they can reach out to moderate Muslims to build a joint initiative against "radical Islam." Such a joint initiative could aim to refute "radical Islam's" tortured interpretations of the Qu'ran and delegitimize its ideological rationale for violent "jihad."

Moderate Islam can potentially be a critical ally for the western world, especially as it is currently engaged in a struggle with more extreme elements for the soul of Islam. Ralph Peters, a retired military officer and author of *Beyond Terror: Strategy in a Changing World* contends, "At present, there is a mighty struggle underway on Islam's frontiers for that religion's soul. Those frontiers should be the focus of our efforts to encourage Islam's humane tendencies…constructive engagement on Islam's social, economic and spiritual frontiers would be…helpful in the long-term."[585] The debate over what kind of Islam will prevail has engulfed Asian Muslims as to whether they need to adopt a new and more extreme model that is foreign to them.[586] Fuller concurs, "The United States…should…engage overseas Muslims vigorously, including those Islamic clerics who enjoy great respect and authority as men of uncompromised integrity…Many of these clerics represent undeniably moderate forces within political Islam, but their own understanding of the West, though far from uniformly hostile is flawed and often initially unsympathetic."[587]

Education in Islamic Countries

Education can be a key vehicle for promoting moderation and tolerance, especially with respect to countries and peoples of different cultures. Education can also serve to de-legitimize terrorists and provide citizens with skills in which to lead productive lives and thus play an important role in unlocking progress in the Islamic world. However, substantial reforms will be required in the Islamic world through education if it is to provide such a needed benign impact. At present, the educational curricula and textbooks in many Islamic countries currently impose a major educational, cultural and political barrier to urgently needed progress and reforms.

Many textbooks in the region, particularly older texts, incorporate anti-Western and anti-Semitic hatred. This makes it easier for extremist elements and terrorists to rationalize violence against the United States, Israel, and other Western states. The Center for Monitoring the Impact of Peace has reviewed a number of Palestinian Authority textbooks (the older ones were published in Egypt and Jordan) and more recently textbooks in Syria. The findings of the survey are shocking.

In the Syrian textbooks referenced by the study, there was not a single positive comment about Jews or Judaism, the Jewish people were called a "false people" and Israel an "imaginary nation," Judaism was described as racist, and both anti-Semitism and the Holocaust were rationalized.[588] Older Palestinian Authority textbooks (particularly those published in Egypt and Jordan) contained similar content. Israel was described as an "evil" enemy to be fought through Jihad; some maps made no reference at all to Israel. Its legitimacy was denied, and some guides even contained passages declaring that "Marytred Jihad fighters are the most honored people, after the Prophets" and that people should strive to compete with each other to "attain Martyrdom in battle."[589] Newer textbooks have removed much of the vile anti-Semitic language, but, they still do not acknowledge Israel's existence or right to exist. During the ongoing Intifada (low-grade conflict), many of the older textbooks were put back into circulation.[590]

In the West Bank and Gaza Strip similar problems exist. Even worse, the Hamas terrorist organization runs a number of schools and mosques and this gives this organization a direct path to the hearts and minds of Palestinian children. Hamas makes no secret that its aim is to "re-educate" the masses in order to support its violent hate-driven cause. The Hamas Covenant declares, "It is necessary that scientists, educators and teachers, information and media people, as well as the educated masses, especially the youth and sheikhs of the Islamic movements, should take part in the operation of awakening (the masses). It further declares that it is important that basic changes be made in the school curriculum, to cleanse it of the traces of ideological invasion that affected it as a result of the orientalists and missionaries who infiltrated the region following the defeat of the Crusaders at the hands of Salah el-Din (Saladin)."[591]

In Saudi Arabia, a textbook available in public high schools contains a lesson on which "good Muslims should be befriended." Using various religious scriptures, it warns against having Jewish and Christian friends concluding, "It is compulsory for the Muslims to be loyal to each other and to consider the infidels their enemy."[592] These intolerant arguments also appear on the Internet. Hamoud al-Shuaibi, a sheik that issued a fatwa (religious ruling) condemning the U.S. military action in Afghanistan declared, "Jihad is allowed against infidels like the Jews, Christians and atheists."[593] A young Saudi Arabian woman wrote to *New York Times* syndicated columnist Thomas Friedman that "Our schools teach religious intolerance, most of our mosques preach hate against any non-Muslims, our media is exclusively controlled by the government and religious people. Our moderate ideas have no place to be presented. Our government is not doing anything really to stop the religious control from paralyzing our lives."[594]

These educational deficiencies are part of what feeds extremism and terrorism. "It is social fanaticism," Jamal Khashoggi, the deputy editor in chief of *The Arab News* said of such curricula, "but it takes just a few small adjustments to turn it into political fanaticism."[595] Against this backdrop, Columnist Thomas Friedman writes, "If you want to understand the milieu that produced Bin Ladenism—and will reproduce it if nothing changes…"[596] Even more frightening, is a warning written by Saad Mehio who regularly contributes to various Arab newspapers. "So what comes after the Taliban and Osama Bin Laden are finished? Probably more Talibans and new Osama Bin Ladens. This is the sad and shocking reality that we must confront. It will happen apart from all the fanfare surrounding America's military triumph in Afghanistan and all the other achievements of this so-called war on terror. Why? Because the Taliban and Mr. Bin Laden are not isolated cases but manifestations of a complex, and potentially durable, sociopolitical phenomenon."[597]

Even the universities in large parts of the Arab world are stricken by serious deficiencies. Eissa Al-Halyan, an Arab progressive leader, recently complained in the Saudi daily *Al-Jazirah*, "Although there are hundreds of educational institutions in our region, they still follow old methods and techniques which were first used several hundred years ago. We continue to use them even though the world beyond our borders is living in—and reacting to—the era of discovery and the age of electronic information."[598] Al-Halyan also added, "Under the pressure of sheer numbers of students and other considerations, including the financial one, our universities have become little more than large buildings full of students. The only thing about them that would indicate they are universities is the banner bearing the magic word 'university' which is displayed everywhere."[599]

The Arab Human Development Report that was released in October 2003 by the United Nations Human Development Program outlines the educational and societal impediments to the production and dissemination of knowledge in the Arab world. The following excerpts from the report highlight the magnitude of the problem currently affecting the Arab world and how it stunts the progress of that part of the world:

> Key knowledge dissemination processes in Arab countries, (socialization and upbringing, education, the media and translation), face deep-seated social, institutional, economic and political impediments…the most important challenge facing Arab education is its declining quality…Arabic culture…finds itself facing the challenges of an emerging global cultural homogeneity and related questions about cultural multiplicity, cultural personalities, the issue of the 'self' and the 'other', and its own cultural character…Arab culture has no choice but to engage again in a new global experiment. It cannot enclose itself, contented with living on history, the past and inherited culture alone in a world whose victorious powers reach into all corners of the earth, dominating all forms of knowledge, behavior, life, manufactured goods and innovation. Undoubtedly, some currents embedded in this culture would prefer a policy of withdrawal of rejection and hostility to all values, ideas, and practices brought about by this global culture. This may appear justified in some ways, but a negative policy of 'non-interaction' can only lead to the weakening and

diminution of the Arab cultural structures rather than their reinforcement and development."[600]

Canadian television journalist and, a Muslim herself, Irshad Manji argues that such problems even confront Muslims outside the Middle East and Islamic world. "Whatever the culture in which Muslims lived, be it rural or digital, and whatever the generation, whether symbolized by a 1970s mosque for immigrants or by a media-connected city for the new millennium, Islam emerged as desperately tribal," she wrote in *The Trouble With Islam* complaining that many contemporary Islamic leaders place a premium on imitation over independent thought and that such an approach is dangerous, "When imitation goes mainstream, most of us fail to explore our prejudices—or even acknowledge that we have any. We believe what we're supposed to believe, and that's that."[601]

Manji also appeals to Muslims to reassert their right to independent thought, noting that classical Islam did not prohibit such independent thought and that their failure to do so will bring harm to Muslims. She explains that classical Islamic philosopher Ibn Rushd (Averroes) observed, "There is no religious stipulation that all such passages [in the Qu'ran] have to be interpreted literally" and that if Muslims won't begin to speak out against the fundamentalists, "these guys will walk away with the show. And their path leads to a dead-end of more vitriol, more violence, more poverty, more exclusion."[602]

The consequences of the above-described situation are dire. First, individuals who learn not to question authority (be it authoritarian leaders or extremist religious leaders) lose the intellectual capacity to make informed choices. Hence, it becomes easier for extremists to peddle a perverted version of Islam in which Qu'ranic prohibitions against the killing of innocents and suicide are turned on their head. Second, illiteracy and a lack of exposure to the outside world makes it more difficult for Arabs to embrace the global lessons that are essential for economic, social, political, and personal success and more difficult for them to reject anti-Western and anti-Semitic conspiracy theories that are disseminated by various extremists.

Media Propaganda

The lack of a quality education is just part of the absence of what can be described as an information infrastructure in the Arab and Islamic worlds. In Arab and Islamic countries, the general lack of an independent media provides another major informational barrier. The Committee for the Protection of Journalists ranks a number of Islamic countries as among the world's worst abusers of the media:

> Bucking a worldwide trend toward democracy in the post-Cold War era, the political landscape of the Middle East and North Africa remained dominated by an assortment of military-backed regimes, police states, autocracies, and oligarchies...Abdel Rahman al-Rashed, chief editor of the influential London-based daily *Al-Sharq al-Awsat*, commented that despite the optimistic predictions of some analysts in recent years, the state of press freedom in the region has remained largely static. 'We...know that what we are allowed to publish is not what the readers want,' al-Rashed wrote. 'The margin that has improved in most Arab countries is just cosmetic and far from the alleged claim of the freedom of the media and political democracy. In the more repressive and centralized states of the region, such as Iraq and Libya, the state owns and controls all media and allows no dissent.[603]

The 2003 Arab Human Development Report augments this finding as it discloses:

> The mass media are the most important agents for the public diffusion of knowledge yet Arab countries have lower information media to population ratios (number of newspapers, radio and televisions per 1000 people) compared to the world average. There are less than 53 newspapers per 1000 Arab citizens, compared to 285 papers per 1000 people in developed countries.

> In most Arab countries, the media operate in an environment that sharply restricts freedom of the press and freedom of expression and opinion. Journalists face illegal harassment, intimidation and even physical threats, censorship is rife and newspapers and television channels are sometimes arbitrarily closed down. Most media institutions are state-owned, particularly radio and television.[604]

Commonplace under such repression of the press is one-sided TV coverage that focuses on graphic violence against Palestinians without providing context into the "historic conflict", portraying the United States and West in often harsh even "Satanic" terms, popularizing myths pertaining to the 9/11 attacks, misleading their publics into believing that the West is at war with Islam, lacking sufficient independence to provide credible and critical information to the public, sometimes serving as the propaganda arms of repressive dictators and portraying suicide bombers as courageous martyrs.

Tim Golden of *The New York Times* reports of the one-sided, saturation coverage of the Palestinian situation in Egypt, "On both private satellite channels and state-run national networks, the plight of the Palestinians—portrayed as victims of barbaric Israeli aggression—has saturated the news. The Palestinian cause has become a staple of religious programming, entertainment shows and even sports talk shows."[605] "It is no coincidence that countries such as Egypt, Saudi Arabia...where the public has little access to outside information or free and independent news media are the very places where terrorism is bred," observes David Hoffman, President of Internews Network.[606] Sentiments such as those expressed by 18-year-old Wisam Rochalina that Muslims have reasons to fear the U.S. and that there is no evidence that Bin Laden was responsible for 9/11 are often propagated by the Arabic Media and can spread to various other parts of the Islamic world such as Indonesia.[607]

The Israeli-Palestinian Dispute

Another major regional challenge that concerns the United States and has been used as a rationalization for Islamist terror in the Middle East and beyond is the long-running Israeli-Palestinian dispute. This dispute has been a banner cause for Middle Eastern and Islamist extremist and terrorist groups and a barrier to improved American public standing in the Middle East.

U.S. support for Israel in its fight against terrorism has turned substantial numbers of Arabs against the United States and proved to be a rallying cause for Islamist terrorist groups. However, Israel remains a vital strategic ally of the United States. It also has much in common with the United States. Among other things, it is a liberal democracy, a market economy, and a Western state in the cultural sense. Consequently, the United States cannot reasonably be expected to abandon Israel.

Due to the fundamental nature of the differences that divide the two sides, the longstanding Arab-Israeli and Palestinian-Israeli disputes will be difficult to resolve. Moreover, they are not matters that can be remedied by quick changes in U.S. foreign policy. The historical narratives of the Israeli, Arab, and Palestinian peoples help explain the dynamics that drive the historic Palestinian-Israeli and Arab-Israeli disputes. Dennis Ross's *The Missing Peace* lays out a seminal summary of the Israeli, Arab, and Palestinian narratives:

> For the Israeli people, Zionism is a natural response to the tragic history of the Jewish people, Arab hostility toward the Jewish people that commenced with the 1920 riots reaffirmed the Jewish people's sense of vulnerability and determination of an independent, self-reliant state, almost 1 percent of Israel's population was killed in the 1948 War, through much of its early existence Israel

was left by the international community to fend for itself, and from 1948–1967 when the Arabs controlled east Jerusalem, Jewish people were denied access to their most important religious site, the Western Wall. For the Arabs, the land in question is viewed as belonging to them and the developments that led to the establishment of Israel were seen as a historic betrayal and product of colonialism. For the Palestinians, internal divisions led to weakness and an environment in which radical groups could compete with one another in pursuing extremes and moderates were undermined, the refugee situation that resulted from the 1948 War became a tool by which Arab states sought to exploit for their own political purposes, and Palestinians suffered the harsh consequences of a lack of competent leadership.[608]

This narrative plays a powerful role in shaping the region's future. For Israel, this narrative will likely continue to translate into:

- Maintaining a strong military capability and taking tough actions against those carrying out acts of terrorism.

- Placing the security of its state ahead of international demands calling for restraint on a wide range of issues ranging from the security fence to counter-terrorism operations.

- Seeking defensible borders to reduce its vulnerability. Thus, Israel is reluctant to give up land, which would compromise its defensible position, in exchange for promises that could easily not be honored.

- The survival of a Jewish state as critical to the survival of the Jewish people.

- Prepared to "tough it out" in a hostile environment rather than make concessions that would signal Israeli weakness.

- Desire to maintain an undivided Jerusalem (which is enshrined in Israel's "Basic Law" or its de facto Constitution).

- Reluctance to reduce settlement activity or eliminate it.

- Actions and not words e.g., an actual security effort by the Palestinians not promises, used to judge progress in order for the peace process to advance.

For the Palestinians, this narrative will likely continue to translate into:

- An environment that is not hospitable to compromise or moderation.

- The continued existence of a number of terrorist organizations ranging from Hamas to the Al Aqsa Martyrs' Brigade.

- An ongoing search for "collaborators."

- Palestinian public support for Palestinian terrorist groups and the chronic unwillingness by the Palestinian leadership to combat terrorism, even as terrorism has become the greatest single obstacle to advancing the peace process.

- The expectation that Israel would have to lead the way in making substantive concessions.

For purposes of further understanding how the dispute evolved to its current situation, a brief historical account is also useful. In response to significant anti-Semitism, during the late 19th century, a movement arose in Europe for the restoration of historic Israel in the Palestine region. Based on archaeological evidence, early historical accounts that pre-date the Zionist movement, and recent pioneering work concerning genetic research[609], there is little doubt of a historic Jewish presence in that region.

In 1917, the British Government issued the Balfour Declaration that proclaimed, "His Majesty's Government view with favor the establishment in Palestine of a national home for the Jewish people, and will use their best endeavors to facilitate the achievement of this object, it being clearly understood that nothing shall be done which may prejudice the civil and religious rights of existing non-Jewish communities in Palestine, or the rights and political status enjoyed by Jews in any other country."[610]

By 1919, it appeared that both the Arab and Jewish people were ready to choose accommodation. Emir Feisal representing the Arab leadership and Chaim Weizmann representing the Jewish side reached an agreement that supported the creation of a Jewish state in the Palestine region. The agreement stated:

> The Arab State and Palestine in all their relations and undertakings shall be controlled by the most cordial goodwill and understanding...Immediately following the completion of the deliberations of the Peace Conference, the definite boundaries between the Arab State and Palestine shall be determined by a Commission to be agreed upon by the parties hereto...In the establishment of the Constitution and Administration of Palestine, all such measures shall be adopted as will afford the fullest guarantees for carrying into effect the British

> Government's Declaration of the 2nd of November, 1917…All necessary measures shall be taken to encourage and stimulate immigration of Jews into Palestine on a large scale, and as quickly as possible to settle Jewish immigrants upon the land through closer settlement and intensive cultivation of the soil. In taking such measures the Arab peasant and tenant farmers shall be protected in their rights and shall be assisted in forwarding their economic development.[611]

The aftermath of World War I led to Britain's inability to devote sufficient effort to this agreement's implementation and the first historic opportunity for accommodation passed.

That mutually accommodative atmosphere did not last too long. By 1936, the Palestine region had experienced several severe outbreaks of civil strife between Arabs and Jews. As a result, the Palestine Royal Commission (also known as the Peel Commission) was appointed to look into the violence and other matters pertaining to the British Mandate. In 1937, the Commission found:

> The Jewish National Home is no longer an experiment…The temper of the Home is strongly nationalist. There can be no question of fusion or assimilation between Jewish and Arab cultures. The National Home cannot be half-national…Arab nationalism is as intense a force as Jewish. The Arab leaders' demand for national self-government and the shutting down of the Jewish National Home has remained unchanged since 1929…

> The position of the Palestine Government between the two antagonistic communities is unenviable. There are two rival bodies—the Arab Higher Committee allied with the Supreme Moslem Council on the one hand, and the Jewish Agency allied with the Va'ad Leumi on the other—who make a stronger appeal to the natural loyalty of the Arab and the Jews than does the Government of Palestine. The sincere attempts of the Government to treat the two races impartially have not improved the relations between them. Nor has the policy of conciliating Arab opposition been successful. The events of last year proved that conciliation is useless. The evidence submitted by the Arab and Jewish leaders respectively was directly conflicting and gave no hope of compromise.[612]

In light of these circumstances, the Peel Commission recommended a partitioning of the land between the Arab and Jewish populations. World War II's onset precluded implementation of this report's recommendations.

After World War II, civil strife was intensifying in the region. The Library of Congress' Country Study on Israel explains:

> By 1947 Palestine was a major trouble spot in the British Empire, requiring some 100,000 troops and a huge maintenance budget. On February 18, 1947, Bevin informed the House of Commons of the government's decision to present the Palestine problem to the United Nations (UN). On May 15, 1947, a special session of the UN General Assembly established the United Nations Special Committee on Palestine (UNSCOP), consisting of eleven members. The UNSCOP reported on August 31 that a majority of its members supported a geographically complex system of partition into separate Arab and Jewish states, a special international status for Jerusalem, and an economic union linking the three members. Backed by both the United States and the Soviet Union, the plan was adopted after two months of intense deliberations as the UN General Assembly Resolution of November 29, 1947. Although considering the plan defective in terms of their expectations from the League of Nations Mandate twenty-five years earlier, the Zionist General Council stated willingness in principle to accept partition. The League of Arab States (Arab League) Council, meeting in December 1947, said it would take whatever measures were required to prevent implementation of the resolution.[613]

Upon Israel's Declaration of Independence on May 15, 1948, Arab armies launched invasions of the new state. Consequently, another historic opportunity for a compromise settlement was missed.

Three more wars followed in 1956, 1967, and 1973. These resulted in Israel gaining control of East Jerusalem (from Jordan), the West Bank (from Jordan), Gaza Strip (from Egypt), and the Golan Heights (from Syria).

Periodic peace efforts to resolve this dispute have all failed so far. The Oslo process which began in 1993 with the signing of the Israel-Palestine Liberation Organization Agreement of 1993 ("Oslo Agreement") moved ahead in spite of continuing terrorist attacks against Israel. On December 28, 2000, Israeli Prime Minister Ehud Barak accepted President Clinton's bridging proposal that would have granted to the Palestinians 97 percent of the West Bank, 100 percent of the Gaza Strip, all of East Jerusalem except for the Western Wall, established a $30 billion fund for Palestinian refugees, and made it possible for all Palestinian refugees to move to the new Palestinian state. Palestinian leader Yasser Arafat rejected the agreement, insisting that Palestinian refugees (all refugees from the 1948 War and all their descendents) be accepted by Israel. In effect, Arafat attempted to use the diplomatic process to repeal the creation of Israel. A third historic opportunity for peace had failed to be realized.

President Bush's Road Map initiative that began in 2002 also floundered largely due to Palestinian unwillingness to disarm and dismantle the terrorist groups as called for in Stage 1 of the Road Map process. During spring 2004, Israeli Prime Minister Ariel Sharon proposed an initiative that would have led Israel to unilaterally withdraw settlements from the Gaza Strip and parts of the West Bank. In 2005, Israel completed its disengagement from the Gaza Strip and portions of the West Bank. Whether or not the post-Arafat period sees the emergence of new Palestinian leadership that is committed to fighting terrorism and compromising in the negotiating process remains to be seen and at this time, one cannot confidently predict any near-term breakthroughs.

In the end, there have been fleeting opportunities for progress in the past that failed to materialize, so a sense of caution is required in the early stages of the evolution of the post-Arafat period. What remains unchanged is that the historic dispute remains a sore point among Arabs and a focal point of Arab anger directed toward the U.S. due to its strategic relationship with Israel. This situation has important ramifications for the United States with regard to international terrorism and it remains likely that resolution of this historic dispute could be one of the keys to successfully waging and winning the war on terrorism.

A Fertile Soil for Terrorism

The backwardness in terms of living standards and combined deficiencies in the education/media in the Islamic World have real consequences in terms of how the people there view themselves, the rest of the world, and the approach they take with regard to the historic Arab-Israeli dispute. Today, distrust and animosity, particularly toward the United States are widespread and extensive.

Recent polling data showed that support for the U.S.-led war on terrorism remained minimal in major Islamic states. By March 2004, just 37 percent of those surveyed in Turkey supported the war on terrorism and 28 percent in Morocco favored it. In Pakistan and Jordan, support came to 16 percent and 12 percent respectively.[614]

In addition, the United States was viewed either somewhat unfavorably or very unfavorably by a majority in all four countries, with 61 percent in Pakistan, 63 percent in Turkey, 68 percent in Morocco, and 93 percent in Jordan holding such views.[615] Worse, 59 percent of Germans and 62 percent of French residents held similar views and in France 54 percent of respondents felt that the world would be safer if another country were as powerful as the United States.[616] With respect to the overall war on terrorism, small majorities in France and Turkey felt that the United States was overreacting to the threat of terrorism, while over-whelming majorities reached the same conclusion in Jordan, Pakistan, and Morocco, all three of which are crucial frontline states in the ongoing war on ter-rorism.[617] Even more disturbing, a majority of respondents in Jordan and Paki-stan viewed Osama Bin Laden favorably and the population was equally divided with respect to Osama Bin Laden in Morocco.[618] Finally, majorities in France, Jordan, Turkey, Morocco, and Pakistan felt that the United States seeks to con-trol Middle East oil and to dominate the world.[619]

In the Islamic world, these results are not surprising when considering the eroding citizen education there. "People try to understand why they feel so pow-erless," Dr. Robert Kramer, a professor of organizational behavior at Stanford Business School explains in discussing why people sometimes adopt conspiracy theories. "[O]ne ready explanation is that since we're good people, there must be powerful, evil forces arrayed against us."[620] When one considers the lack of inde-pendent media sources and lack of education combined with the past pre-emi-nence in the region, the picture grows even clearer. "Paranoia often springs up when information is lacking, filling a basic human urge to connect the dots and form a coherent picture," reports Erica Goode of *The New York Times.* "Abroad, conspiracy theories gain purchase from basic misconceptions about American society."[621] Friedman concurs. "[T]his negative view of America as a nation that achieved wealth and power without any spiritual values is also deliberately nur-tured by governments and groups in the Middle East. It is a way of explaining away their own failures to deliver a better life for their own people: The Ameri-cans are powerful only because they stole from us or from others—not because of anything intrinsically spiritual or humane in their society," he states.[622]

This latest UNDP report demonstrates clearly that the retreat from democra-tization and embrace of repression that now pervades Islamic societies and their institutions is largely responsible for the feeling of a lack of well-being that is so prevalent in many parts of the Islamic World.

Global Strategies for Winning the 21st Century War Against Terrorism

Given the historic, social, and political dynamics in play with regard to the war on terrorism, winning this war will require that the West develop a comprehen-sive strategy that includes military, financial, economic, political, and communi-cations resources. Understanding the history and the general causes of terrorism will be essential to crafting effective strategies for combating terrorism in various parts of the world.

In addition, a reasonable profile for state sponsors of terrorists or states in which terrorist movements are likely to take root can be developed. In general, many if not all of the following conditions exist: (1) political repression, (2) a lack of economic freedom, (3) a sufficiently large base of uneducated or undereducated persons, (4) a strong secular or religious-based ideology, (5) access to a ready supply of weapons, bombs, etc.[623]

Political repression tends to "close the door" to the ability of people to make changes through the political process and deprives them of their civil liberties and political rights. Unfortunately a rogue state-authoritarian ruler autocracy is the model, which has led to political repression and poverty in much of the Islamic world. A lack of economic freedom combined with the absence of individual property rights has reduced or minimized opportunities for these populations to improve their economic well-being realize job opportunities, develop employment skills that can create a productive economy providing middle-class incomes. A lack of economic and political freedom greatly curtails the ability to improve the standard of living that is possible in any given country. Conversely, a broad base of uneducated or undereducated people living in poverty will make it much easier for terrorist leaders to recruit followers to their cause. This is especially the case when the people lack the knowledge and ability to obtain information needed to challenge their lack of opportunity and ability to find more productive endeavors as well as achieve change through the political process.

This combination of factors has led to a sub-standard level of living across wide parts of the Islamic world, particularly in the Middle East and North Africa. It has been particularly jarring to Muslims in these regions. They have found it humiliating that an Islamic culture that had been preeminent for a millennium has now become backward and inferior to a Western civilization, which Islam had conquered and exceeded for many centuries.

Daniel Pipes has written the following description of this decline in Islamic culture and of the anger and humiliation it has fostered among many Muslims contributing to their contemporary resentment of the West.

> This anger has deep roots. From the Islamic religion's origins in the seventh century and for roughly the next millennium, the career of Muslims was one of consistent worldly success. By whatever standard one judged—power, wealth, health, or education—Muslims stood at the pinnacle of global achievement. This connection between accepting the Islamic message and apparent reward by God endured in so many aspects of life in so many places

for such a long time that Muslims readily came to assume that mundane well-being was their due as a sign of God's favor. To be Muslim meant to be on the winning team.

But then, starting about 1800, things went awry. Power wealth, health, and education moved elsewhere, and specifically to Europe, a place long scorned as backward. For two centuries, Muslims have watched as other peoples, especially Christians surged ahead. Not only did France, England, and the United States do so on the grandest scale, but more recently East Asia has outpaced the Muslim world. As a result, a sense of failure has suffused Muslim life. If Islam brings God's grace, many Muslims have asked themselves, why do Muslims fare so poorly? This traumatic of things going all wrong is key to understanding modern Islam.[624]

The Cato Institute's Brink Lindsey similarly concludes, "Modernity thus came as a humiliation, a shocking realization that the local culture was hopelessly backward compared with that of the new foreign masters."[625]

This falling behind of the Islamic world in the Middle East and North Africa has led to many of the states attempting various schemes to regain lost ground, albeit unsuccessfully as the fundamental factors needed for a successful shift to market economics and political democracy have not been present in a large part of this area. "Despite extensive soul-searching, Muslims have not found an answer to the question 'what went wrong?' Instead, they have bounced from one scheme to another, finding satisfaction in none of them. A succession of false starts have left Muslims deeply perplexed about their predicament, and not a little frustrated. In all, Muslims sense their own conspicuous lack of success in emerging from the humiliation of current circumstances," Pipes explains.[626]

Another major reason for the Middle East's lack of development may well have been the discovery of oil in the Middle East. In a lecture at a lecture at the Greenwich Library in Greenwich, Connecticut, historian Bernard Lewis explained that the discovery of oil and its increasing importance as an energy source proved particularly damaging in spite of its economic benefits. Its discovery and rise in importance largely allowed the region to avoid a "no taxation without representation" debate. As oil revenue funded Arab governments due to their control over the region's oil wealth, these governments had little need to be concerned with representation. Hence, the dependable stream of oil income as a substitute for taxation helped strengthen autocracy in the region.[627]

In his recent book, *Jihad: The Trail of Political Islam*, Gilles Kepel explains that "Petro-Islam" and the expansion of the extreme Wahhabist movement was greatly aided by the 1973 Arab-Israeli War. In the aftermath of the war, the world's oil supply had been reduced, the price of oil had risen and Saudi Arabia "now had unlimited means with which to further its ancient ambition of hegemony over the Community of the Faithful."[628]The rise in oil-based incomes also had indirect benefits for non-oil producers. Kepel explains that migrant workers from such states were able to send money back home to their families and this helped insulate the regimes of non-oil producers from public accountability for their inability to generate and sustain meaningful economic growth.[629]

This repression-driven absence of economic growth, and the lack of political accountability and Wahhabite expansion made possible by the discovery and importance of oil is also undercutting the possibilities for the Islamic states to offer a quality education to their citizens. "The boxes of catalogue cards scattered on the floor [Cairo University Library] are emblematic of the way that poverty has caused higher education to unravel in the once proud universities in most parts of the Muslim world," states Roy Mottahedeh, professor of Islamic Studies at Harvard University, adding that undergraduate education in such societies needs to be a priority "Because the enormous bulge of populations under 21 in these countries are hungry for education and understanding, and they are the future interpreters of their cultures."[630] He also concludes that access to a liberal education for students in Islamic states is essential because a 'liberal' education teaches us to think critically and write intelligently about both the human and scientific spheres which is a value that the Muslim and Western cultures have shared for more than a thousand years."[631]

The United Nations Development Program's 2003 Arab Human Development Report concluded that the region's dependence on oil has caused significant harm to its capacity for knowledge production. "One of the main features of the production pattern prevailing in Arab countries, which influences knowledge acquisition, is a high dependence on the depletion of raw materials, chiefly oil, and reliance on external rents. This rentier economic pattern entices societies to import expertise from outside because this is a quick and easy resort that however ends up weakening local demand for knowledge and forfeiting opportunities to produce it locally and employ it effectively in economic activity," [632] the report stated.

Free Market, Democratic, and Legal Reforms will be necessary in the Arab and Islamic world

Western assistance alone cannot change the adverse fortunes of contemporary Islamic states. Rather, those countries will need to undertake substantial internal reforms. They will need to embrace both democratic governance and economic freedom.

Currently, it is the absence of both that is significantly hindering progress in the Middle East and other parts of the Islamic world. In the Middle East, there is a substantial difference in citizen well-being between those states that are economically and politically free and those that are not. For example, entering the 21st century, average global annual per capita GDP was approximately $8,200. In economically-free states, the figure rises to $15,704. In politically-free states, it reached $16,449. States that are both economically and politically free fare best with an average figure of $17,073. Those that lacked economic freedom had an average annual per capita GDP of $3,198 and those that lacked political freedom were at only $4,433.[633]

The Middle East has sizable gaps in well-being that are masked by significant endowments in oil reserves. The average annual per capita GDP figure overall is $10,586. Economically-free states enjoy a higher average annual GDP of $13,785 and politically-free states have an even higher per capita GDP of $18,723 (all politically free states are also have market-based economies). States lacking economic freedom suffer with a yearly GDP of only $4,955. Those countries restricting only political freedom have an annual GDP of $9,335.[634]

These gaps are not surprising and did not spring up overnight. It has been widely understood that "democratizaton" used in its broadest sense to include greater economic and/or political freedoms can put nations on a path toward substantially higher and sustained economic growth. States, however, that retreat from "democratization" moves to a path of greatly diminished growth, which can persist for years and even decades.[635] Yet, democratization seems largely absent in the Islamic world. Freedomhouse.org reports in *Freedom in the World 2001–2002*, "Since the early 1970s, when the third major historical wave of democratization began, the Islamic world, and in particular, its Arab core, have seen little evidence of improvements in political openness, respect for human rights and transparency."[636]

A study by the UN Development Programme (UNDP) has found the GDP in Spain to be greater than all 22 Arab states combined, whose total factor productivity declined at an average annual rate of 0.2 percent between 1960–1990. In 1960, the productivity of labor in the Arab world was 32 percent that of North America. By 1990, it had declined to 19 percent. The region overall did not develop as quickly as comparable regions and its achievements as measured by the UNDP's Human Development Index also lagged the world's average. Causes of these disproportionate results include a lack of emphasis on political rights, shortage of opportunities for obtaining quality educations, and the differing treatment accorded women.[637]

The 2003 Arab Human Development Report offers additional insight into the lack of development within the Arab world. It ties together culture, education, and media in explaining the region's lack of knowledge production and dissemination. This lack of knowledge production and dissemination ensures a lower standard of living than would otherwise be the case.

The report states, "Turning knowledge assets into knowledge capital requires the production of new knowledge in all areas: in the physical and social sciences, arts, humanities and all other forms of social activity and data in the report tell a story of "stagnation in certain areas of knowledge production, especially in the field of scientific research. In addition to think production, scientific research in Arab countries is held back by weak basic research and the almost total absence of advanced research in fields such as information technology and molecular biology."[638]

Given the region's lack of knowledge infrastructure, importing foreign technology also is not a panacea for the region's technological deficiencies. The report adds, "Arab countries' experiments with the transfer and adoption of technology have neither achieved the desired technological advancement nor yielded attractive returns on investments. Importing technology has not led to its adoption and internalization in the host country, let alone to its diffusion and production."[639]

The Al Qaeda terrorist group has a deliberate and longstanding strategy aimed at winning the hearts and minds of the Arab/Islamic world. In addition to the obstacles presented by lack of educational opportunity and lack of an independent media, etc., Al Qaeda's competing propaganda/disinformation effort complicates the U.S. effort to win the hearts and minds of the region's peoples. According to a November 2004 Congressional Research Service paper entitled, "Al Qaeda: Statements and Evolving Ideology," Al Qaeda has "conducted a sophisticated public relations and media communication campaign…designed to elicit psychological reactions and communicate complex political messages to a global audience as well as to specific populations in the Islamic world, the United States, Europe, and Asia."[640]

Al Qaeda's public relations strategy employs among the following elements:

- It utilizes "the sensitive historical and religious imagery of Islamic resistance to the European Crusades" to define the war on terrorism as an existential struggle between the U.S., Israel, and Islam. The wars in Iraq and Afghanistan are portrayed as the West's new crusades against Islam.

- It employs modern ideas and issues e.g., Samuel Huntington's theory on the "clash of civilizations" to articulate the message that the war on terrorism is really a war on Islam.

- It calls for Muslims to unite against what it seeks to define as the global threat against Islam and calls for a government based on Islamic law (the weakness on this point is that in practice Al Qaeda has touted the Taliban rule as an ideal model and the disastrous consequences of that rule can potentially be employed to drive moderate Muslims away from extremists).

- It employs a concept of "collective guilt" to justify attacks on American civilians, asserting that American society is "morally corrupt" and that because America's civilians choose their government, by extension they are responsible for its decisions.

- It seeks to create divisions. In April 2004, Bin Laden offered Europeans a conditional "truce" if they abandoned their support for the U.S. in both Iraq and Afghanistan. There were no takers. It also attempted to create divisions among Americans just prior to the 2004 Election.[641]

The report also noted, "Al Qaeda has displayed a pragmatic willingness to adapt its statements to changing circumstances while retaining a messianic commitment to its ideological agenda."[642] This adaptive capability makes the vital battle for hearts and minds especially difficult.

The Long-Term Global War on Terrorism: The Critical Battle for Hearts and Minds

Perhaps the most important battlefield in the "war on terrorism," likely will not occur in any military battlefield involving sophisticated and lethal weapons of war. Rather, it will most likely be spread out across classrooms, television sets and computers in the "battle for hearts and minds" both internationally and domestically. "The military struggle is a part of the struggle we face, but the far greater struggle we face is the war of ideas. As much as we worry about Bin Laden and Al Qaeda…we worry far more about the attitudes of tens of millions of young Arabs and hundreds of millions of young Muslims," Thomas Kean and Lee Hamilton, the Chairman and Vice-Chairman of the 9/11 Commission told the U.S. House of Representatives, "Those who sympathize with Bin Laden represent, in the long-term, a far greater threat to us. They represent the well-spring to refresh the doctrine of hate and destruction, no matter how many Al Qaeda members we capture or kill."[643] Given the very real barriers to the production and dissemination of knowledge in the Arab world, this battle might also be the more difficult one to wage.

The West's success in this battle would be greatly facilitated if it can join forces with mainstream Islam. "It must also strengthen the education of its own citizens and improve the accuracy and balance of reporting by Western-based media...At the same time, the Western world must immediately strengthen the education of its citizens, as well as the Islamic world, on the benefits, virtues, values and freedoms of Western civilization. The success of this initiative will be important to winning the 'war for hearts and minds.' Focus on youth [and]...give students an alternative to the fundamentalist groups that are breeding grounds for terrorism."[644]

Winning this critical battle will be a daunting challenge. As the war on terrorism remains ongoing, its magnitude is becoming increasingly clear. One sees military, political, religious, historical, and economic factors all at play. In the Islamic World, not to mention various other parts of the world, there is significant resentment or distrust expressed toward the United States.

Following a survey of Arab attitudes and U.S. public diplomacy with regard to the Arab World, The Advisory Group on Public Diplomacy for the Arab and Muslim World, which was established by the United States Department of State to address U.S. public diplomacy challenges as they relate to the Arab and Islamic world, issued a report to the that indicated much remained to be done in winning hearts and minds in the war on terrorism. Among other things, the report declared, "At a critical time in our nation's history, the apparatus of public diplomacy has proven inadequate, especially in the Arab and Muslim world...Our adversaries' success in the struggle of ideas is all the more stunning because American values are so widely shared. As one of our Iranian interlocutors put it, 'Who has anything against life, liberty and the pursuit of happiness?' We were also told that if America does not define itself, the extremists will do it for us..."[645]

The importance of effective public diplomacy extends beyond the war on terrorism. Public diplomacy will need to address the growing perception among some states that the United States is an empire. Failure to dispel that notion could lead to adverse consequences or at least foreign policy complications for the United States. Dimitri K. Simes, President of the Nixon Center, explains:

> [M]ost of the world sees the United States as a nascent imperial power...Whether or not the United States now views itself as an empire, for many foreigners it increasingly looks, walks, and talks like one, and they

respond to Washington accordingly…Empires cannot escape the laws of history. One of the most salient of these laws is that empires generate opposition to their rule, ranging from strategic realignment among states to terrorism within them. Another is that empires have never been cost free and that the level of opposition to them depends on the costs that the imperial power is willing to shoulder…An empire that displays weakness and is not taken seriously is an empire in trouble. Being perceived as capricious or imperious, however, is also dangerous.[646]

Broad Reforms to Jointly Win and Retain the Hearts and Minds of the West and Traditional Islamic States

A multifaceted strategy will be required to win and retain the "hearts and minds" of people in the West and in the Islamic World. "Today, the youth of the Muslim world, deeply confused about their identity and critical of their own corrupt and autocratic rulers, seek refuge in another extreme ideology that promises a better and more dignified life. The United States, heeding its past successes, must offer a more compelling alternative," former U.S. diplomat Helena Finn explains.[647] Its cornerstones will be communications and education initiatives coupled with political and economic reforms needed for the Islamic world to overcome its grinding poverty and lack of personal freedoms.

Based on the ideological nature of the war on terrorism and issues concerning education and the media in the Arab and Islamic worlds, some of the communication strategies employed during the Cold War offer useful approaches that could prove applicable today. The rise of the Internet makes such a task even more readily achievable than it was during the time of the Cold War.

Misleading statements issued in the name of Islam should be challenged. Qu'ranic verses that prohibit the killing of innocents and suicide need to be highlighted. People in the West should be informed that individuals and groups who exploit Islam are not representative of Islam in general or the vast majority of Muslims in particular.

In terms of education in Islamic states, the United States and Pakistan have recently entered into a partnership aimed at improving Pakistan's educational system and thereby eroding the incentive for Pakistani youth to enter madrasas as an alternative to Pakistan's public schools. The U.S. Agency for International Development (USAID) is implementing a 5-year, $100-million agreement aimed at increasing access to quality education throughout Pakistan.[648] With regard to the challenges confronting education in Pakistan, not unlike those in other Islamic states, the Congressional Research Service recently noted, "[R]esistance to the reform of Pakistan's madrassas is fierce, and the schools identified as the most immediately threatening to Pakistani society and U.S. interests—though small in number—may be immune to governmental pressure due to their access to external funding sources and their close connections to powerful Islamist politicians. One nongovernmental report identifies centralized and 'deeply politicized' control of Pakistan's public education system—perhaps most especially of curriculum and textbooks—and an over-emphasis on Urdu-medium instruction to be important causes and exacerbators of the country's ongoing ethnic and sectarian divisions. The report also criticizes centralized curricular decision-making as bringing about a rise in the Islamization of public syllabi, an outcome that may be the intent of national leaders seeking to manipulate religious fervor in pursuit of foreign policy goals in Kashmir and Afghanistan."[649]

What are we Fighting for? Is it Worth the Cost?

To be sure, the war against terrorism will be a long and difficult struggle. At times it might well prove tempting for political leaders and citizens to cut short the struggle. In the face of sometimes difficult sacrifices, some might even advance the notion that the struggle could be pursued through wholly non-military means. However, in the past, efforts founded solely on trade assistance, financial credits, and diplomacy have not always achieved the objectives of such policies.[650]

Consequently, no task will be more vital than ensuring that the West's citizens and political leaders understand what they are fighting for. A letter written in 2002 by David Blankenhorn, president of the Institute for American Values, to global intellectuals and leaders, and signed by influential and respected academics and civic leaders across the United States concisely articulates the paramount values that are being defended by the U.S.-led coalition carrying out the global "war on terrorism."

"At times it becomes necessary for a nation to defend itself through force of arms. Because war is a grave matter, involving the sacrifice and taking of precious human life, conscience demands that those who would wage the war state clearly the moral reasoning behind their actions, in order to make plain to one another, and to the world community, the principles they are defending," the letter states.[651] It then outlines the case for the U.S. led coalition "war on terrorism" affirming that it satisfies the traditional criteria for a "just" war in protecting innocents from harm, fighting against a great danger, being conducted by a legitimate authority having a responsibility for public safety, and is conducted only against combatants.[652]

Preemptive military action in this instance is consistent with the principles outlined above, because all efforts in the military campaign are being made to secure the safety of innocent persons. Given the unprovoked nature of such attacks as those that occurred on 9/11 creating a "destroy or be destroyed" nature to the conflict.

A non-military dimension in the battle for hearts and minds must also be waged in the Islamic world (countries whose populations are predominantly Muslim), where the educational and media institutions are held captive by repressive governments or political extremists and used for indoctrination and propaganda purposes against the West.

The challenge posed by the "forced ignorance" of the populations in the Islamic world will not be easy to overcome. David Hoffman warns, "…slick marketing techniques and legions of U.S. spokespersons on satellite television will not be sufficient to stem the tide of xenophobia sweeping through the Islamic' world. When antiterrorist ads produced by the U.S. government were shown recently to focus groups in Jordan, the majority of respondents were simply puzzled, protesting, 'But Bin Laden is a holy man.' The widespread antagonism to U.S. regional policies further limits what public diplomacy can achieve."[653]

All areas of common ground should be seen as opportunities where the West can constructively engage the Islamic world in surmounting fundamental disagreements to combat terrorism. The West can also assist in bringing political and economic reforms essential to improving the well-being of the Islamic world without abandoning traditional Islamic culture, religion and values.

Conclusion

Following the 9/11 attacks, the U.S. finds itself in yet another giant struggle with enormous stakes. This is likely to be a long-term, widespread struggle, as the July 7, 2005 coordinated terrorist attacks on the London transit system[654] indicate that the terrorists aim to make the entire Western world their battlefield.

Such a struggle is consistent with the periodic turns in the cycles of history. This fight against radical Islam as promoted by the new generation of totalitarians is not unlike the Cold War against Communism in which the U.S. and its Western allies endured for 45 years until the ideological struggle concluded with a U.S. and Western victory. Given the quasi-religious nature of the current conflict, the differences are even more basic and likely enduring than those pertaining to conflicting political ideologies at play in the Cold War.

If the U.S. and its allies are to ultimately prevail, the role that their citizens and institutions play will be decisive. The health of the United States' culture and institutions, the quality of the education received by its citizens, and their willingness to participate and sacrifice will be essential to sustaining the long struggle against terrorism and weapons of mass destruction. Toward that end, it will be important that the U.S. and its coalition partners "stay the course" and remain rooted in virtue. Primary, secondary and higher education will need to strengthen their curricula to include more comprehensive courses in Western Civilization, U.S. and World history, as well as, civics, geography and religion so that citizens will understand and effectively carry out their basic responsibilities. A well-functioning media with First Amendment freedoms that gathers and transmits needed and often complex information in a fair and objective manner with requisite background context will be important and needed by the citizens to understand the challenges that they are facing.

U.S. culture since the last decades of the 20th century has been corroded by a self-absorbed philosophy based on moral relativism (which asserts that there is no such thing as "right" or "wrong") and has seen its institutions of marriage family and religion weakened. The education of its citizens all too often embraces the principles of multiculturalism and political correctness. These are serious institutional matters that if not quickly and effectively addressed can lead the U.S. into a dangerous decline and citizens' loss of freedom in the process. That is the lesson of the cycles of history and the 20th century experience with utopian socialistic and communist rule.

Weariness and apathy must not be options. They can only lead to aggressors exploiting both actual and perceived weakness to their advantage with a grave loss to Western Civilization. The 21st century war on terrorism is much different from World War II and the Cold War. The United States "homeland" is a battleground with its civilians the targets. The terrorist enemy does not respect the Geneva Conventions or other norms that treat civilians during war as "protected" persons. Terrorists seek to deliberately attack and murder civilians to spread fear, inflict economic and social costs, and weaken a country's resolve to fight such as to lose the war.

A combination of heroic virtue, a sound culture and engaged citizens with the strong educational-informational background is required if the United States and its allies are to prevail. The ability of the residents of London to withstand the heavy aerial bombardment from Nazi Germany's Luftwaffe at a critical point in

World War II demonstrates that free people who know what they are fighting for and are prepared to sacrifice greatly cannot be defeated.

A similar challenge currently confronts 21st century America. America's destiny now rests in the hands of its citizens, culture, and institutions together with those of its allies. They have already endured a difficult two-year period of trial and have emerged stronger and prepared to stay the course. It will not be easy and a significant additional sacrifice will likely be required. The ultimate outcome turns on the citizen's ability to address and promptly repair the damages inflicted on the culture and the quality of the education of its citizens.

Iraq: What's Next?

Following months of inconclusive weapons inspections, on March 17, 2003, in a nationally-televised address, President Bush issued a blunt ultimatum for Saddam Hussein and his leadership to vacate Iraq. "Saddam Hussein and his sons must leave Iraq within 48 hours. Their refusal to do so will result in military conflict, commenced at a time of our choosing," Bush declared.[655] Since the end of the major military campaign, a low-level uprising led principally by the deposed Hussein dictatorship's remnants and foreign terrorist elements has been ongoing. Initially, the focus of such hostilities had been narrowly confined for the most part, though sporadic sabotage has occurred against critical Iraqi infrastructure. Later, it was directed against the emerging new Iraqi Government, even after elections had been held.

There is little doubt that the challenge of Iraq's democratic transformation and reconstruction will be enormous. "The reality is that Arab civil society on the whole has not been a force for democratization. Civil society, as the zone of voluntary associative life beyond family ties but separate from the state and the market, fulfills a variety of functions. Like elsewhere, the zone of civil society in Arab countries can be a source of democratic change, but it is not inherently one. The bulk of Arab civil society is made up of organizations, associations, and movements that support the status quo, advocate conservative reforms, or are simply apolitical,"[656] Amy Hawthorne of the Carnegie Endowment for International Peace explains.

To date, Arab reform initiatives have not provided significant positive results. "Worst of all are the political results: the long quest for freedom has left a string of shabby tyrannies, ranging from traditional autocracies to dictatorships that are modern only in their apparatus of repression and freedom," Bernard Lewis explains.[657] These results suggest that the United States and its allies will need to play an intensive role in helping Iraqis develop governing institutions, a constitution that protects the rights of women and ethnic and religious minorities, and provides for a strong legislature, and preparing those who will be charged with governance, upholding the rule of law, and providing security.

Historically, the success rate for such nation-building projects has been low. Just 4 of 15 such projects have led to democracy after a decade. These projects are West Germany (1945–49), Japan (1945–52), Grenada (1983) and Panama (1989).[658] In all these successes, each of the countries had at least some earlier experience with regard to democracy or democratic institutions. Moreover, the larger-scale nation-building projects (Germany and Japan) required a commitment of several years.

Second, few Presidents have ever embarked on the number of mega projects currently being pursued by President Bush: war on terrorism, rebuilding of Afghanistan and Iraq, and pursuit of a resolution of the Israeli-Palestinian dispute. Only President Wilson and President Truman undertook multiple projects of a similar scale.

All of these projects will require a significant time commitment, financial resources, and in the cases of Iraq, Afghanistan, and the war on terrorism, U.S. military manpower. With the federal budget deficit now reaching $450 billion, the economy emerging from a period of weakness and the recurring casualties in Iraq, there will likely be abundant temptations for the nation to abandon at least some of these projects.

On the other hand, the recent experience of the consequences of post-Soviet Afghanistan's falling into the hands of the Taliban and Al Qaeda serves as a vivid reminder of the dangers of pursuing a half-hearted reconstruction effort, particularly in Iraq.

At this time, Iraq likely faces at least three possible medium-term scenarios. It could evolve into a stable and self-sustaining democracy, its democratic experiment could proceed only to fizzle in the longer-term due to institutional, constitutional, and factional difficulties, or possibly sparked by a key assassination or terrorist attack, the democratic experiment could be derailed.

In a May 24, 2004 national address at the U.S. Army War College in Carlisle, Pennsylvania, President Bush vowed not to allow Iraq's democratic experiment to fail.

> These two visions, one of tyranny and murder, the other of liberty and life, clashed in Afghanistan. And thanks to brave U.S. and coalition forces and to Afghan patriots, the nightmare of the Taliban is over, and that nation is com-

ing to life again. These two visions have now met in Iraq, and are contending for the future of that country. The failure of freedom would only mark the beginning of peril and violence. But, my fellow Americans, we will not fail. We will persevere, and defeat this enemy, and hold this hard-won ground for the realm of liberty,[659]

However, Iraq is making progress even in the face of enormous challenges and the Iraqi people are beginning to take greater charge of their destiny. Following the election, there was an unprecedented case where civilians fought back against the terrorists that have been attempting to hinder the country's democratic transformation and economic reconstruction. The story also highlighted additional evidence that Iraq's civilians are turning against the terrorists. "Ordinary Iraqis rarely strike back at the insurgents who terrorize their country. But just before noon on Tuesday, a carpenter named Dhia saw a troop of masked gunmen with grenades coming toward his shop here and decided he had had enough. As the gunmen emerged from their cars, Dhia and his young relatives shouldered their Kalashnikov rifles and opened fire, the police and witnesses said. In the fierce gun battle that followed, three of the insurgents were killed, and the rest fled just after the police arrived," [660] *The New York Times* reported, "It was the first time that private citizens are known to have retaliated successfully against the insurgents. There have been anecdotal reports of residents shooting at attackers after a bombing or an assassination…The battle was the latest sign that Iraqis may be willing to start standing up against the attacks that leave dozens dead here nearly every week." If such a trend is sustained, the long-run prospects for the country's future could be substantially improved.

Iraq's democratization has also become a pivotal focus of the United States' forward strategy of advancing freedom to repressed parts of the world. The effort remains under stiff challenge from an assortment of terrorist organizations and remnants of the deposed Ba'athist regime of Saddam Hussein. However, the stakes in the outcome are so great that the United States can ill-afford to shrink from the necessary sacrifices entailed. "…if the United States loses in Iraq, the repercussions will seriously weaken America everywhere. If we lose in Iraq, neo-isolationism in both the Republican and Democratic parties the disposition is actually stronger on the left than on the right—will in all probability skyrocket. And if such a retreat could be catastrophic for the West—Bin Ladenism and other nefarious forces in the Middle East would be supercharged; Beijing might make a play to squash once and for all democratic Taiwan—then failure in Iraq could conceivably define the post-Cold War world, replacing 9/11 as the signal event of our era,"[661] American Enterprise Institute scholar Reuel Marc Gerecht explained.

Iraq's elected government prepared a draft constitution that was approved in a referendum held on October 15, 2005, though sizable sectors of Iraq's Sunni population rejected it.[662] In addition, Sunni voters turned out in much higher figures than they did in the January 2005 election.[663] Nationwide, Iraqis approved the draft constitution by a 79 percent–21 percent margin with 63 percent of Iraqis voting.[664]

In the wake of the referendum, evidence continued to point to a growing Sunni embrace of the democratic political process. Following the results of the referendum, leaders of three Sunni political parties joined together to participate in the December 15, 2005 parliamentary elections.[665] Sunni participation increased dramatically, with an estimated 88 percent turning out to vote in the Anbar Province, which has been the heart of the Sunni-led campaign of insurgency and terrorism.[666] Overall, 10.9 million Iraqis—or 70 percent of eligible voters—turned out to vote.[667] This represented a 20 percent increase in voter participation over the January 2005 turnout.[668] Violence during the election was much lower than that in the January 2005 election in which a transitional Parliament had been elected.[669]

With Sunni participation increasing, the December parliamentary elections could result in a more diverse slate of political leaders, who will then make possible amendments to the preliminary draft of the constitution that was just approved. Afterward, if Sunnis are satisfied with the process and outcome, their viewing the democratic process and constitution in terms of increased legitimacy could strengthen Sunni support for the final stages of Iraq's democratic transformation. If so, this development might well mark a major development against the largely Sunni-led insurgency and its terrorist groups.

Finally, even as Iraq undergoes its transition toward democracy, its Kurdish province offers a case study for Iraq and also Middle East democracy. Kurdistan undertook a shift toward democracy following the 1991 Iraq War under the protection of American and British no-fly zones. Since then, it has achieved sustained economic progress, begun to attract highly-skilled professionals from elsewhere in Iraq, and seen the rise of construction financed by the private sector, particularly Kurdish businessmen who live abroad. Kurdistan is also secular in nature where women enjoy equal rights in government employment.[670]

6

Ready or Not, It's Here

As the 20th century drew to a close, the United States appeared triumphant economically, politically, and militarily. It had successfully led the Free World's victory over communism in the Cold War. America's burgeoning annual federal budget deficits had been replaced by large and growing budget surpluses. The unemployment rate had fallen to levels approaching what some economists considered full employment. The U.S. was at peace and was defended by the strongest military in the world. To many, it appeared that the 21st century might turn out to be another "American Century."

However, shortly after the beginning of the 21st century, the United States and thousands of its citizens became the victims of suicide hijackers who flew commercial jets into the World Trade Center and Pentagon. Since then it has become clear that the new century will not be a paradise of unbroken peace and prosperity. The massive terrorist attacks in New York City and Washington, DC on September 11, 2001, which killed nearly 3,000 people, starkly demonstrated that the Free World's Cold War victory had not vanquished for all-time the kind of great global dangers that earlier had periodically tested the will and resolve of the world's free and democratic societies. Just a decade after the last great global ideological struggle ended, a new ideological war between totalitarianism and freedom was again underway.

This renewed struggle, however, occurs in an environment markedly different from that in which the 20th century Cold War was waged. The nation-state, which has remained the preeminent organizing governance principle for the world's peoples since the Treaty of Westphalia in 1648, at the beginning of the 21st century is in a period of transition with indications that this state-based system may be in decay.

The United States now finds itself in the early stages of a new period of "testing." Against the dangerous backdrop of dramatic global and domestic changes that have taken place and are still evolving, the United States now faces the formidable task of expediting the development of a global strategy capable of its helping lead the Free World to triumph over a quasi-religious and totalitarian challenge. Moreover, in a world accustomed to pursuing tight deadlines and focusing little farther than the near future, its strategy will likely have to stretch into the indefinite future.[671]

The 21st Century Global Environment

Chapter 1 introduced the reader to the concept of the cycles of history. It conveyed that while history has a linear nature; it also has a cyclical component. In the context of history's cycles, the 21st Century presents a new period of challenge.

Chapter 1 also discussed the waxing and waning of Great Powers. Although the United States has experienced at least some of the characteristics of a Great Power moving toward maturity and no Great Power to date has escaped over the long-run a subsequent period of decline. The United States, however, is fundamentally different from past empires and capable of avoiding their fate in that it was established with a republican form of government, which it retains today.

Chapter 1 also provided the reader with a survey of the major forces that are currently challenging and transforming the 21st century's global landscape and introducing dangerous risks. Such forces are capable of and likely to generate and promote both order and disorder. These risks of disorder are greatest during periods of transition and uncertainty such as those presented at the opening of the 21st century.

Globalization and technology are bringing enormous opportunities, but also are generating costs and risks. Technological innovation and the information revolution are making possible and available broadly opportunities for increased living standards, which can transcend borders and distance. Terrorists are already leveraging these forces for their own benefit through quasi-religious indoctrination and corruption. After all, technological advances are justified as having the benefit of reducing the costs of destruction according to historian Niall Ferguson writes.[672]

As globalization advances and the technology and information revolutions steam ahead, a rising tide of massive demographic change and ideological challenge also looms ahead. Gigantic demographic changes already are substantially increasing the pension and healthcare financial burdens of some countries from an expanded aging share of the population. These growing burdens can greatly magnify the scale of the ongoing struggle between democratic states and those under totalitarianism.

Chapters 1 and 4 provide a glimpse of the demographic future based on the U.S. Department of Census' newly released *Global Population Profile: 2002*. During the 2000–2050 half-century, the populations of underdeveloped and developing countries are expected to grow significantly faster than those of developed states. The world's poorest countries—those with a per capita GDP of one-third of the world average or below—are projected to account for nearly 70 percent of the world's population increase, with an increase of almost 2 billion persons.[673] Almost a third of that increase, just over 650 million persons, is likely to occur in states that are largely disconnected from the globalized world and at particularly high risk of becoming ungovernable or failed states.[674] If the ongoing efforts at economic development in China, India, and Russia should fail, the population increase attributed to states potentially at risk of becoming ungovernable would more than double to 1.33 billion persons.[675]

A closer look at the Islamic world, namely countries in which 50 percent or more of the population is comprised of Muslims, shows both robust, if not spectacular population growth, especially in the poorest countries. More than 90 percent of the Islamic world's predicted 1.2 billion person increase will occur in countries whose per capita GDP is below the world's average and two-thirds of that growth is expected to take place in countries whose per capita GDP is one-third or less of the world average.[676]

Several states that are near the epicenter of the ongoing war on terrorism are expected to see explosive population growth. Saudi Arabia's and Yemen's populations are predicted to nearly quadruple to 91.1 million and 71.1 million respectively by 2050.[677] Even as the world's population ages, those in Saudi Arabia and Yemen will remain remarkably youthful. Each of these two countries will see more than 50percent of their population comprised of persons under 20-years-old by 2025 (the latest year for which such projections are available).[678] In contrast, just 31.7 percent of the world's population and 21.6 percent of the developed countries' populations will be made up of persons younger than age 20.[679] Other states that are major battlegrounds in the war on terrorism such as Afghanistan and Pakistan will also remain significantly more youthful than the world as a whole.[680] This youth advantage will result in these countries continuing to experience population growth that exceeds that of the world, on average, and especially developed countries, an increasing number of which are expected to experience the onset of negative population growth during the 2002–2050 timeframe.

A Call to Citizens

Chapter 2 introduced the reader to the role and responsibility of U.S. citizens. It briefly explained the conception of the United States' unique form of republican government. Colonial America launched its revolution for independence on a simple, yet radical at the time, powerful proposition: *We hold these truths to be self-evident, that all men are created equal, that they are endowed by their Creator with certain unalienable Rights, that among these are Life, Liberty and the pursuit of Happiness.—That to secure these rights, Governments are instituted among Men, deriving their just powers from the consent of the governed...*[681] This proposition defined the principles, values and character that the United States' Founders set for its citizens: People's natural rights are beyond the reach of government. People create governments to protect these fundamental rights. Governments derive their authority from the consent of the people. Inherent in the principle that governments derive their authority from the consent of their people is also the recognition that the citizen has both rights and responsibilities.

The United States Constitution, adopted on September 17, 1787, established a federal government on the basis of the mission articulated in the Declaration of Independence. This new government was accorded significant but also limited powers. It contained a strong safeguard combined with a system of checks and balances against an undue accumulation of power in the form of a separation of powers among the major branches of government. In addition, the Constitution specifically reaffirmed that the states and the people were given the largest share of authority and protection over their own affairs.

Chapter 2 draws upon the *Federalist Papers* to explain the responsibilities that the Founders left for the nation's citizens. It was the Founders belief that, if the nation's democratic experiment was to succeed and endure, citizens must be informed and engaged in the affairs of their country.

The Knowledge and Skills 21st Century Citizens Require

In the 21st century environment, the skills, knowledge and fortitude required for citizens to effectively carry out their global role and responsibilities are more demanding than ever before. With the United States now having an array of critical and vital interests around the world, there is now a greater than ever premium on the kind of skills and knowledge that citizens must have to understand the growing number of diverse countries, cultures, peoples, policies, and their relationship to the United States.

Set forth below are a number of general principles and understandings that are highly relevant in forming a part of the framework by which citizens can consider in evaluating current and alternative U.S. options and policies.

Non-intervention/Isolationism is not a viable foreign policy.[682] Today, the United States has widespread and significant global interests. Neglecting or ignoring the realities of these interests and failing to take diplomatic, economic, and sometimes military steps to safeguard these interests could prove dangerous to the nation's security and well-being. Chapter 4 highlights the experience of pre-World War II disarmament and appeasement. Such approaches, while well-intended, could well signal to enemies and other would-be aggressors that a given country is weak or lacks resolve. Such calculations, whether or not accurate, could reduce the disincentives for such hostile elements to refrain from targeting American interests at home or abroad.

Toward that end, the American public will need to be vigilant against the siren call of those who advocate retreat or disengagement for the sake of peace. The ideal of "peace on any terms available" is little more than repackaged appeasement and it offers little prospect of offering any kind of enduring peace, much less security.

Such a radical outlook is not without precedent in American history. During times of difficulty or challenge, such siren calls have arisen in the past. Such a situation arose when President Harry Truman launched his effort to protect free Europe from the spread of communism. Then, former Vice President Henry Wallace vigorously fought such a new policy approach arguing that it would only make the world more dangerous, that the U.S. was undermining the United Nations and would "become the most hated nation in the world", and incredibly enough, that it was actually in the U.S. national interest for communism to succeed in the Soviet Union.[683] Today, in the early stages of the 21st century war on terrorism, one hears similar echoes of these earlier appeals.

The strength of America's culture is important in shaping its foreign policy and determining its outcomes: A nation's cultural grounding is an important factor that helps it define its destiny. Former Secretary of State Henry Kissinger observed, "[A] view of the future is too often submerged in tactics. The problem is not the inadequacy of individual leaders but rather the systemic problem of their cultural preparation."[684] In Chapter 3, the book provides a broad sketch of the state of the nation's culture and the underlying forces that shaped it into its present form.

The importance of the nation's broader internal situation cannot be underestimated. Arguably, internal decay could pose the greatest long-term threat to the nation's well-being. British historian Niall Ferguson explained, "The question Americans must ask themselves is just how transient they wish their predominance to be. Though the barbarians have already knocked at the gates—once, spectacularly—imperial decline in this case seems more likely to come, as it came to Gibbon's Rome, from within."[685]

Chapter 3 also introduces the PC culture concepts of moral and cultural relativism. This relativism lies at the root of any "peace at any price" movement, which rests on assumptions that there are essentially no distinguishing moral and cultural differences between the United States and its opponents. Were such fundamental differences to be acknowledged, they would preclude such an approach to formulating U.S. foreign policy, as those differences would suggest that America's offer of "peace at any price" might still be found unacceptable to those arrayed against it.

King George III's milder form of tyranny was an unbearable price that led America's Founders to "pledge to each other our Lives, our Fortunes and our sacred Honor."[686] Similarly, today's and tomorrow's citizens, must prepared to make the same kind of commitment and persevere in that cause against the international terrorists of the ilk of Osama Bin Laden and his allies, and in the future similar great challenges, if the nation's freedom, democracy, and economic prosperity are to be sustained for the long-term.

Access to quality information combined with an education that creates an ability to understand the world and employ that information will be required for optimal decision-making: To better understand the world and people around them, U.S. citizens will need a journalism media that provides timely and credible information. They will need an educational system—both at the primary and secondary levels and at the university level—that provides them with an intellectual framework that includes philosophy, mathematics, science, economics, history, geography, and languages, among others.

The role of education in preparing Americans for the responsibilities of citizenship is an essential role. In his 1953 Nobel Lecture, George Marshall told his audience, "Because wisdom in action in our Western Democracies rests squarely upon public understanding, I have long believed that our schools have a key role to play. Peace could be advanced through careful study of all the factors which have gone into the various incidents now historical that have marked the breakdown of peace in the past. As an initial procedure our schools, at least our colleges but preferably our senior high schools, as we call them, should have courses which not merely instruct our budding citizens in the historical sequence of events of the past, but which treat with almost scientific accuracy the circumstances which have marked the breakdown of peace and have led to the disruption of life and the horrors of war."[687]

During the 20th century, the nation's schools increasingly distanced themselves from this mission. Diana Ravitch, one of America's leading historians of education, observed, "Time and again, experts urged the schools to de-emphasize reading, writing, history, mathematics, and science; to drop foreign languages; to replace history with social studies; to eliminate high-quality literature and substitute for it uninspired scraps from textbooks; and to teach only what was useful and immediately functional."[688] "The study of history and philosophy, the disciplines most relevant to perfecting the art of statesmanship, are neglected everywhere or given such utilitarian interpretations that they can be enlisted in support of whatever passes for conventional wisdom,"[689] Kissinger adds.

> This development, if not corrected, could impose an incalculable adverse cost on American citizens. A society that turns its back on the teaching of history encourages mass amnesia, leaving the public ignorant of the important events and ideas of the human past and eroding the civic intelligence needed for the future. A democratic society that fails to teach the younger generation its principles of self-government puts these principles at risk…A society that is racially and ethnically diverse requires, more than other societies, a conscious effort to build shared values and ideals among its citizenry."[690]

The Global War Against Terrorism

Early in the 21st century, the United States is threatened by an expanding fundamentalist terror movement fueled by Islamic radicalism. This terrorism is a product of a combination of an ongoing internal struggle that is being waged in the Islamic world between liberal Islam and Islamic fundamentalism, the oppression of the authoritarian states that predominate the Islamic world and deprive their citizens of political and economic opportunities only found in free and democratic states, and the hazardous environments that exist in failed or failing states.

Chapter 4 provides readers with a broad survey of the overall war on terrorism. It highlighted historical information that has shaped the modern-day Arab and Islamic worlds and drew upon lessons from history in setting out a broad approach for addressing the challenge of terrorism. It also discussed the role of state sponsors of terrorism and the dangers posed by a possible convergence of weapons of mass destruction (WMD) and terrorism.

Winning the "hearts and minds" of the Islamic world was described as an important part of the comprehensive strategy for winning the war on terrorism set forth in Chapter 4. A declassified Department of Defense memo dated October 1, 2001 explained of the then forthcoming war in Afghanistan,

> This war has been a long time in incubation and now hatched is not the war between nation states we are familiar with. It is a war fought on two fronts: one against material assets and the other in the minds of men…The minds of men front. Ultimately this is the largest front, the hardest to fight, and the hardest to win.[691]:

U.S. and UN Roles In Addressing "State Failure:"

State failure is another element that has bearing on the outcome of the war on terrorism and can have an adverse impact on critical U.S. interests. Basically, a failed state is one that is no longer capable of handling the most basic functions of governance: maintaining law and order, providing for its own defense, or sustaining a viable economy. Chester Crocker, a professor of Strategic Studies at Georgetown University's School of Foreign Service explains, "State failure directly affects a broad range of U.S. interest, including the promotion of human rights, good governance, the rule of law, religious tolerance, environmental preservation, and opportunities for U.S. investors and exporters. It contributes to regional insecurity, weapons proliferation, narcotics trafficking, and terrorism."[692]

The process that leads to state failure is often a gradual process and the decay might not be readily apparent for an extended period of time. However, Crocker notes, "When state failure sets in, the balance of power shifts ominously against ordinary civilians and in favor of armed entities operating outside the law (or with tacit official approval)."[693]

Crocker then adds, "State failures (and associated conflicts) overwhelmingly occur in wretchedly poor countries, not in wealthy industrial or post-industrial states."[694] In his February 24, 2004 testimony before the Senate Select Committee on Intelligence, Vice Admiral Lowell E. Jacoby expressed concern over the world's various "ungoverned spaces." He told the Committee:

> "We are…increasingly concerned over Ungoverned Spaces, defined as geographic areas where governments do not exercise effective control. Terrorist groups and narcotic-traffickers use these areas as sanctuaries to train, plan and organize, relatively free from interference. There are numerous Ungoverned Spaces around the world such as the western provinces in Pakistan, portions of

the southern Philippines, Indonesian islands, Chechnya, rural areas in Burma, several areas in Africa and areas in South America. Ungoverned Spaces included densely populated cities where terrorists can congregate and prepare for operations with relative impunity. I believe these areas will play an increasingly important role in the war on terrorism as Al Qaeda, its associated groups and other terrorist organizations use these areas as bases for operations."[695]

Failing states, failed states, or ungoverned spaces are typically disconnected for globalization. Thomas P.M. Barnett of the U.S. Naval War College explains, "[W]here globalization is thick with network connectivity, financial transactions, liberal media flows, [there is]collective security...stable governments and rising standards of living...where globalization is thinning or just plain absent...regions [are] plagued by politically repressive regimes, widespread poverty and disease, routine mass murder, and—most important—the chronic conflicts that incubate the next generation of global terrorists."[696]

If permitted to fester for long in their disconnected state, these global backwaters can give rise to threats that impact the United States, its allies, and their interests. Occasionally such situations can make it necessary for the United States to deploy its armed forces there. Barnett writes, "If a country is either losing out to globalization or rejecting much of the content flows associated with its advance, there is a far greater chance that the U.S. will end up sending forces at some point," and, "a country's potential to warrant a U.S. military response is inversely related to its globalization connectivity."[697]

The reason such situations can threaten U.S. or allied interests and even require U.S. military intervention is that such conditions are difficult to isolate or contain. Rather, state failure is tied to internal strife and humanitarian crises and such situations can spread beyond an affected area's borders to destabilize entire regions.[698] Trends in indicators such as the Heritage Foundation's Index of Economic Freedom, the World Bank's Governance Indicators, and Freedomhouse.org's indices of political rights and civil liberties, among other tools, can help identify countries that are vulnerable to state failure or have begun to evolve down that path.

The key challenge for the United States is not to confront state failure after it occurs. By then, the costs and risks are already enormous and damage to U.S. or allied interests has likely been inflicted. It is important that the United States and its allies together with the UN, where it is capable, be able to recognize and reverse the process before states fail.[699] Such candidates for future state failure include Saudi Arabia, Russia, Colombia, and North Korea, among others.[700] The UN Security Council could also play an important role in working proactively to assist states in danger of failure e.g., with regard to helping provide stabilization forces as needed.

Far from treating the state failure process as being an inappropriate demand on American foreign policy, policymakers need to recognize the importance of addressing such situations. Barnett warns that such challenges can only be ignored at the nation's peril. "History is full of turning points like that terrible day [9/11], but no turning-back-points. We ignore the gap's existence at our own peril, because it will not go away until we as a nation respond to the challenge of making globalization truly global."[701]

To meet these challenges will require that the United States maintain robust economic and military power and remain engaged in such areas of global affairs even as some critics assert without solid proof that U.S. hegemony is harmful to the world. What is harmful to the world's interests is the failure of a majority of European countries to maintain the level of military resources needed to create a successful deterrent, as would be an erosion of U.S. economic and military strength and a reduced willingness on the part of the United States to involve itself in major global matters.

In the July/August 2004 edition of Foreign Affairs, Johns Hopkins University Professor of Strategic Studies, Eliot Cohen explains,

> The United States today…has less choice about its role in world affairs than its worried leaders and their critics, or its anxious friends and numerous enemies, think. The logic of empire is a logic of extension, and the strategic conundrum of empire is that of over commitment and overstretch. Despite the wishes of French and Chinese politicians, no countervailing state or federation will restore a balance-of-power system akin to that of Europe in the eighteenth and nineteenth centuries, at least not in the near future. Despite the wishes of idealists, no international institution has proven capable of effective action in the absence of the power generated and exercised by states. And a third possibility—anarchy unleashed after a disgusted United States recalls its legions in a spurt of democratic disgust at and indifference to the rest of the planet—is too horrifying to contemplate.[702]

Some pundits suggest that a world without U.S. power would likely become the kind of multi-polar, balance-of-powers type arrangement that prevailed during the 19th century. British historian Niall Ferguson asserts that such thinking could prove disastrously incorrect. "What if, instead of a balance of power, there is an absence of power?"[703]

A world populated by numerous failed or failing states, along with the robust demographic growth projected for such states, could be especially dangerous. Ferguson warns that it could evolve into a new "Dark Ages." He then describes just what such a world might be like:

> Waning empires. Religious revivals. Incipient anarchy. A coming retreat into fortified cities. These are the Dark Age experiences that a world without a hyper-power might quickly find itself reliving. The trouble is, of course, that this Dark Age would be an altogether more dangerous one than the Dark Age of the ninth century. For the world is much more populous—roughly 20 times more—so friction between the world's disparate "tribes" is bound to be more frequent. Technology has transformed production; now human societies depend not merely on freshwater and the harvest but also on supplies of fossil fuels that are known to be finite. Technology has upgraded destruction, too, so it is now possible not just to sack a city but to obliterate it…The alternative to unipolarity would not be multipolarity at all. It would be apolarity—a global vacuum of power. And far more dangerous forces than rival great powers would benefit from such a not-so-new world disorder.[704]

The National Security Strategy unveiled by President Bush in September 2002 seeks to help avoid such problems. It establishes the following as long-term goals for the United States: the promotion of human dignity, the strengthening of alliances aimed at defeating international terrorism, working with other states to help defuse regional conflicts, championing free markets and free trade, and working cooperatively with the world's leading states.[705]

The U.S. National Security Strategy reaffirms the Nation's basic values declaring, "our first imperative is to clarify what we stand for: the United States must defend liberty and justice because these principles are right and true for all people everywhere" and seeks to ensure that the United States Military must be able to "decisively defeat any adversary if deterrence fails."[706]

Targeted foreign aid is an important part of the National Security Strategy. The Strategy notes that in order for the United States to prevail in the ongoing war on terrorism, it will take steps "diminishing the underlying conditions that spawn terrorism by enlisting the international community to focus its efforts and resources on areas most at risk" and "using effective public diplomacy to promote the free flow of information and ideas to kindle the hopes and aspirations of freedom of those societies ruled by the sponsor of global terrorism."[707] For such a strategy to be implemented and effective, it will require continuing broad-based support from American citizens.

Currently, there is a substantial mismatch between the foreign policy challenges that confront the nation and its expenditures on foreign assistance. A comparison of the 21st century U.S. involvement in the early years of the war on terrorism to the 20th century challenge of the early years of the Cold War reveals that U.S. foreign assistance in the opening years of the global war on terrorism is just one-tenth of its level during the first decade of the Cold War.[708] At the beginning of the Cold War era, U.S. foreign assistance amounted to 1.87 percent of GDP compared to 0.18 percent of GDP in 2004.[709]

The United States also requires cooperation and participation from among its allies and support from the United Nations. Unfortunately, as was discussed in Chapter 4, significant barriers have been created to block such participation and support, which need to be overcome. The United Nations also is in need of significant structural reforms to address problems that hinder its effectiveness. At the same time, fundamental policy differences led by France have limited Europe's willingness to join with the U.S. in several important areas, particularly in the post-Saddam Hussein era in Iraq.

Can U.S. Citizens Stay the Course?

More than two hundred years ago, America's Founders gave the nation its enduring mission as described in the American Declaration of Independence. That idea defined the relationship between the U.S. citizen and the state for the nation that emerged and that idea is embodied in the Constitution that was drafted in 1787.

Much about the world has changed since the United States declared and won its independence, fought a civil war to maintain its unity and thereafter rose to increasing economic and military preeminence. On January 8, 1918, President Woodrow Wilson extended America's founding principles to U.S. foreign policy. On that occasion, he asserted that the United States had entered World War I to see "that the world be made fit and safe to live in; and particularly that it be made safe for every peace-loving nation which, like our own, wishes to live its own life, determine its own institutions, be assured of justice and fair dealing by the other peoples of the world as against force and selfish aggression. All the peoples of the world are in effect partners in this interest, and for our own part we see very clearly that unless justice be done to others it will not be done to us."[710] President Bush's National Security Strategy and quest to end world tyranny reflects this Wilsonian idealism.

These are not easy objectives. Just as had been the case at the beginning of the United States' last great struggle, the Cold War, U.S. citizens must avoid becoming distracted by the gravity of the challenge so as not to become vulnerable to those who advocate the "easy" retreat of the United States from the world stage. In fact, many of the same arguments one hears today are extraordinarily similar to those made at the time President Harry Truman launched his doctrine of contesting Soviet expansionism and declared that the United States would assist Greece and Turkey in the effort proclaiming, "I believe that it must be the policy of the United States to support free peoples who are resisting attempted subjugation by armed minorities or by outside pressures."[711]

In response, former Vice President Henry Wallace launched a series of bitter attacks on President Truman's policy both in the United States and on a tour of Europe. "When Truman offers unconditional aid to King George of Greece, he is acting as the best salesman communism ever had. In proposing this reckless adventure Truman is betraying the great tradition of America and the leadership of the great American who preceded him," Wallace snarled.[712] Wallace also warned that Truman's aid to anti-Soviet governments would "unite the world against America and divide America against herself."[713] Rather, he asserted that the success of Soviet communism was in the American interest. At Paris, Wallace told a group of American veterans, "I believe that it is in the interest of America that communism should prosper in Russia."[714]He also launched into arguments that the United States was undermining the United Nations and that the Truman Administration was launching on a reckless course while withholding facts from the public. "America is asked to ignore the world tribunal of the United Nations and take upon herself the role of prosecutor, judge, jury—and sheriff—what a role!...In the name of crisis, facts are withheld, time is denied, hysteria is whipped up. The Congress is asked to rush through a momentous decision as if great armies were already on the march. I hear no armies marching. I hear a world crying out for peace."[715]

Wallace also condemned evolving efforts that ultimately led to the establishment of the NATO alliance that endures to this day. He dismissed prospects of such an alliance predicting that it would result in "catastrophe, violence and bloodshed in Europe."[716] Finally, he asserted that U.S. foreign policy was "on the road to ruthless imperialism."[717]

Wallace's robust and loud opposition was not lost on America's rising communist foes. *Pravda*, the official Soviet media organ, hailed Wallace a "sincere friend."[718] Similarly, Chinese Communist radio also praised Wallace while describing the Truman Administration as "a reactionary clique" acting "in the old Hitlerite way."[719] Chile's Communist Party called Wallace the "most legitimate successor" to President Franklin Roosevelt.[720]

While Wallace was obtaining rich praise from the Soviet and Chinese communist governments, Winston Churchill, Republican opposition leaders in the U.S. and the American public were rallying behind Truman.

On April 19, Wallace ridiculed Churchill's perspective that strength preserves peace complaining, "It is a source of sorrow that Britain's great fighting leader cannot use his genius in fighting for peace."[721] With the carnage of World War II still fresh in mind, Churchill fired back declaring, "War isn't but inevitable, but it would be inevitable if Britain and the United States were to follow the policy of appeasement and one-sided disarmament which brought about the last war."[722]

American citizens also understood the realities that governed the world and were in general support of the President. In New England, a March 1947 poll showed that respondents supported the Truman Doctrine by a 7-to-1 margin with such support "crossing political party lines and without respect to the economic position of individuals."[723] General approval was also reported on the west coast where there was also "a complete renunciation of isolationism."[724] In the south, early sentiment was "tentatively favorable" for President Truman's ambitious program to oppose the expansion of Soviet-style communism.[725] Even in the Midwest, once "a hotbed of isolationism"[726] there were mixed views rather than flat-out opposition that had been the case in the past.

Just as then, when the Communist leadership in the Soviet Union and China took comfort from Wallace's message, the same can hold true today in the war against global terrorism, which could provoke a dangerous situation much as the pre-World War II appeasement and disarmament did on the eve of World War II.

Thus, at this crucial juncture in the ongoing war on terrorism, American citizens are confronted with the question as to whether they can and will stay the course so that the U.S. and its allies will prevail against the great challenge that now confronts it. Armed with a keen understanding of history, firm commitment to the nation's founding principles, a willingness to make the kind of sacrifices, if necessary, undertaken by past generations, and access to timely and quality information, the prospects of citizens staying the course can only be greatly augmented.

The early Cold War experience is not unique in that American citizens were "tempted" with "short cuts" or "simple solutions." During periods of long challenge, such issues can often arise. They become dangerous when citizens lack sufficient information and education to make informed judgments, as such a situation can make it more than likely that at least some would yield to such temptations. In the complex global war on terrorism, of which Iraq is an important part, citizens should not be tempted to engage in rash decision-making just as they withstood similar siren calls at the onset of the Cold War. In the 21st century, there are no simple and expedient solutions that would bring about peace and security for the United States and its allies.

Maintaining U.S. Sovereignty

Finally, in the complex and dynamic 21st century global environment, the recent United Nations paralysis over the issue of the Iraq war provided a glimpse of another big issue that could have an important impact in defining the future: the role of the sovereign state vs. global governance.

During the 1990s, a number of scholars argued that the principle of state sovereignty was becoming increasingly less relevant in world politics.[727] Among these scholars, it was increasingly thought that a stable, secure and peaceful world could best be realized if global governance with the United Nations as its centerpiece could take on an enlarged role once understood to be left to its sovereign states. In their view, sovereignty was outdated.

Yet, even if one views the role of the United Nations through the prism of the 1990s and first years of the 21st century, its performance leaves much to be desired. It was unable to summon the will and resources to head off the 1994 genocide in Rwanda, it could not reach a consensus to bring about Iraq's compliance with a host of Security Council resolutions that dated to the early 1990s, and it remains unable to bring an end to the genocidal conduct currently underway in Sudan. State sovereignty continues to offer a relevant if not potentially more effective approach. Cornell Professor of Government Studies, Jeremy Rabkin explains:

> [A]s a political doctrine, sovereignty was never simply a celebration of force. It was precisely about the control of force. If physical compulsion were required to make every person obey every law, then even the strongest government would find law enforcement an impossible challenge. Sovereignty is about establishing which authorities have the last word on the legal resort to force—that is, who is entitled to make rightful claims for compliance, at least among the citizens of a particular territory. Different constitutional arrangements might provide different answers to this question in different states. A sovereign entity would not be sovereign in its own territory if it could not exclude claims by outsiders against its own citizens—or if it could not rely on its own people to ignore such claims when raised against heir own government.[728]

The U.S. Founders embraced the principle of sovereignty in laying out constitutional authority for U.S. foreign policy. "Certainly, the historic American view was that sovereignty offered the best hope of preserving peace. No alternative arrangement seems a more assured path to peace, even today,"[729] Rabkin states. In the years ahead, the debate as to the proper balance between global governance and state sovereignty is likely to continue. American citizens will need to understand that sovereignty is the singular principle that gives them authority over their own destiny. Global governance, well-intended as it might seem, has not proved very effective in addressing some of the world's paramount threats to international peace and security. Moreover, in a sovereign state, citizens can choose their leaders and hold them accountable for their actions. Such accountability is lost in reliance on global governance. There, citizens have at best only an indirect voice in choosing a limited number of those charged with governance and consequently surrender control over their own destiny. Such a world would be at odds with the Founding principles that granted only limited powers to the federal government and left most of the authority with the nation's citizens so as to best preserve the basic freedoms on which the American republic was established.

21st Century U.S. Foreign Policy

On January 20, 2005, President Bush was sworn into office for a second term. The keynote of his Inaugural address charged the U.S. and the Free World with a bold mission for the 21st century: advance liberty and bring an end to tyranny. "[I]t is the policy of the United States to seek and support the growth of democratic movements and institutions in every nation and culture, with the ultimate goal of ending tyranny in our world…The best hope for peace…is the expansion of freedom in all the world."[730]

President Bush asserted that the global realities of the 21st century demanded that U.S. foreign policy promote our democratic founding values overseas. Otherwise, the dangers created by regions and peoples living in tyranny could pose a threat to the United States, its Free World allies, and national interest. In further documenting the many factors underlying the central thesis of this case, President Bush explained to America's citizens:

> We have seen our vulnerability—and we have seen its deepest source. For as long as whole regions of the world simmer in resentment and tyranny—prone to ideologies that feed hatred and excuse murder—violence will gather, and multiply in destructive power, and cross the most defended borders, and raise a mortal threat. There is only one force of history that can break the reign of

hatred and resentment, and expose the pretensions of tyrants, and reward the hopes of the decent and tolerant, and that is the force of human freedom…America's vital interest and our deepest beliefs are now one. From the day of our Founding, we have proclaimed that every man and woman on this earth has rights, and dignity, and matchless value, because they bear the image of the Maker of Heaven and earth. Across the generations we have proclaimed the imperative of self-government, because no one is fit to be a master, and no one deserves to be a slave. Advancing these ideals is the mission that created our Nation. It is the honorable achievement of our fathers. Now it is the urgent requirement of our nation's security, and the calling of our time.[731]

Recognizing the critical role that U.S. allies also have to play in this 21st century mission, President Bush reached out to them stating, "And all the allies of the United States can know: we honor your friendship, we rely on your counsel, and we depend on your help. Division among free nations is a primary goal of freedom's enemies. The concerted effort of free nations to promote democracy is a prelude to our enemies' defeat."[732]

Tying the advance of democracy to the well-being of the world's community of nations and national security is not an overreach. A large body of research has increasingly demonstrated that democracy and freedom provide large benefits to free nations in terms of economic, social and political outcomes. Chapter 4 provides a reasonable profile of how a state that is at risk of either becoming a state sponsor of terrorism or already has experienced the rise of a significant terrorist movement. Such states often experience political repression and/or an absence of economic freedom, among other autocratic political factors.

Researchers at UCLA found that the institutional framework that is at the heart of a free and democratic society is a powerful contributor to a country's wealth creation. Conversely, the absence of such a framework significantly impairs a country's ability to raise living standards. "More than eighty percent of the cross-country variation in wealth (GNI/capita) can be explained by nine separate influences. The most significant and consistent positive influences are strong property rights, political rights, civil liberties, press freedom, and government expenditures," their report disclosed.[733] They also found that steps toward democratization increased a country's ability to accelerate its growth while a retreat from democratization set it back substantially. In the first five years after a country advanced toward democratization or undertook a democratic event, on average, its annual growth rate rose to 2.2 percent from an average of 0.3 percent the preceding five years. The next five years saw annual growth rate increase to 2.8 percent and the following ten years saw a further acceleration to 3.8 percent.[734] In contrast, for countries that stepped back from democracy or underwent an anti-democratic event e.g., suspended elections, average economic growth shrank from 1.2 percent the five years preceding the event to 1.0 percent the next five years. Afterward, economic growth almost evaporated to less than 0.1 percent per year before rising somewhat to a sluggish 0.4 percent for the following decade.[735] Given these contrasting rates of economic growth, 20 years after a country undertook a democratic event; its economy would have grown almost 70 percent faster than that of the state moving away from democracy.

In its April 2003 *World Economic Outlook*, the International Monetary Fund found that a nation's democratic institutions, which tended to limit the concentration of power that is typical in authoritarian regimes, played an important role both with respect to economic growth and the quality of governance. "[T]he aggregate governance measure of institutions is alone capable of explaining nearly three-fourths of the cross-country variation in income per head,"[736] the report found. "[P]oor institutions may lead to more volatile, crisis-prone economies compared with situations where institutions are better developed...Furthermore, the impact of institutions appears to be significant even when policy measures such as differences in inflation, exchange rate overvaluation, openness, and government deficits are taken into account,"[737] the report continued.

Later in its report, the IMF made clear that the kind of reforms it had in mind was democratization and economic freedom. The report declared that a successful market-based economy would require institutions that "protect property rights, uphold the rule of law, and rein in corruption.[738]

The lack of political and economic freedom found in the Middle East and Islamic World is described as having contributed to suboptimal living standards. In these regions, significant terrorist movements are currently present. The IMF's findings highlight the paramount importance of democratization and economic freedom in building better and more capable institutions and generating more positive outcomes.

Under President Bush, the United States has reaffirmed its understanding that there is a key tie between freedom and its own national security just as President Wilson did in 1918 when calling for the world to be made "fit and safe to live in; and particularly that it be made safe for every peace-loving nation which, like our own, wishes to live its own life, determine its own institutions, be assured of justice and fair dealing by the other peoples of the world as against force and selfish aggression."[739] At the beginning of 2005, then outgoing Secretary of State Colin Powell described the Bush understanding as follows, "The United States cannot win the war on terrorism unless we confront the social and political roots of poverty. We want to bring people to justice if they commit acts of terrorism, but we also want to bring justice to people. We want to help others achieve representative government that provides opportunity and fairness. We want to unshackle the human spirit so that entrepreneurship, investment, and trade can flourish. This goal is the indispensable social and political precondition for sustainable development; it is the means by which we will uproot the social support structures of terrorism."[740]

A recent report by the National Intelligence Council highlights the importance of this strategy for the Middle East and Islamic World in addressing the threat posed by Islamic radicalism. "[P]olitical Islam will have a significant global impact leading to 2020, rallying disparate ethnic and national groups and perhaps even creating an authority that transcends national boundaries....Even as the world gets richer, globalization will profoundly shake up the status quo, generating enormous economic, cultural, and consequently political convulsions."[741]

Emergent Opportunities and Promising Developments for Democratization and Peace

Over the past year, there have been a number of promising developments in the Middle East that suggest that President Bush's democratization strategy has the potential to make progress in this crucial geopolitical region. In the wake of Yasser Arafat's death, Palestinians elected Mahmoud Abbas (Abu Mazen), a relative moderate, as their new President. In spite of threats by terrorists and Ba'athist insurgents in Iraq and some attacks on voters, Iraqi citizens successfully elected a government to lead them. In Lebanon, the assassination of a popular reformist leader led to an upwelling of popular support that compelled Syria to end its longstanding occupation of Lebanon.

Palestinian Elections/Palestinian-Israeli Situation

On January 9, 2005, Palestinians returned to the democratic process, which had been suspended when Yasser Arafat canceled elections that had been scheduled for January 2003. In those elections, Mahmoud Abbas won a decisive victory.[742]

Following the election, Abbas employed the legitimacy conferred by his electoral mandate to begin to chart a course that was radically different from that of his predecessor Yasser Arafat. Just days after the election, Palestinian terrorists carried out an attack on Israelis near the Gaza Strip's Karni Crossing[743] and

Abbas deployed Palestinian police in the Gaza Strip with orders to prevent terrorists from firing mortar rounds and Qassam rockets at Israel and Israeli settlements.[744] In February, during a political impasse over the new Palestinian Cabinet that would work with Prime Minister Ahmed Qurei, Abbas intervened behind-the-scenes to help bring about a Cabinet largely devoid of old-line Arafat loyalists.[745]

Should President Abbas succeed in shifting the focus of Palestinian governance, the emphasis on promoting the general welfare of Palestinian society, by creating a law-based society in which wealth creation and economic development could progress, it would likely entail dismantling and disarming the terrorist groups whose existence hinder such development. That kind of approach could create the kind of stability that would facilitate peacemaking with Israel.

Iraqi Elections/New Government

On January 30, 2005, Iraq's people held elections and chose a transitional government that would be charged with drafting the nation's new constitution.[746] In spite of threats and attacks carried out by terrorists that killed more than 30 persons, millions of Iraqis risked their lives to vote.[747]

Ahead of the election, terrorist leader Abu Musab al Zarqawi had attempted to compel Iraqis into making a false choice between Islam and democracy with charge that elections and democracy constitute "heresy."[748] These efforts to intimidate Iraqis and deprive them of their free will through violence backfired. "In some cases, the violence seemed to goad the Iraqis on. In the predominantly Shiite neighborhood of Khadamiya in northern Baghdad, where nearly 100 people were killed in terror attacks the preceding year, the turnout was said to approach 80 percent,"[749] *The New York Times* reported.

The Iraqi election was especially significant as it reaffirmed the universality of free thought, a premise on which President Bush's democratization efforts are based. In the long-run, this repudiation of the terrorists' claim to speak for Islam could undermine the claims to authority made by other quasi-religious totalitarian movements in the Islamic world. By May, Iraq's elected government had formed a Cabinet and was poised to have its Sunni representative's reach out to disaffected Sunnis in a bid to foster a stronger sense of national unity and improve the nation's security.[750]

The Restoration of Lebanon's Sovereignty

Following the assassination of former Lebanese Prime Minister Rafik Hariri, Lebanon's various opposition elements joined together and brought about the fall of the country's pro-Syrian Prime Minister, Omar Karami and later Syria's full military withdrawal from Lebanon in April 2005.[751] As the winds of freedom gained strength in Lebanon, both the Lebanese and Arab press took notice of the region's changing climate. "Electricity is in the air. Beirut is a sea of excitement, and activity and turmoil. The word 'revolution' is on many lips...It was a momentous event, and it led to the resignation of the pro-Syrian government of Prime Minister Omar Karami...Syria should consider what is happening in a sober manner and not thwart the ideals demonstrated by Lebanon's youth: it is, indeed, the time for change."[752] Columnist Fuad Abu Hijila wrote in the West Bank's *Al-Hayat Al-Jadida* on March 3, "The Lebanese experience proves that we cannot separate ourselves from the rest of the world. What is going on in Lebanon may very well be repeated in other Arab countries under different banners and slogans but certainly under the same motivation, namely, the people's desire to live in freedom."[753] A day earlier, Saudi Arabia's *Arab News* reported, "People power has come to Lebanon...The events on the streets of Beirut are comparable to the recent 'orange' revolution in Ukraine and earlier 'velvet' revolutions in Georgia and in Eastern Europe. They are not over yet, but are going to go down in the country's history as a turning point as seminal as the civil war...The Middle East is ready for change."[754]

On March 1, the *Jordan Times* declared, "In scenes reminiscent of bygone eras in Berlin and Bucharest, tens of thousands of Lebanese thronged the streets of Beirut in defiance of a ban on popular protests and in a display of massive popular will and mourning in the wake of the assassination of Rafik Hariri...And so the first major peaceful blow for the future of Lebanon has been landed and the people's will has prevailed without a shot fired in anger."[755] Ahmed Al-Jarallah, Editor-in-Chief of Kuwait's *Arab Times* observed, "The Lebanese regime has been caught between the decisions of Damascus and demands of its people, who want Syria to leave their soil taking the puppet regime along with it...The people of Lebanon have made their demands clear. They want Syrians to leave their country along with its followers."[756] The Arab media's response underlined the notion that the Middle East thirsts for democracy and freedom and that a U.S. foreign policy that emphasizes democratization is on a correct course.

Conclusion

As 2005 concluded, the ongoing war on terrorism and the continuing need to improve the nation's domestic security remained pressing issues. Iraq was continuing to move toward becoming a parliamentary democracy in the face of continuing violence brought on by Ba'athists and Al Qaeda terrorists. In the U.S., the 9-11 Public Discourse Project, comprised of members of the 9/11 Commission, found that critical tasks of providing adequate radio spectrum for first responders, risk-based allocation of funding, development of effective pre-screening of airline passengers, and a new mission for the CIA Director that reflects the realities of the war on terrorism remained to be completed.[757]

As had been expected by the Nation's Founders, the role that American citizens play in the political process—sharing their views with their elected representatives, participating in the electoral process, providing their expertise in areas in which they could assist—will likely prove crucial in shaping the course the nation takes. If the nation's citizens can help restore the health of the country's vital educational institutions and media from the weakening that had occurred as the U.S. popular culture underwent major changes beginning in the 1960s, the United States will again have the chance to overcome history's latest challenge.

A Look Forward to the U.S. Citizens 21ˢᵗ Century Role

The preceding chapters outline the major forces—demographics, culture, liberty, the proliferation of technology, and globalization—that have created a 21ˢᵗ century world that is quite different from that of the 20ᵗʰ century. At the same time, the cyclical nature of history with recurrent broad themes, including the rise and fall of great powers and underlying dynamics, is also detailed. Hence, the United States finds itself in the midst of an historic crossroads in terms of its global standing and in an economic and political environment in which it is likely to be subjected on many continents to severe tests.

How the United States ultimately fares will be largely a function of how well its citizens carry out their role and how well the nation's culture and education support their role. This book lays out the role America's Founders envisioned and reaffirms their notion of an empowered, informed, and engaged citizenry as the nation's primary basis on which it surmounts its latest great challenges. Nevertheless, to succeed, U.S. citizens need to be prepared and take a closer look at their culture and institutions. Reforms are needed if the nation's schools and media are to be capable of providing citizens with the knowledge framework (particularly history, geography, and civics) necessary for them to understand the 21ˢᵗ century global environment that confronts their country and recognize their role and responsibilities based on credible information which they can effectively rely on to perform their role as set forth by the Founders some two centuries ago.

Therefore, the book provides U.S. citizens with background information on the current preeminent threat that confronts their country: Islamist terrorism. It provides an historic framework from which U. S. and global citizens can understand the rise of this threat, the current cultural and religious environment in the Islamic world that creates an hospitable environment for extremists, and the needed broad solutions through which the United States, its allies, and moderate Muslims could employ to mitigate such extremism that underpins 21ˢᵗ century Islamist terrorism. Later, the book identifies the dangers presented by failed states and the challenges established by the new U.S. foreign policy objective of spreading democracy as a means for creating a more stable and peaceful global environment.

A number of other factors will be important in helping to determine how well the United States will be able to succeed in its objectives of eliminating the threat of Islamist terrorism and bringing about a more democratic, prosperous and peaceful world. One of the more crucial factors that can contribute to such an American success would be a willingness of its European allies to again play the effective role they did within NATO during the Cold War.

Role of European Allies:

As the 21st century's great challenge presented by rogue states and international terrorism continues to evolve, the United States' leadership in the international war on terrorism will be indispensable. Support from American allies, particularly the NATO states, and effectively-performing international institutions could facilitate success in this vital struggle. At this point in time, the United States also will need to work primarily in partnership with sovereign states to address the fundamental needs for reforms that are hindering the United Nations' ability to play a meaningful role with regard to the many threats posed by international terrorism, rogue states, and nuclear proliferation.

Recently, the United States and its European allies have been moving slowly apart in terms of both their philosophical outlooks and diplomatic approaches. Some of the consequences of this drift were visible in the UN Security Council's difficult deliberations concerning what to do about Iraq and also Germany's blunt declaration that it would not support any war against Iraq. In addition, recent developments in which voters in France and the Netherlands rejected the EU's proposed regional constitution could lead to Europe adopting a more inward-orientation as the Continent's states wrestle with the aftermath of the decision and seek to chart a new course.

In addition, Europe's nations combined do not have nearly the military resources and technology held by the United States. At the same time a relatively larger share of Europe's budgetary resources are tied up by heavy social welfare obligations. Consequently, Europe's situation is tantamount to one where it is increasingly "harvesting" its economic wealth, while the U.S. position is akin to "growing" more of it. This situation could tend to accelerate the ongoing trans-Atlantic drift by feeding and reinforcing emerging philosophical and diplomatic differences.

Presently, there is a growing schism between how European and American leaders consider the question of power where arguably the EU increasingly wants influence without paying for it (which would require building the military strength needed to offer credibility through power). Consequently, Europe is retreating from the use of power even in today's highly dangerous global environment. The U.S. continues to remain willing and able to exercise it.

However, the situation is somewhat more complex. In Europe, the polling seems to suggest that a growing divide over the legitimacy of the use of power and aspirations for a strong European Union might be helping drive results. In France, Germany, and Russia, the majority of respondents felt that it would be a good thing if the European Union were as strong as the United States and that Europe should be more independent from the United States.[758] In Britain, France, and Germany more than 60 percent of respondents felt that a country needs UN approval prior to using military force.[759]

In an article published in the June 2002 edition of Policy Review, Robert Kagan details the trans-Atlantic drift and touches on some of the fundamental aspects involved. In an opening caricature aimed at providing some context of where things stand, Kagan writes:

> On the all-important question of power—the efficacy of power, the morality of power, the desirability of power—American and European perspectives are diverging….It is entering a post-historical paradise of peace and relative prosperity, the realization of Kant's "Perpetual Peace." The United States, meanwhile, remains mired in history, exercising power in the anarchic Hobbesian world where international laws and rules are unreliable and where true security and the defense and promotion of a liberal order still depend on the possession and use of military might[760]

Kagan argues that the drift that has led to these differing perceptions is not new, has been shaped by Europe's historical experience and may also be partly a product of the protection that was provided to Europe by the United States during the Cold War, and that Europe's increased preference for social welfare programs could make it unrealistic for Europe to seek to rebuild its former power.

> Europe, because of its unique historical experience of the past half-century—culminating in the past decade with the creation of the European Union—has developed a set of ideals and principles regarding the utility and morality of power different from the ideals and principles of Americans, who have not shared that experience. Not only were Europeans unwilling to pay to project force beyond Europe after the Cold War, they would not pay for suffi-

cient force to conduct even minor military actions on the continent without American help…the collapse of the Soviet Union was an opportunity to flex global muscles, Europeans took it as an opportunity to cash in on a sizable peace dividend. Average European defense budgets gradually fell below 2percent of GDP, and European military capabilities steadily fell behind those of the United States throughout the 1990s.[761]

There is also some argument that the philosophical divide between the United States and European Union is increasingly of a more fundamental nature. Specifically, a fault-line appears to exist over the issue of the role of religion in society and its relationship to freedom. French philosopher Bernard-Henri Lévy explained that "Americans and Europeans hold differing notions of the relationship between freedom and religion. In Europe less religion generally means more freedom, he said, adding that de Tocqueville was prescient in observing that in America the two travel on the same road."[762]

In addition, ongoing demographic changes could also further widen the trans-Atlantic divide. Recently, renowned Middle East historian Bernard Lewis predicted, "At the latest, following current trends, Europe will have Muslim majorities in the population at the end of the 21st century."[763] Whether or not Europe's Muslim population integrates into the Continent's Western-oriented culture or fundamentally re-orients itself will have important policy implications given Europe's democratic governance. Questions as to whether Europe's interests and values would increasingly have less in common with those of the United States would influence the overall nature of the trans-Atlantic relationship. For now, that is far into the future and there are many possibilities. Still, the demographic changes will become increasingly significant over time and arguably Europe's possible future tilt may well be increasing the urgency of the United States to win the "hearts and minds" of the world's Muslims.

Europe's perceived exposure to the impact of Middle East instability and terrorism and its growing demographic ties to the Middle East may also accelerate the drift away from the United States. Leon T. Hadar of the Cato Institute explained, "Even in the European countries that supported the United States on Iraq, most elites and the public at large are concerned that the American policy in the Middle East will create political instability in the region and could inflame anti-Western sentiment in the Arab world, spurring more terrorism directed, not just at the United States, but at all Western states. Under these circumstances, Europe, with its geographical proximity and close economic and demographic ties to the Middle East, could become the first victim of American policy."[764]

The growing divide and ongoing demographic changes in Europe described in the preceding pages could also impact the future of NATO, particularly as it relates to NATO's mission in the 21ˢᵗ century. Presumably, it would make good sense for NATO to play a larger role in combating terrorism and acting as a defensive bulwark against rogue states. Yet, increasing philosophical differences between Europe and the United States could hinder NATO's ability to take on such a role.

Finally, recent developments with respect to European integration through a draft EU Constitution could have implications for the United States. In late spring 2005, almost 55 percent of French voters rejected the draft constitution[765] and approximately 63 percent of Dutch voters did the same.[766] Following the votes, Europe's leaders and states will need to resolve a number of issues. One such question concerns how much "broadening" or admittance of new members will take place, as a key reason for the French defeat of the draft constitution was concern among the French that an influx of "cheap labor from new EU members" could be facilitated by the proposed constitution.[767] What will be the balance between "top-down" (Europe-wide) and "bottom-up" (national) governance? Will this balance lend itself to a continuation of Europe's sovereign states maintaining independence with regard to major foreign policy matters or will it lead toward a common EU foreign policy on significant issues? Given that economic concerns played a role in the defeat of the draft constitution, will trade liberalization be slowed or sustained in the EU? Will the defeat of the constitution make efforts to reform enormously costly social welfare programs more difficult and will such added difficulty impede the Continent's long-run economic growth prospects? How responsive to their nation's citizens will Europe's national governments be in the post-constitution transition?

How Europe resolves these issues will likely play an important role in determining what capacity Europe will have to contribute to helping the United States advance matters that are of common interest e.g., the prosecution of the international war on terrorism. Ultimately how quickly the EU addresses the near-term challenges posed by the referenda in the Netherlands and France and what changes in governments/policies result could be significant in determining how effective the trans-Atlantic partnership would be in helping the U.S. wage the war on terrorism.

Role of International Institutions

Prior to the 2003 war in Iraq, President Bush warned that the UN was at a historic crossroads. It could take the path of the League of Nations and be rendered irrelevant. Or it could act to uphold international peace and security and its potentially valuable role toward that end. He reminded the General Assembly that Iraq represented the very kind of problem the UN was established to address.[768] On November 8, 2002, the United Nations Security Council unanimously adopted Security Council Resolution 1441 granting Iraq "a final opportunity to comply with its disarmament obligations under existing UN resolutions". Tragically, when it came to enforcement, the United Nations Security Council proved unable or unwilling to enforce its "final" resolution. As a result, as the world advances in the opening decade of the 21st century, its ability to depend on the UN Security Council to play a leading role in addressing the major threats of the age—those presented by international terrorism, rogue states, and nuclear proliferation—is not assured.

Although some have argued that the UN is an indispensable[769] multilateral organization, its indispensability cannot by itself ensure its success or long-term legitimacy. In order for the UN to be successful as a credible institution, it is going to have to evolve its organizational structure to reflect resource and power realities of the 21st century. At the same time, it will need to inject a degree of flexibility into its structure whereby periodic changes can be made as warranted.

The UN will also need to reform its voting and committee processes. With regard to committees, any country may contest a committee slot. This is where serious problems can emerge. For example, the UN Commission on Human Rights has in its ranks, chronic human rights abusers such as Saudi Arabia who have gained sufficient power to block other human rights abusers such as Iran from being cited for their human rights abuses. For the sake of consistency, it would be reasonable to expect that members of this Commission follow the UN's Universal Declaration of Human Rights as a minimum condition of eligibility.

At the same time, the United Nations will also need to address the issue of funding inequities. At present, 10 countries account for 77.7 percent of the budget while 3 (the United States, Japan, and Germany) contribute 51.4 percent of the budget. At the same time, 42 states (most of which are not island states with very small populations) fund just .001 percent each or less than $12,300 per year.[770] There is no good reason for this level of inequity that can be described as approaching the absurd. In addition, the fact that some states pay almost nothing denies them an important incentive for accountability when it comes to their performance in the UN, as in general, one who contributes little or nothing toward the maintenance of an organization has a far smaller stake in the ultimate success of a given organization.

Moreover, one also finds startling inequities among the permanent members of the Security Council. While it might be reasonable to expect that those with the largest economies contribute most toward the budget (another reason for bringing the organizational structure in line with present-day realities), as the Security Council plays the leading role on issues of international peace and security, perhaps the permanent members should also be expected to contribute a larger amount than non-permanent members e.g., perhaps 5 percent or more. In any case, the U.S., France, and Britain meet this threshold. Russia and China barely contribute more than 1 percent of the budget yet retain permanent member status.

At the same time, there are growing questions as to the United Nations' ability to oversee its own major programs in an effective and impartial fashion. Toward the end of 2004, the United States Congress was investigating the United Nations' long-running Oil-for-Food program that had been the centerpiece of the Iraq sanctions regime. The early findings point to a potentially colossal management failure and possibly pervasive corruption.

On November 15, 2004, Senator Norm Coleman, Chairman of the Senate Permanent Subcommittee on Investigations, who later publicly called upon UN Secretary-General Kofi Annan to resign[771], revealed that Saddam Hussein may have generated personal profits in excess of $20 billion between 1991–2002 under the Oil-for-Food program.[772] Even worse, the magnitude of the scandal could be even greater. "The extent to which UN officials personally benefited from Saddam's influence pedaling has not been fully explored. We need substantially greater cooperation from the United Nations to answer these and other questions,"[773] Coleman explained while complaining that the UN was obstructing the investigation.

According to Coleman, Saddam Hussein generated personal profits through the Oil-for-Food program from oil smuggling that was facilitated through trade protocols and unauthorized sales of oil, surcharges on oil purchases, kickbacks on humanitarian goods, the purchase of substandard goods under the Oil-for-Food program, abuses in the Kurdish region of Iraq, and investment of illicit revenues.[774] At least some of the corruption uncovered so far appeared to have been deliberate and that such corruption undercut the main purpose of the Iraq sanctions regime, which was to preclude Iraq from developing or obtaining weapons systems by which it could pose a threat to its neighbors.

Even some well-known corporations were involved in the corrupt practices of the program. According to Coleman, one such organization, the Weir Group, agreed to a "kickback" arrangement in order to receive contracts even as the prices of such contracts were "inflated by 30percent to 40percent" under the deal.[775] The Banque Nationale de Paris, one of the banks that held proceeds from Iraq's oil sales for the Oil-for-Food program may also have been "noncompliant" in its administration.[776] A spokesman for the Bank argued that the Bank had relied on the UN's controls and only processed transactions that had been approved by the Sanctions Committee.[777]

In an indication that the United Nations recognizes that its organization needs to readapt to be effective in the 21st century, a panel appointed by the Secretary-General released a comprehensive report in December 2004 that summarized the organization's performance and suggested possible reforms, some of which would be significant. This report also addressed the UN's possible role with respect to contemporary issues such as terrorism, the proliferation of weapons of mass destruction, and the use of force for self-defense.

From the onset, the report reaffirms that the sovereign state remains the world's principal actor. "If there is to be a new security consensus, it must start with the understanding that the front-line actors in dealing with all the threats we face, new and old, continue to be individual sovereign states, whose role and responsibilities, and right to be respected are fully recognized in the Charter of the United Nations."[778] The report argues for the relevance of collective security, a principle on which the United Nations was established observing, "Today's threats recognize no national boundaries, are connected, and must be addressed at the global and regional as well as the national levels. No state, no matter how powerful, can by its own efforts alone make itself invulnerable to today's threats. And it cannot be assumed that every state will always be able or willing to meet its responsibility to protect its own peoples and not to harm its neighbors."[779]

The report also highlights some key deficiencies with regard to the UN's performance. According to the report, the UN General Assembly "has lost vitality and often fails to focus effectively on the most compelling issues of the day, the Security Council will need to be more proactive in the future…the Commission on Human Rights suffers from a legitimacy deficit that casts doubts on the overall reputation of the United Nations."[780]

When it comes to promoting or protecting international peace and security or combating terrorism, the report offers a number of observations, recommendations, and guidance. Speaking to the effectiveness of Chapter VII sanctions efforts, it notes, "Sanctions failed when they were not effectively targeted and when the Security Council failed to enforce them."[781] It also explains that the United States' decision to consult the Security Council prior to the recent war in Iraq was an exception for a superpower and not a long-established norm, with such consultation proving rare in the past.[782] In order to address gathering threats and better apply its mandate for protecting international security, the report offered the Security Council guidance for authorization of military force. The criteria that should be employed concern the seriousness of the threat, the proper purpose of the intervention, that the use of force constitutes a last resort, that the force employed would respect the principle of proportionality, and that the decision would consider the balance of consequences from employing military force or refraining from doing so.[783]

Of particular relevance to current affairs in which the United States and its allies are waging an ongoing war on terrorism, the report addresses terrorism and takes a notably tougher stance than that applied by some of the UN's member states. The report proclaims, "Terrorism attacks the values that lie at the heart of the Charter of the United Nations: respect for human rights; the rule of law; rules of war that protect civilians; tolerance among peoples and nations; and the peaceful resolution of conflict."[784] The threat of terrorism has become especially urgent due to the fact that Al Qaeda is a terrorist organization with global reach, not likely to be the last such entity, and that terrorists seek to inflict mass casualties.[785]

The report notes that many states remain outside the international conventions on terrorism and asserts that the Security Council might need to take additional steps against such states if they fail to undertake their obligation to combat terrorism.[786] The report also rejects the two principal arguments that have been employed by states to avoid agreeing to a universal definition of terrorism[787]:

At the same time, the report introduces a suggested definition of terrorism, defining it as "any action, in addition to actions already specified by the existing conventions on aspects of terrorism, the Geneva Conventions and Security Council resolution 1566 (2004), that is intended to cause death or serious bodily harm to civilians or non-combatants, when the purpose of such act, by its nature or context, is to intimidate a population, or to compel a Government or an international organization to do or to abstain from doing any act."[788]

Nevertheless, one should not expect immediate changes in how the UN conducts business much less how it addresses the threat of terrorism. After all, the UN has proved largely unable or unwilling to enforce longstanding conventions such as the Universal Declaration of Human Rights to the point where the report warns that this lack of credibility on the human rights issue is undermining the credibility of the entire institution.

For now, and likely well into the opening decade or more of the 21st century, U.S. citizens and policymakers will need to recognize the role that the UN can potentially play is likely limited when it comes to addressing the great challenges of the day. Instead, the role played by the United States together with its partners acting in the capacity of sovereign states is likely to be more effective. After all, even in the 21st century global environment, AEI's Jeremy Rabkin argues that the concept of state sovereignty is far from obsolete. "No people can trust others to care about their security as much as their own government does. A world of sovereign states will have disagreements, but international institutions have no better record than states in preventing war—or assuring victory over nations that have threatened peace. The ultimate issue is not peace but the moral right of nations to hold different views."[789]

The Rise of China as a Great Power

Finally, it makes sense to discuss briefly a few of the other major countries that could play an influential role in shaping the coming years of the 21st century and beyond. One in particular stands out: the rise of China as an economic and military great power. How China evolves could well have a direct and/or indirect influence on the United States' world standing and it is useful to provide a short briefing to America's citizens

At the current point in time, there is a broad consensus among geo-strategists that the rise in China could be among the most important developments of the 21st Century. The widely-respected Congressional Research Service explained.[790]

The economic rise of China and the growing network of trade and investment relations in northeast Asia are causing major changes in human, economic, political, and military interaction among countries in the region. This is affecting U.S. relations with China, China's relations with its neighbors, the calculus for war across the Taiwan Straits, and the basic interests and policies of China, Japan, Taiwan, and South Korea.

In its annual report to Congress on China's military power, the U.S. Department of Defense stated:

> The rapid rise of the People's Republic of China (PRC) as a regional political and economic power with global aspirations is one of the principal elements in the emergence of East Asia, a region that has changed greatly over the past

quarter of a century. China's emergence has significant implications for the region and the world. The United States welcomes the rise of a peaceful and prosperous China, one that becomes integrated as a constructive member of the international community. But, we see a China facing a strategic cross-roads. Questions remain about the basic choices China's leaders will make as China's power and influence grow, particularly its military power. [791]

Although China considers its economic development to be of paramount importance, the idea that Taiwan is an inseparable part of China, even as Taiwan is currently a sovereign entity, to be reunited in the future is a doctrine that trumps all others. At present, China continues to adhere to a policy objective of peaceful reunification but, according to the Pentagon report, "continues to see the threat and possible use of force as integral to its policy of dissuading Taiwan from pursuing independence..."[792] The report adds, "The prospect of large-scale conflict, such as a war between China and Taiwan that included direct U.s. involvement would likely prompt China's leaders to place the reestablishment of a favorable 'strategic configuration of power' ahead of national development."[793] Needless to say, such a war would have catastrophic consequences for East Asia and for the global economy.

According to the Pentagon's report, there are three major scenarios for China's evolution: (1) It could choose a course of peaceful integration and benign competition; (2) it could seek to exercise dominance in a growing sphere of influence; or (3) it could emerge with reduced confidence and an internal focus aimed at preserving both national unity and the Chinese Communist Party's claim to legitimacy.[794] At the same time, the report also outlines a number of developments that could divert China from a beneficial course of peaceful integration and benign competition; nationalistic fervor bred by expanding economic power and political influence, structural economic weaknesses that could undermine economic growth, an inability to accommodate the forces of an open market economy, a government that has difficulty adapting to a great power role or an expanding military-industrial complex that proliferates advanced arms. [795]

Given the importance of economic growth in helping promote the evolution of a peaceful China, perhaps modeled after the political transformations that followed economic revolutions in South Korea and Taiwan, American citizens will need to be cognizant of the risks involved with any attempts at protectionism aimed at curbing the United States' currently massive annual trade deficits with China, which amounted to $162 billion in 2004.[796]

Current U.S. policy with China is based on the principles of "idealism" and "realism" with economic relations tending to be idealistic and military ones realistic.[797] Among the policy options available to the United States with respect to China are those that entail sustaining the status quo, containing China, counter-balancing the rising economic influence of China, and facilitating globalization and democratization in China.[798] The Congressional Research Service advises a continuing blend of realism and idealism. "A key for U.S. policy seems to be to pursue policies with a sufficient dose of realism to account for long-term idealistic goals of fostering more representative government in Beijing and inducing countries to pursue peaceful relations, not only because of the U.S. military deterrent, but out of their own self interests," [799] the CRS report states. Indeed, if the United States could work in partnership with China so that China evolves along the benign path of peaceful integration that could prove highly beneficial in an already very challenging 21st century. Kishore Mahbubani, Dean of the Lee Kuan Yew School of Public Policy in Singapore, observed in the September/October edition of *Foreign Affairs*, "...if Beijing continues to abide by Washington's rules, peace and stability could reign, and the United States, as both a society and an economy, could benefit a great deal from the renaissance of Chinese civilization."[800]

From the brief sketches provided above, it should be readily apparent that China's evolution has important long-term consequences for the United States. Appropriate U.S. policies could prove helpful in facilitating a peaceful evolution for China. In contrast, short-term oriented ones aimed at retaliating for trade deficits could cause far more harm than good economically, both for the U.S. and China, and put China on a path that might lead away from a peaceful evolution. Such a path would further tax the U.S. at a time when it is facing a substantial challenge in the ongoing global war on terrorism. As a result, informed and educated citizens could play a constructive role in helping guide policymakers in navigating the challenges and opportunities presented by China's current economic transformation.

Russia

Although it has been almost two decades since the breakup of the Soviet Union and end of the Cold War, Russia's evolution remains among the United States' critical interests. Russia remains a nuclear power, possesses abundant natural resources, and lies along the periphery of the Islamic world in Central Asia and could play a potentially important role in the war on terrorism and in helping combat the spread of weapons of mass destruction. A May 2005 report from the Congressional Research Service states

With the dissolution of the U.S.S.R. and a diminished Russia taking uncertain steps toward democratization, market reform and cooperation with the West, much of the Soviet military threat has disappeared. Yet developments in Russia are still important to the United States. Russia remains a nuclear superpower. It will play a major role in determining the national security environment in Europe, the Middle East, and Asia. Russia has an important role in the future of arms control, nonproliferation, of weapons of mass destruction, and the fight against terrorism. Such issues as the war on terrorism, the future of NATO, and the U.S. role in the world will all be affected by developments in Russia. Also, although Russia's economy is distressed, it is recovering and is potentially an important trading partner. Russia is the only country in the world with more natural resources than the United States, including vast oil and gas reserves. It has a large, well-educated labor force and a huge scientific establishment. Also, many of Russia's needs—food and food processing, oil and gas extraction technology, computers, communications, transportation, and investment capital—are in areas in which the United States is highly competitive.[801]

Nonetheless, Russia's evolution also has the potential to offer adverse foreign policy consequences. The CRS report also observes, "Russian foreign policy has grown more assertive, fueled in part by frustration over the gap between Russia's self-image as a world power and its greatly diminished capabilities. Russia's drive to reassert dominance in and integration of the former Soviet states is most successful with Belarus and Armenia but arouses opposition in Georgia, Ukraine, Azerbaijan, and Moldova. The Commonwealth of Independent States (CIS) as an institution is failing."[802]

North Korea and Iran

North Korea and Iran pose the most significant imminent threats to the effort to curb the spread of nuclear weapons. North Korea is believed to possess a handful of nuclear weapons and has acknowledged embarking on a uranium enrichment program. Iran has been seeking to leverage the Nuclear Nonproliferation Treaty's provisions concerning the peaceful use of nuclear energy to possibly pursue a crash nuclear weapons development program. How the international community responds to each of these developments will prove crucial in determining how well the international institutions can perform in helping mitigate the world's most preeminent threats. Although North Korea recently agreed to a draft agreement that, if fulfilled, would lead to its eventual nuclear disarmament, a closer inspection finds that this agreement might offer little or no substantive assurances that North Korea would actually disarm. In fact, it could represent a dangerous strategy on the part of various states to pursue expediency and isolate the United States in its tough stance against North Korea's nuclear weapons.

The United States gave ground and accepted the draft agreement while continuing to insist that disarmament precede any rewards. As discussed in Chapter 1, history has a cyclical nature. Iran is widely believed to be pursuing the development of nuclear weapons. Since October 2003, the foreign ministers of Britain, France, and Germany have been attempting to negotiate an agreement with Iran whereby Iran would receive incentives to restrict its nuclear program.[803] To date, progress in those negotiations has been limited.

In addition, June 2005 saw a hardliner, Mahmoud Ahmadinejad, win Iran's presidential election on a platform of a "Second Islamic Revolution."[804] Afterward, Ahmadinejad called for Israel to be "wiped off the map" and repeatedly denied the Holocaust.[805] Holocaust denial was also disseminated through Iran's media with the Jaam-e Jam 2 TV station rejecting the existence of the crematoria at Auschwitz and proclaiming, instead, that Jewish rabbis in Europe killed children as Passover sacrifices.[806]

With Ahmadinejad's increasingly aggressive anti-Semitic and anti-Israel rhetoric and Iran's pursuit of nuclear weapons, Iran could, in the medium-term, pose a grave new threat to international peace and security. Well prior to World War II, Adolf Hitler began putting his *Mein Kampf* into practice, provision by provision, while the world stood by even as some warned that Hitler was pursuing a new German Empire that could threaten the "undoing" of those who stood aside.[807] As a result, the United States and its allies will likely face the difficult choice between expediency and persistence, even as some clamor for the tempting path of least resistance as occurred prior to World War II.

The Iranian and North Korean challenges present two specific issue on which the temptation for "easy" but non-viable solutions could arise. Citizens need to be willing to help sustain the resolve of their leaders when such choices arise. If so, the United States could well continue to prosper in freedom. If not, it could be tested by severe challenges even as the long-term war on terrorism continues.

For more information on these and other important issues please visit:
www.bridgesburning.com

Endnotes

Preface

[1] Will and Ariel Durant, *The Lessons of History*, Pleasantville, NY: The Reader's Digest, 1968, pp.92-93.

[2] Os Guinness, *The American Hour*, New York: The Free Press, 1993, p.4.

[3] Os Guinness, *The American Hour*, New York: The Free Press, 1993, p.4.

Chapter 1

[4] William Strauss and Neil Howe, *The Fourth Turning*, New York: Broadway Books, 1997, p.14.

[5] B.G. Brander, *Staring Into Chaos*, Dallas: Spence Publishing Company, 1998, p.388.

[6] Arnold J. Toynbee, *A Study of History*-Abridgement of Volumes I-IV (Abridgement by D.C. Somervell), New York: Oxford University Press, 1947, p.253.

[7] William Strauss and Neil Howe, *The Fourth Turning*, New York: Broadway Books, 1997, p.3.

[8] William Strauss and Neil Howe, *The Fourth Turning*, New York: Broadway Books, 1997, p.3.

[9] William Strauss and Neil Howe, *The Fourth Turning*, New York: Broadway Books, 1997, p.208.

[10] Sir John Glubb, *The Fate of Empires and Search for Survival*, Edinburgh, Scotland: William Blackwood & Sons, Ltd., 1981, p.2.

[11] Sir John Glubb, *The Fate of Empires and Search for Survival*, Edinburgh, Scotland: William Blackwood & Sons, Ltd., 1981, p.2.

[12] Sir John Glubb, *The Fate of Empires and Search for Survival*, Edinburgh, Scotland: William Blackwood & Sons, Ltd., 1981, pp.1-25.

[13] Sir John Glubb, *The Fate of Empires and Search for Survival*, Edinburgh, Scotland: William Blackwood & Sons, Ltd., 1981, pp.1-25.

[14] Os Guinness, *The American Hour*, New York: The Free Press, 1993, p.4.

[15] Os Guinness, *The American Hour*, New York: The Free Press, 1993, p.4.

[16] Donald Kagan and Frederick W. Kagan, "Peace for Our Time?" *Commentary*, September 2000, p.42.

[17] Excellent texts that deal with these causes include Arnold Toynbee's *A Study of History*, Paul Johnson's *Modern Times*, Jack F. Matlock, Jr's, *Autopsy On An Empire*, and Paul Kennedy's *The Rise and Fall of the Great Powers*.

[18] Legitimacy concerns a level of ideas. It "is not justice or right in an absolute sense; it is a relative concept that exists in people's subjective perceptions. All regimes capable of effective action must be based on some principle of legitimacy," notes author Francis Fukuyama formerly of the State Department (Francis Fukuyama, *The End of History and The Last Man*, New York: The Free Press, 1992, p.15).

[19] Charles Diehl, *Byzantium: Greatness and Decline* (Translated from French by Naomi Walford), New Brunswick, New Jersey: Rutgers University Press, 1957, p.139.

[20] U.S. recognition of the Soviet Union's overextension and ability to exploit that situation hastened the end of the Cold War. "We believed that Judgment Day could be speeded up by challenging the Soviets on the fringes of the empire, where they were overextended," observes AEI's Michael Ledeen in describing the reasoning behind the Reagan Doctrine (Michael A. Ledeen, *Freedom Betrayed*, Washington, DC: The AEI Press, 1996, p.46).

[21] Will and Ariel Durant, *The Lessons of History*, Pleasantville, NY: The Reader's Digest, 1968, pp.92-93.

[22] Newt Gingrich, *Winning the Future*, Washington, DC: Regnery Publishing, Inc., 2005, p.xii.

[23] U.S. Census Bureau, *Statistical Abstract of the United States: 2003*, Washington, DC: 2002, Table 12.

[24] U.S. Census Bureau, *Statistical Abstract of the United States: 2003*, Washington, DC: 2002, Table 12.

[25] U.S. Census Bureau, *Statistical Abstract of the United States: 2003*, Washington, DC: 2002, Table 12.

[26] U.S. Census Bureau, *Statistical Abstract of the United States: 2003*, Washington, DC: 2002, Table 12.

[27] U.S. Census Bureau, *Statistical Abstract of the United States: 2003*, Washington, DC: 2002, Table 12.

[28] U.S. Census Bureau, *Statistical Abstract of the United States: 2003*, Washington, DC: 2002, Table 12.

[29] Social Security Administration, "OASDI Trustees Report," March 23, 2005, Tables V1.F7 and V1.F9.

[30] Congressional Budget Office, "The Future Growth of Social Security: It's Not Just Society's Aging," July 1, 2003.

[31] The Boards of Trustees of the Federal Hospital Insurance and Federal Supplementary Medical Insurance Trust Funds, "2005 Annual Report," March 23, 2005.

[32] Social Security and Medicare Board of Trustees, "Status of the Social Security and Medicare Programs: A Summary of the 2004 Annual Reports."

[33] Social Security Administration, "OASDI Trustees Report," March 23, 2005, Table V1.F9.

[34] Congressional Budget Office, "Comparing Budgetary and Trust Fund Measures of the Outlook for Social Security and Medicare," October 10, 2003.

[35] Congressional Budget Office, "Comparing Budgetary and Trust Fund Measures of the Outlook for Social Security and Medicare," October 10, 2003.

[36] "Strengthening Social Security for the 21st Century," February 2005, http://www.whitehouse.gov/infocus/social-security/200501/strengthening-socialsecurity.html

[37] Estelle James, "Social Security Reform Around the World: Lessons from Other Countries," National Center for Policy Analysis, August 2002, p.2.

[38] U.S. Census Bureau, *Statistical Abstract of the United States: 2002*, Washington, DC: 2001, Table 5.

[39] Jeffrey S. Passel, Randolph Capps, Michael E. Fix, "Undocumented Immigrants: Facts and Figures," The Urban Institute, January 12, 2004.

[40] Daniel T. Griswold, "Willing Workers: Fixing the Problem of Illegal Mexican Migration to the United States," The Cato Institute, October 15, 2002, p.5.

[41] Jeffrey S. Passel, Randolph Capps, Michael E. Fix, "Undocumented Immigrants: Facts and Figures," The Urban Institute, January 12, 2004.

[42] Patrick Buchanan, *The Death of the West*, New York: St. Martin's Press, 2002, pp.3-4.

[43] Thomas Sowell, *Migrations and Cultures*, New York: Basic Books, 1996, pp.376-377.

[44] Thomas Sowell, *Migrations and Cultures*, New York: Basic Books, 1996, p.385.

[45] Samuel P. Huntington, "The Hispanic Challenge," *Foreign Policy*, March/April 2004.

[46] Jagdish Bhagwati, "Coping with Anti-Globalization: A Trilogy of Discontents," *Foreign Affairs*, January/February 2002.

[47] Daniel Yergin, *The Commanding Heights*, New York: Simon and Schuster, 1998, p.14.

[48] Daniel Yergin, *The Commanding Heights*, New York: Simon and Schuster, 1998, p.16-17.

⁴⁹ Ana I. Eiras, "Advancing Free Trade in Latin America at the Québec Summit of the Americas," *The Heritage Foundation Backgrounder*, April 12, 2001.

⁵⁰ Jagdish Bhagwati, *In Defense of Globalization*, New York: Oxford University Press, 2004, pp.1-308.

⁵¹ Osama Bin Laden's "Letter to the American People," November 2002.

⁵² Samuel P. Huntington, *The Clash of Civilizations*, New York: A Touchstone Book, 1996, pp.208.

⁵³ Samuel P. Huntington, *The Clash of Civilizations*, New York: A Touchstone Book, 1996, pp.208.

⁵⁴ Samuel P. Huntington, *The Clash of Civilizations*, New York: Touchstone, 1996, p.19.
On p.21 Huntington argues, "In the post-Cold War world, the most important distinctions among peoples are not ideological, political, or economic. They are cultural. Peoples and nations are attempting to answer the most basic question humans can face: Who are we? And they are answering that question in the traditional way human beings have answered it…People define themselves in terms of ancestry, religion, language, history, values, customs, and institutions." This cultural dimension played an important role in the conflict between the orthodox Christian Serbs and Muslim ethnic Albanians over the fate of Kosovo during 1998 and 1999. In that conflict in which NATO intervened, all parties frequently drew upon history to assert their legitimacy in the matter.

⁵⁵ Samuel P. Huntington, *The Clash of Civilizations*, New York: Touchstone, 1996, p.13.

Chapter 2

⁵⁶ Samuel P. Huntington, *The Clash of Civilizations*, New York: Touchstone, 1997, p.20.

⁵⁷ Samuel P. Huntington, *The Clash of Civilizations*, New York: Touchstone, 1997, p.43.

⁵⁸ Samuel P. Huntington, *The Clash of Civilizations*, New York: Touchstone, 1997, pp.45-46.

[59] Samuel P. Huntington, *The Clash of Civilizations*, New York: A Touchstone Book, 1996, pp.213.

[60] Samuel P. Huntington, *The Clash of Civilizations*, New York: A Touchstone Book, 1996, pp.213.

[61] Samuel P. Huntington, *The Clash of Civilizations*, New York: A Touchstone Book, 1996, pp.213.

[62] Richard K. Betts, "The New Threat of Mass Destruction," *Foreign Affairs*, January-February 1998.

[63] National Commission on Terrorist Attacks Upon the United States, *The 9/11 Commission Report*, July 2004, Executive Summary, p.2.

[64] Samuel P. Huntington, *The Clash of Civilizations*, New York: Touchstone, 1996, pp.84-85.

[65] Henry Kissinger does a good job discussing the relationship between power, weakness, aggression, and common values and the need for strength. "Equilibrium works best if it is buttressed by an agreement on common values. The balance of power inhibits the capacity to overthrow the international order; agreement on shared values inhibits the desire to overthrow the international order. Power without legitimacy tempts tests of strength; legitimacy without power tempts empty posturing." (Henry Kissinger, *Diplomacy*, New York: Simon & Schuster, 1994, p.77).

[66] Federalist No.70 in Alexander Hamilton, James Madison, John Jay, *The Federalist Papers* (with an Introduction by Clinton Rossiter), New York: A Mentor Book, 1961, p.424.

[67] U.S. Declaration of Independence.

[68] Alexander Hamilton, James Madison, John Jay, *The Federalist Papers* (with an Introduction by Clinton Rossiter), New York: A Mentor Book, 1961, pp.35, 226, 253, 256, 279, 280, 510, and 521.

[69] "The internal effects of a mutable policy are…calamitous. It poisons the blessings of liberty itself. It will be of little avail to the people that the laws are made by men of their own choice if the laws be so voluminous that they cannot be read, or so incoherent that they cannot be understood; if they be repealed or revised

before they are promulgated, or undergo such incessant changes that no man, who knows what the law is today, can guess what it will be tomorrow. Law is defined to be a rule of action; but how can that be a rule, which is little known, and less fixed?" Madison wrote in Federalist No. 62 in Alexander Hamilton, James Madison, John Jay, *The Federalist Papers* (with an Introduction by Clinton Rossiter), New York: A Mentor Book, 1961, p.381.

[70] "[T]he vigor of government is essential to the security of liberty," Hamilton observed in Federalist No. 1 in Alexander Hamilton, James Madison, John Jay, *The Federalist Papers* (with an Introduction by Clinton Rossiter), New York: A Mentor Book, 1961, p.35.

[71] Federalist No.41 in Alexander Hamilton, James Madison, John Jay, *The Federalist Papers* (with an Introduction by Clinton Rossiter), New York: A Mentor Book, 1961, p.256.

[72] Federalist No. 55 in Alexander Hamilton, James Madison, John Jay, *The Federalist Papers* (with an Introduction by Clinton Rossiter), New York: A Mentor Book, 1961, p346.

[73] Federalist No. 52 and 57 in Alexander Hamilton, James Madison, John Jay, *The Federalist* Papers (with an Introduction by Clinton Rossiter), New York: A Mentor Book, 1961, pp. 327, 352.

[74] Federalist No. 51 in Alexander Hamilton, James Madison, John Jay, *The Federalist Papers* (with an Introduction by Clinton Rossiter), New York: A Mentor Book, 1961, pp.321-322.

[75] Federalist No. 51 in Alexander Hamilton, James Madison, John Jay, *The Federalist Papers* (with an Introduction by Clinton Rossiter), New York: A Mentor Book, 1961, p.323.

[76] Federalist No. 57 in Alexander Hamilton, James Madison, John Jay, *The Federalist Papers* (with an Introduction by Clinton Rossiter), New York: A Mentor Book, 1961, p.353.

[77] Federalist No. 46 in Hamilton, Madison, and Jay, *The Federalist Papers* (with an Introduction by Clinton Rossiter), New York: A Mentor Book, 1961, p.294.

[78] Federalist No. 49 in Hamilton, Madison, and Jay, *The Federalist Papers* (with an Introduction by Clinton Rossiter), New York: A Mentor Book, 1961, p.313.

[79] Federalist No. 41 in Hamilton, Madison, and Jay, *The Federalist Papers* (with an Introduction by Clinton Rossiter), New York: A Mentor Book, 1961, p.256.

[80] "Gallup believed polling could help democracy to work better. He never argued that politicians should slavishly follow polls, but he preached relentlessly that they should listen to the polls. The poll could put the siren calls of pressure groups in perspective. In fact, they are 'almost the only present check on the growing power of pressure groups.' The polls could put elections in perspective since the policy implications of elections are often misinterpreted. Polls help to remove power from political parties, too. They limit the power of 'political bosses to pick presidential candidates in smoke-filled rooms.' They do what open primaries were intended to do: put the nomination of candidates in the people's hands," University of California at San Diego Professor Michael Schudson observes in his *The Good Citizen*, New York: The Free Press, 1998, p.225. For additional information, one can consult Kiku Adatto's *Picture Perfect* (New York: Basic Books, 1993), Michael Schudson's *The Power of News* (Cambridge, Massachusetts: Harvard University Press, 1995), and Mary Ann Glendon's *Rights Talk* (New York: The Free Press, 1991).

[81] Alexis de Tocqueville, *Democracy in America* (J.P. Mayer, ed.), New York: Perennial Library, 1988, pp.58, 60.

[82] Alexis De Tocqueville, *Democracy in America* (translated by George Lawrence and edited by J.P. Mayer), New York: Perennial Library, 1988, p.72.

[83] Os Guinness, *The American Hour*, New York: The Free Press, 1993, p.148.

[84] Alexander Hamilton or James Madison, Federalist No. 51.

[85] http://www.usflag.org/american.creed.html

[86] Thomas A. Bailey, *A Diplomatic History of the American People—Tenth Edition*, Englewood Cliffs, New Jersey: Prentice-Hall, Inc., 1980, p.974.

[87] Noel V. Lateef, "Great Decisions: 2005 Edition," Foreign Policy Association.

[88] Noel V. Lateef, "Great Decisions: 2005 Edition," Foreign Policy Association.

[89] Michael Schudson, *The Good Citizen*, New York: The Free Press, 1998, pp.301-306.

[90] Benjamin Wallace-Wells, "The Oblivious Voter," *Policy Review*, April-May 2003.

[91] Of those voting in the 2004 election, 22 percent cited moral values as the most important issue, 20 percent cited the economy/jobs, 19 percent terrorism, and 15 percent Iraq. "Election Results," CNN.com.

[92] For those who said that they attended Church services more than weekly, Bush won 64 percent–35 percent; for those who said that they attended Church services on a weekly basis, President Bush on 58 percent–41 percent. Bush prevailed by a narrow 50 percent–49 percent margin among those who attended Church services monthly. Kerry won among those who attended Church services a few times a year (54 percent–45 percent) and among those who never attended Church services (62percent–36percent). "Election Results," CNN.com.

[93] Among married voters, Bush won 57 percent–42 percent but lost narrowly among those without children (51 percent–48 percent) while easily winning among those with children (59 percent–40percent); Kerry won among unmarried ones by a 58 percent–40 percent margin. "Election Results," CNN.com.

[94] Bob Herbert, "Voting Without The Facts," *The New York Times*, November 8, 2004.

[95] Adam Nagourney, "Baffled in Loss, Democrats Seek Road Forward," *The New York Times*, November 7, 2004.

[96] Adam Nagourney, "Baffled in Loss, Democrats Seek Road Forward," *The New York Times*, November 7, 2004.

[97] Adam Nagourney, "Baffled in Loss, Democrats Seek Road Forward," *The New York Times*, November 7, 2004.

[98] James Q. Wilson, "Why Did Kerry Lose? Answer: It Wasn't' 'Values,'" AEI, November 2004.

[99] James Q. Wilson, "Why Did Kerry Lose? Answer: It Wasn't' 'Values,'" AEI, November 2004.

[100] "Election Results," CNN.com.

[101] "Election Results," CNN.com.

[102] Everett Carll Ladd and Karlyn H. Bowman, *What's Wrong*, Washington, DC: The AEI Press, 1998, pp.83-84, 99, 101-108, 115-144.

[103] "Election Results," CNN.com.

[104] John Samples and Patrick Basham, "Election 2002 and the Problems of American Democracy," Policy Analysis, The Cato Institute, September 5, 2002, pp. 3, 9-10, 14.

[105] John Samples and Patrick Basham, "Election 2002 and the Problems of American Democracy," Policy Analysis, The Cato Institute, September 5, 2002, pp. 3, 9-10, 14.

[106] John Samples and Patrick Basham, "Election 2002 and the Problems of American Democracy," Policy Analysis, The Cato Institute, September 5, 2002, pp. 3, 9-10, 14.

[107] Diane Ravitch & Joseph P. Viteritti (eds.), *Making Good Citizens: Education and Civil Society*, New Haven: Yale University Press, 2001, pp.5-6.

[108] "Dumbing of America," *The Washington Times Weekly Edition*, March 1–7, 1999, p.6.

[109] Hugh Heclo, "Is the Body Politic Dying?" *Political Science Quarterly*, Number 3 2003, p.491.

[110] Rick Hampson, "The invisible voter is everywhere," *USA Today*, October 28, 1998, p.A2.

[111] Nicholas Lemann, "The New American Consensus," *The New York Times Magazine*, November 1, 1998, pp.68.

[112] Nicholas Lemann, "The New American Consensus," *The New York Times Magazine*, November 1, 1998, pp.70,72.

[113] Fareed Zakaria, "The Rise of Illiberal Democracy," *Foreign Affairs*, November-December 1997, p.32.

114 "Because they wield the power of language and symbols, their values and ideas are broadcast by the press, movies, television, universities, primary and secondary schools, books and magazines, philanthropies, foundations, and many churches. Thus, intellectuals are influential out of all proportion to their numbers," writes Judge Robert H. Bork (Robert H. Bork, *Slouching Towards Gomorrah*, New York: ReganBooks, 1996, p.84).

115 Daniel J. Boorstin, *Democracy And Its Discontents*, New York: Vintage Books, 1975, p.59.

116 Alexander Hamilton, *Federalist No. 84.*

117 Jean Bethke Elshtain, *Just War Against Terror*, New York: Basic Books, 2003, p.161.

118 Jean Bethke Elshtain, *Just War Against Terror*, New York: Basic Books, 2003, p.168.

119 "[W]hat has become clear is that democratic predispositions need to be nurtured—that they do not develop so spontaneously that it can be taken for granted that every new generation will be as supportive of America's political and civic traditions and institutions as were previous generations," reports the NCES in (Richard G. Niemi and Chris Chapman, U.S. Department of Education. National Center for Education Statistics. "The Civic Development of 9th-Through 12th-Grade Students in the United States", Washington, DC: 1998, p.1.

120 Diane Ravitch & Joseph P. Viteritti (eds.), *Making Good Citizens: Education and Civil Society*, New Haven: Yale University Press, 2001, p.30.

Chapter 3

121 "A Call to Civil Society," Institute for American Values, 1998, pp.7-13.

122 Emily Morison Beck (ed.), *Bartlett's Familiar Quotations*, Boston: Little, Brown and Company, 1980, p.389.

123 Demolition Man, p.302

[124] Alexis de Tocqueville, *Democracy in America* (Translated by George Lawrence and edited by J.P. Mayer), New York: Harper & Row, Publishers, 1988, p.72.

[125] John O' Sullivan, "A Principality in Utopia," AEI Bradley Lecture, March 1, 1997.

[126] John O' Sullivan, "A Principality in Utopia," AEI Bradley Lecture, March 1, 1997.

[127] Charles Murray, *The Underclass Revisited*, Washington, DC: The AEI Press, 1999, pp.36-37.

[128] Charles Murray, *The Underclass Revisited*, Washington, DC: The AEI Press, 1999, p.37.

[129] John D. Fonte, "Post-West Syndrome," American Enterprise Institute, October 27, 1997.

[130] Todd Gitlin, *The Twilight of Common Dreams*, New York: Metropolitan Books, 1995, p.151.

[131] Arthur M. Schlesinger, Jr., *The Disuniting of America*, New York: W.W. Norton & Company, 1992, p.134.

[132] Arthur M. Schlesinger, Jr., *The Disuniting of America*, New York: W.W. Norton & Company, 1992, p.102.

[133] Samuel Huntington, "One Nation Out of Many," *The American Enterprise*, September 2004.

[134] Thomas L. Krannawitter, "The Intellectual Errors and Political Dangers of Multiculturalism," *The Proposition*, the Claremont Institute, March 2003.

[135] William Bennett, Letter dated Fall 2003.

[136] John D. Fonte, "Post-West Syndrome," American Enterprise Institute, October 27, 1997.

[137] Jacques Barzun, *From Dawn to Decadence*, New York: HarperCollins Publishers, 2000, p.604.

138 Jacques Barzun, *From Dawn to Decadence*, New York: HarperCollins Publishers, 2000, p.593.

139 James W. Ceaser, "Toward a New Public Philosophy," AEI Bradley Lecture Series, March 8, 1999.

140 John A. Howard, "Democratic Values Are Being Lost to Self-Interest," in David L. Bender (ed.), *American Values*, San Diego, CA: Greenhaven Press, Inc., 1989, p.55.

141 Jacques Barzun, *From Dawn to Decadence*, New York: HarperCollins Publishers, 2000, p.598.

142 Jacques Barzun, *From Dawn to Decadence*, New York: HarperCollins Publishers, 2000, p.598.

143 U.S. Constitution

144 Steven Greenhut, "New book documents how many of our freedoms have eroded," *The Greenwich Times*, May 20, 1999, p.A15.

145 Monroe C. Beardsley (ed.), *From Descartes to Nietzsche*, New York: The Modern Library, 1962, p.318.

146 George Boas, *Dominant Themes of Modern Philosophy*, New York: The Ronald Press Company, 1957, p.385.

147 George Boas, *Dominant Themes of Modern Philosophy*, New York: The Ronald Press Company, 1957, pp.387-388.

148 George Boas, *Dominant Themes of Modern Philosophy*, New York: The Ronald Press Company, 1957, p.389.

149 George Boas, *Dominant Themes of Modern Philosophy*, New York: The Ronald Press Company, 1957, p.391, 393-394.

150 George Boas, *Dominant Themes of Modern Philosophy*, New York: The Ronald Press Company, 1957, pp.389-390.

151 George Boas, *Dominant Themes of Modern Philosophy*, New York: The Ronald Press Company, 1957, p.395.

[152] George Boas, *Dominant Themes of Modern Philosophy*, New York: The Ronald Press Company, 1957, p.401.

[153] George Boas, *Dominant Themes of Modern Philosophy*, New York: The Ronald Press Company, 1957, pp.399, 404.

[154] George Boas, *Dominant Themes of Modern Philosophy*, New York: The Ronald Press Company, 1957, p.401.

[155] Monroe C. Beardsley (ed.), *From Descartes To Nietzsche*, New York: The Modern Library, 1992, p.332.

[156] George Boas, *Dominant Themes of Modern Philosophy*, New York: The Ronald Press Company, 1957, p.402.

[157] Bryan Magee, *The Story of Philosophy*, New York: DK Publishing, Inc., 1998, pp.165-166.

[158] Bryan Magee, *The Story of Philosophy*, New York: DK Publishing, 1998, pp.165-166.

[159] Bryan Magee, *The Story of Philosophy*, New York: DK Publishing, Inc., 1998, p.168.

[160] Bryan Magee, *The Story of Philosophy*, New York: DK Publishing, Inc., 1998, p.170.

[161] John Fonte, "Why There is a Culture War," <u>Policy Review</u>, December 2000–January 2001, p.31.

[162] John Fonte, "Why There is a Culture War," <u>Policy Review</u>, December 2000–January 2001, p.31.

[163] "The power of moral prejudices has penetrated deeply into the most intellectual world, the world apparently most indifferent and unprejudiced, and has obviously operated in an injurious, obstructive, blinding, and distorting manner," he wrote in *Beyond Good and Evil* (Monroe C. Beardsley (ed.), *From Descartes To Nietzsche*, New York: The Modern Library, 1992, p.820); In Nietzsche's mind, the major values and mores of his day had to be discarded because they were primarily of religious origin and tradition, both of which he considered irrelevant. In fact, he argued that Socrates, Jesus and others had, in the

values they promoted given the "weak" preference over the "strong"(e.g. justice not strength should reign) which was a reversal of the natural course of events that had allowed man to rise above the animals in the first place. In his opinion, the typical values of slaves had been glorified as virtues. Consequently, he felt the "slave-moralities" as he called them were in need of radical change (Bryan Magee, *The Story of Philosophy*, New York: DK Publishing, Inc., 1998, pp.173-174).

[164] Camille B. Wortman, Elizabeth F. Loftus, and Marey E. Marshall, *Psychology*, New York: Alfred A. Knopf, 1988, p.346.

[165] Camille B. Wortman, Elizabeth F. Loftus, and Mary E. Marshall, *Psychology*, New York: Alfred A. Knopf, 1988, p.347.

[166] Camille B. Wortman, Elizabeth F. Loftus, and Mary E. Marshall, *Psychology*, New York: Alfred A. Knopf, 1988, pp.348-351.

[167] Roger Kimball, "The Marriage of Marx & Freud," *The New Criterion*, December 1997, pp.4-5. For more detailed information, one can read Wilhelm Reich's *The Mass Psychology of Fascism and The Function of Orgasm*.

[168] Bryan Magee, *The Story of Philosophy*, New York: DK Publishing, Inc. 1998, p.205-206.

[169] Roger Kimball, "Virtue gone mad," *The New Criterion*, September 1997, p.9.

[170] Roger Kimball, "Virtue gone mad," *The New Criterion*, September 1997, pp.8-9.

[171] James Miller, *Democracy Is In The Streets*, New York: Simon and Schuster, 1987, p.14.

[172] The Port Huron Manifesto in James Miller, *Democracy Is In The Streets*, New York: Simon and Schuster, 1987, p.333.

[173] The Port Huron Statement in James Miller, *Democracy Is In The Streets*, New York: Simon and Schuster, 1987, p.332.

[174] The Port Huron Statement in James Miller, *Democracy Is In The Streets*, New York: Simon and Schuster, 1987, p.338.

[175] The Port Huron Statement in James Miller, *Democracy Is In The Streets,* New York: Simon and Schuster, 1987, pp.339-340.

[176] The Port Huron Statement in James Miller, *Democracy Is In The Streets,* New York: Simon and Schuster, 1987, pp.334-335, 374.

[177] Douglas A. Jeffrey, "The American Civil Liberties Union v. The Constitution," Claremont, California: The Claremont Institute, 1998, p.4.

[178] Robert H. Bork, *The Tempting of America,* New York: Touchstone, 1990, pp.42-43.

[179] Robert H. Bork, *The Tempting of America,* New York: Touchstone, 1990, p.45.

[180] Robert H. Bork, *The Tempting of America,* New York: Touchstone, 1990, p.49.

[181] Robert H. Bork, *The Tempting of America,* New York: Touchstone, 1990, pp.56-61.

[182] Robert H. Bork, *The Tempting of America,* New York: Touchstone, 1990, p.61.

[183] Dinesh D'Souza, *The End of Racism,* New York: The Free Press, 1995, pp.290-291.

[184] John H. McWhorter, *Losing The Race: Self-Sabotage in Black America,* New York: The Free Press, 2000, p.229.

[185] John H. McWhorter, *Losing The Race: Self-Sabotage in Black America,* New York: The Free Press, 2000, p.229.

[186] John H. McWhorter, *Losing The Race: Self-Sabotage in Black America,* New York: The Free Press, 2000, pp.233.

[187] John H. McWhorter, *Losing The Race: Self-Sabotage in Black America,* New York: The Free Press, 2000, pp.235-238.

[188] Jay P. Greene and Greg Forster, "College Diversity: Fix the Pipeline First," *The Washington Post,* January 7, 2004.

[189] *Grutter v. Bollinger*, June 23, 2003.

[190] *Grutter v. Bollinger*, June 23, 2003.

[191] *Grutter v. Bollinger*, June 23, 2003.

[192] *Gratz v. Bollinger*, June 23, 2003.

[193] *Gratz v. Bollinger*, June 23, 2003.

[194] Roger Kimball, *The Long March*, San Francisco: Encounter Books, 2000, p.7.

[195] Roger Kimball, *The Long March*, San Francisco: Encounter Books, 2000, p.19.

[196] John Fonte, "Why There is a Culture War," *Policy Review*, December 2000–January 2001, p.19.

[197] Joshua Muravchik, *Heaven on Earth: The Rise and Fall of Socialism*, San Francisco: Encounter Books, 2002, p.4.

[198] Joshua Muravchik, *Heaven on Earth: The Rise and Fall of Socialism*, San Francisco: Encounter Books, 2002, p.4.

[199] Joshua Muravchik, *Heaven on Earth: The Rise and Fall of Socialism*, San Francisco: Encounter Books, 2002, p.17.

[200] Diane Ravitch, *The Language Police*, New York: Alfred A. Knopf, 2003, pp.41-42, 52.

[201] Diane Ravitch, *The Language Police*, New York: Alfred A. Knopf, 2003, pp.164-165.

[202] Balint Vazsonyi, *America's 30 Years War*, Washington, DC: Regnery Publishing, Inc., 1998, p.233.

[203] Joshua Muravchik, "Socialists of America, Disunited," *The Weekly Standard*, August 28–September 4, 2000, p.40.

[204] Jonathan Rauch, *Kindly Inquisitions*, Chicago: The University of Chicago Press, 1993, pp.28-29.

[205] Jonathan Rauch, *Kindly Inquisitions*, Chicago: The University of Chicago Press, 1993, p.27.

[206] Jonathan Rauch, *Kindly Inquisitions*, Chicago: The University of Chicago Press, 1993, p.19.

[207] Robert Locke, "Why University Politics Matter," in Center for the Study of Popular Culture's "Political Bias in America's Universities," pp.21-22.

[208] David Horowitz, "Missing Diversity," in the Center for the Study of Popular Culture's "Political Bias in America's Universities," p.10.

[209] David Horowitz, "Missing Diversity," in the Center for the Study of Popular Culture's "Political Bias in America's Universities," pp.12-13.

[210] The Port Huron Statement in James Miller, *Democracy Is In The Streets*, New York: Simon and Schuster, 1987, pp.334-335, 374.

[211] The Port Huron Statement in James Miller, *Democracy Is In The Streets*, New York: Simon and Schuster, 1987, pp.334-335, 374.

[212] George Comstock, *Television in America*, Beverly Hills, CA: Sage, 1980, p.123.

[213] Committee of Concerned Journalists, http://www.journalism.org/ccjabout.html.

[214] Committee of Concerned Journalists, http://www.journalism.org/lastudy3.htm.

[215] Source: Committee of Concerned Journalists, http://www.journalism.org/lastudy2.htm.

[216] Source: Committee of Concerned Journalists, http://www.journalism.org/lastudy2.htm.

[217] Source: Committee of Concerned Journalists, http://www.journalism.org/lastudy2.htm.

[218] Source: Committee of Concerned Journalists, http://www.journalism.org/lastudy2.htm.

[219] Source: Committee of Concerned Journalists, http://www.journalism.org/lastudy2.htm.

[220] "Return to Normalcy? How the Media Have Covered the War on Terrorism," January 28, 2002, at http://www.journalism.org/resources/research/reports/normalcy/default.asp.

[221] Bernard Goldberg, "Networks Need a Reality Check," *The Wall Street Journal*, February 13, 1996.

[222] Leonard Downie Jr. and Robert G. Kaiser, *The News About The News*, New York: Alfred A. Knopf, 2002, pp.4-5.

[223] U.S. Census Bureau, *Statistical Abstract of the United States: 2004–05*, Washington, DC, 2005, Table 1150.

[224] U.S. Census Bureau, *Statistical Abstract of the United States: 2004–05*, Washington, DC, 2005, Table 1150.

[225] U.S. Census Bureau, *Statistical Abstract of the United States: 2004–05*, Washington, DC, 2005, Table 1150.

[226] U.S. Census Bureau, *Statistical Abstract of the United States: 2004–05*, Washington, DC, 2005, Table 1152.

[227] U.S. Census Bureau, *Statistical Abstract of the United States: 2004–05*, Washington, DC, 2005, Table 1152.

[228] U.S. Census Bureau, *Statistical Abstract of the United States: 2004–05*, Washington, DC, 2005, Table 1152.

[229] U.S. Census Bureau, *Statistical Abstract of the United States: 2004–05*, Washington, DC, 2005, Table 1152.

[230] Katherine Q. Seelye, "Newspaper Daily Circulation Down 2.6 percent," *The New York Times*, November 8, 2005.

[231] Katherine Q. Seelye, "Newspaper Daily Circulation Down 2.6 percent," *The New York Times*, November 8, 2005.

[232] Tom Zeller, Jr., "The Lives of Teenagers Now: Open Blogs, Not Locked Diaries," *The New York Times*, November 3, 2005.

[233] Tom Zeller, Jr., "The Lives of Teenagers Now: Open Blogs, Not Locked Diaries," *The New York Times*, November 3, 2005.

[234] Nielsen Media Research, 1998.

[235] Nielsen Media Research, 1998.

[236] Valerie Fahey, "TV by the Numbers," *Health*, December/January 1992, p.35.

[237] Valerie Fahey, "TV by the Numbers," *Health*, December/January 1992, p.35.

[238] Valerie Fahey, "TV by the Numbers," *Health*, December/January 1992, p.35.

[239] Nielsen Media Research, 1998.

[240] Billy Tashman, "Sorry Ernie, TV Isn't Teaching," *The New York Times*, November 12, 1994.

[241] "Strong Families, Strong Schools, Building Community Partnerships for Learning," U.S. Department of Education, 1994.

[242] *Harper's* "Index," September, 1996.

[243] Survey conducted by the National Constitution Center (NCC), Philadelphia, 1998 reported in "Television Statistics and Sources," TV-Free America, http://www.tvfa.org/stats.html.

[244] *Consumer Reports*, February 1998.

[245] Don Feder, "So far to the left, Hollywood off map," *The Boston Herald*, March 17, 1999.

[246] John W. Cones, F.I.R.M.-Book Excerpts, http://www.homevideo.net/FIRM/myths.htm, pp.3,5 of 7.

[247] Cherly Wetzstein, "Sex obsessed: Television's depictions are distorted, critics say," *The Washington Times*-National Weekly Edition, February 15–21, 1999.

248 "Unintended Consequences," Parents Television Council, *Special Report*, May 26, 1999.

249 "Is Newman Your Mail Carrier?" *CMPA Press Release*, May 4, 1999.

250 "Video Villains: The TV Businessman 1955–1986," Center for Media and Public Affairs-*Archive*, http://www.cmpa.com/archive/vidvilns.htm.

251 Anita Gates, "Men on TV: Dumb as Posts And Proud of It," *The New York Times*, April 9, 2000, Section 2-p.1.

252 Anita Gates, "Men on TV: Dumb as Posts And Proud of It," *The New York Times*, April 9, 2000, Section 2-pp.1, 35.

253 Source: *Sending Signals: Kids Speak Out about Values in the Media,"* http://www.media-awareness.ca/eng/issues/stats/contv.htm.

254 Michael Medved, *Hollywood vs. America*, New York: HarperCollins Publishers, 1992, p.183.

255 "Violence on Television," American Psychological Association Public Communications, http://www.apa.org/pubinfo/violence.html.

256 "Bennett, Lieberman Outline Concerns About Television Content in Letter to NAB President," *Press Release*, April 17, 1998.

257 MTV national survey, *Chicago Tribune*, August 15, 1993.

258 Michael Medved, *Hollywood vs. America*, New York: HarperCollins Publishers, 1992, p.109.

259 Michael Medved, *Hollywood vs. America*, New York: HarperCollins Publishers, 1992, p.259.

260 Michael Medved, *Hollywood vs. America*, New York: HarperCollins Publishers, 1992, p.184.

261 Source: International Adult Literacy Survey, http://www.media-awareness.ca/eng/issues/stats/usetv.htm.

262 Coalition for Marriage, Family and Couples Education, Institute for American Values, Religion, Culture, and Family Project at the University of Chicago

Divinity School, "The Marriage Movement: A Statement of Principles," 2000, p.3.

[263] "Love & Marriage," *USA Today*, January 7, 1999, p.1D.

[264] U.S. Bureau of the Census, *Statistical Abstract of the United States: 2002*, Washington, DC: 2001, Table 46.

[265] U.S. Bureau of the Census, *Statistical Abstract of the United States: 1989*, Washington, DC: 1989, p.61-Table 83.

[266] By 1996, the number of marriages had declined 26 percent from its 1984 peak of 2,477,000. At the same time, 1,840,000 marriages that took place in 1996 was the lowest number since the late 1960s
(U.S. Bureau of the Census, *Statistical Abstract of the United States: 1998*, Washington, DC: 1998, p.76-Table 92).

[267] Nick Jans, "Student Problems begin at Home, *USA Today*, September 2, 2003.

[268] Maggie Gallagher, *The Abolition of Marriage*, Washington, DC: Regnery Publishing, Inc., 1996, p.44.

[269] Maggie Gallagher, *The Abolition of Marriage*, Washington, DC: Regnery Publishing, Inc., 1996, p.42; "The persistently lagging well-being of inner-city children—from low birthweight to school failure—is inextricably linked to the prevalence of teen pregnancies and illegitimate births," observes the Manhattan Institute's Heather MacDonald (Heather MacDonald, "Giuliani Tackles Illegitimacy," *The Wall Street Journal*, January 16, 1998, p.A??).

[270] Maggie Gallagher, *The Abolition of Marriage*, Washington, DC: Regnery, Publishing, Inc., 1996, p.47.

[271] Elizabeth Weller, MD, "Adolescent Exposure to Violence," http://www. medscape.com.

[272] Judith P. Siegel, Ph.D., *What Children Learn from Their Parents' Marriage*, New York: HarperCollins Publishers, 2000, p.xvi.

[273] Judith P. Siegel, Ph.D., *What Children Learn from Their Parents' Marriage*, New York: HarperCollins Publishers, 2000, pp.1-2.

274 Edward Shils, *The Virtue of Civility* (Steven Grosby, ed.), Indianapolis, Liberty Fund, 1997, pp.197-198.

275 Edward Shils, *The Virtue of Civility* (Steven Grosby, ed.), Indianapolis, Liberty Fund, 1997, pp.197-198.

276 Patrick F. Fagan, "How Broken Families Rob Children of Their Chances for Future Prosperity," *The Heritage Foundation Backgrounder*, June 10, 1999, pp.1-24.

277 Judith P. Siegel, Ph.D., *What Children Learn from Their Parents' Marriage*, New York: HarperCollins Publishers, 2000, p.203.

278 Judith P. Siegel, Ph.D., *What Children Learn from Their Parents' Marriage*, New York: HarperCollins Publishers, 2000, p.204.

279 Judith P. Siegel, Ph.D., *What Children Learn from Their Parents' Marriage*, New York: HarperCollins Publishers, 2000, pp.206-207.

280 Julia Heath, "Determinants of Spells of Poverty Following Divorce," *Review of Social Economy*, Volume 49, 1992, pp.305-315.

281 Patrick F. Fagan, "How Broken Families Rob Children of Their Chances for Future Prosperity," *The Heritage Foundation Backgrounder*, June 10, 1999, p.3.

282 Linda J. Waite and Maggie Gallagher, *The Case for Marriage*, New York: Doubleday, 2000, p.180.

283 Patrick F. Fagan, "How Broken Families Rob Children of Their Chances for Future Prosperity," *The Heritage Foundation Backgrounder*, June 10, 1999, p.4.

284 Dinesh D'Souza, *The Virtue of Prosperity*, New York: The Free Press, 2000, p.40.

285 Patrick F. Fagan, "How Broken Families Rob Children of Their Chances for Future Prosperity," *The Heritage Foundation Backgrounder*, June 10, 1999, p.5.

286 Larry L. Bumpass, "What's Happening to the Family?" Presidential Address to the Population Association of America, *Demography*, November 1990, pp.483-498.

[287] Patrick F. Fagan, "How Broken Families Rob Children of Their Chances for Future Prosperity," *The Heritage Foundation Backgrounder*, June 10, 1999, p.7.

[288] Linda J. Waite and Maggie Gallagher, *The Case for Marriage*, New York: Doubleday, 2000, p.112.

[289] Linda J. Waite and Maggie Gallagher, *The Case for Marriage*, New York: Doubleday, 2000, p.111.

[290] Linda J. Waite and Maggie Gallagher, *The Case for Marriage*, New York: Doubleday, 2000, p.99

[291] Linda J. Waite and Maggie Gallagher, *The Case for Marriage*, New York: Doubleday, 2000, p.25.

[292] Linda J. Waite and Maggie Gallagher, *The Case for Marriage*, New York: Doubleday, 2000, p.27.

[293] Linda J. Waite and Maggie Gallagher, *The Case for Marriage*, New York: Doubleday, 2000, p.30.

[294] Linda J. Waite and Maggie Gallagher, *The Case for Marriage*, New York: Doubleday, 2000, pp.31-32.

[295] Linda J. Waite and Maggie Gallagher, *The Case for Marriage*, New York: Doubleday, 2000, p.33.

[296] Catherine E. Ross, John Mirowsky, and Karen Goldsteen, "The Impact of the Family on Health: Decade in Review," *Journal of Marriage and the Family*, 1990, p.52.

[297] Linda J. Waite and Maggie Gallagher, *The Case for Marriage*, New York: Doubleday, 2000, p.48.

[298] Linda J. Waite and Maggie Gallagher, *The Case for Marriage*, New York: Doubleday, 2000, p.53.

[299] Linda J. Waite and Maggie Gallagher, *The Case for Marriage*, New York: Doubleday, 2000, p.52.

[300] Institute for American Values, "Why Marriage Matters," 2005, pp.10-11.

[301] Hugh Hewitt, *Searching for God in America*, Dallas: Word Publishing, 1996, p.33.

[302] Hugh Hewitt, *Searching for God in America*, Dallas: Word Publishing, 1996, p.83.

[303] Father Paul A. Duffner, "Theology For The Laity," The Rosary Light & Life Rosary Center, Portland, OR.

[304] Father Paul A. Duffner, "Theology For The Laity," The Rosary Light & Life Rosary Center, Portland, OR.

[305] Inside cover page, Hugh Hewitt, *Searching for God in America*, Dallas: Word Publishing, 1996.

[306] Declaration of Independence.

[307] Declaration of Independence.

[308] Declaration of Independence.

[309] Michael Novak, "God's Country: Taking the Declaration Seriously," AEI: Francis Boyer Lecture, 1999.

[310] Michael Novak, "God's Country: Taking the Declaration Seriously," AEI: Francis Boyer Lecture, 1999.

[311] For more details concerning the weather during the American Revolution, one can consult David Ludlum's *Early American Winters: 1604–1821* (Boston, MA: American Meteorological Society, 1966).

[312] Federalist No. 38 in Hamilton, Madison, and Jay, *The Federalist Papers* (with an Introduction by Clinton Rossiter), New York: A Mentor Book, 1961, p.137.

[313] Declaration of Independence.

[314] Quoted in Michael Novak, "God's Country: Taking the Declaration Seriously," AEI: Francis Boyer Lecture, 1999.

[315] William J. Bennett, *The De-Valuing of America*, New York: Summit Books, 1992, p.207.

[316] Federalist No. 20 in Hamilton, Madison, and Jay, *The Federalist Papers* (with an Introduction by Clinton Rossiter), New York: A Mentor Book, 1961, p.137.

[317] The Gettysburg Address in Robert Famighetti (ed.), *The World Almanac: 1996*, Mahwah, NJ: Funk & Wagnalls Corporation, 1995, p.464.

[318] Robert D. Putnam, *Bowling Alone*, New York: Simon and Schuster, 2000, pp.66-67.

Chapter 4

[319] U.S. Bureau of the Census, <u>Statistical Abstract of the United States: 1997</u>. Washington, DC, 1997, p.163-Table 250.

[320] U.S. Bureau of the Census, <u>Statistical Abstract of the United States: 1997</u>, Washington, DC, 1997, p.163-Table 250, p.170-Table 262.

[321] John Taylor Gatto, <u>*Dumbing Us Down*</u>. Philadelphia, PA: New Society Publishers, 1992, pp.47-50.

[322] Approximately 11 million children, roughly 25 percent of public school children, attend an urban school. This figure accounts for 43 percent of minority children and 35 percent of the poor (Ethan Bronner, "Report Shows Urban Pupils Fall Far Short in Basic Skills," *The New York Times*, January 8, 1998, p.B1).

[323] A coalition of Florida civil rights groups filed a lawsuit in Tallahassee alleging that the state was violating the rights of tens of thousands of children by failing to provide them with an adequate education. The lawsuit seeks educational improvements rather than monetary damages. "All schools are required to provide adequate education and many of these schools are not meeting the state's own minimal standards," said Laura Besvinick, an attorney representing the plaintiffs (Ethan Bronner, "Rights Groups Suing Florida For Failure to Educate Pupils," <u>The New York Times</u>, January 9, 1999, p.A8).

[324] The National Commission on Excellence in Education, *A Nation At Risk*, Cambridge, Massachusetts: USA Research, March 1984, p.5.

[325] John Taylor Gatto, *Dumbing Us Down*, Philadelphia, PA: New Society Publishers, 1992, pp. 30-31.

326 John Taylor Gatto, *Dumbing Us Down*, Philadelphia, PA: New Society Publishers, 1992, p.31.

327 E. D. Hirsch, Jr., *Cultural Literacy*, New York: Vintage Books, 1988, p.xiii.

328 E. D. Hirsch, Jr., *Cultural Literacy*, New York: Vintage Books, 1988, p.xiii.

329 Education was a particularly important theme during the 1998 political campaign. "It's all about our schools," read Democratic candidate for governor of South Carolina Jim Hodges' campaign logo; "No goal is more important than making sure all Texas schoolchildren are able to read," declared Governor George W. Bush, Jr; "If there is a single motivating force in my public life," said Congressman Glenn Poshard of Illinois, "it is to provide a meaningful education to every child in this state." (Ethan Bronner, "Better Schools Is Battle Cry for Fall Elections," The New York Times, September 20, 1998, p.A1); Education was either the most frequently cited issue (the Northeast and West) or second most frequently cited issue (the South and the Midwest) by voters who came to the polls on November 3, 1998 (The New York Times-Election Section, November 5, 1998, pp.B5-B7).

330 The student-teacher ratio has dropped from 18.6 students per teacher in 1980 to 17.1 in 1996. For public schools alone, the ratios have fallen from 18.7 to 17.4 respectively (U.S. Bureau of the Census, *Statistical Abstract of the United States: 1997*, Washington, DC, 1997, p.164-Table 251.

331 Diane Ravitch credits the change in SAT scores for sparking the national debate on education reform which is still ongoing. "This time of ferment and reform was directly stimulated by the impact of the SAT score decline. No other single indicator had the power to alert the public to a national erosion of educational quality, nor the power to elicit research focusing on problems of educational quality...the SAT score drop dramatically raised the level of public attention to education," she observed. (Diane Ravitch, The Schools We Deserve, New York: Basic Books, Inc., Publishers, 1985, pp.177-178.

332 David Boaz, "The Public School Monopoly: America's Berlin Wall," in David Boaz (ed.), *Liberating Schools*, Washington, DC: the Cato Institute, 1991, p.2.

333 Between 1962 and 1994, the mean math score fell from 502 to 479. The mean verbal score fell from 478 to 423 during that same period. Since 1984, the

math score has risen 8 points, but the verbal score has fallen another 3 points according to The College Board which administers the exam.

334 David Harmer, *School Choice*, Washington, DC: Cato Institute, 1994, pp.18-19.

335 In the 1962–63 school year 19,099 students scored above 700 on the verbal section of the exam. In 1982–83, that number dove 39% to 11,638. More students were taking the SAT, but fewer were excelling (Seymour Itzkoff, *The Decline of Intelligence in America*, Westport, Connecticut: Praeger, 1994, p.55).

336 Charles J. Sykes, *Dumbing Down Our Kids*, New York: St. Martin's Press, 1995, p.17.

337 E. D. Hirsch, Jr., *Cultural Literacy*, New York: Vintage Books, 1988, p.5.

338 Diane Ravitch, *The Schools We Deserve*, New York: Basic Books, Inc., Publishers, 1985, p.176.

339 J.R. Campbell, K. Voelkl, and P.L. Donahue, *Report in Brief, NAEP 1996 Trends in Academic Progress*, Washington, DC: National Center for Education Statistics, 1997, p.4.

340 J.R. Campbell, K. Voelkl, and P.L. Donahue, *Report in Brief, NAEP 1996 Trends in Academic Progress*, Washington, DC: National Center for Education Statistics, 1997, pp.5-6.

341 Incremental Changes in Proficiency Test Scores: 1990 vs. 1996

Area	Group	1990 Change	1996 Change
Science	Ages 14–17	+ 35 points/14%	+ 40 points/16%
	Ages 10–13	+ 26 points/11%	+ 26 points/11%
	Through Age 9	+229 points/—	+230 points/—
Math	Ages 14–17	+ 35 points/13%	+ 33 points/12%
	Ages 10–13	+ 40 points/17%	+ 43 points/19%
	Through Age 9	+230 points/—	+231 points/—

Area	Group	1990 Change	1996 Change
Reading	Ages 14–17	+ 33 points/13%	+ 28 points/11%
	Ages 10–13	+ 48 points/23%	+ 47 points/22%
	Through Age 9	+209 points/—	+212 points/—
Writing	Grades 9–11	+ 30 points/15%	+ 19 points/7%
	Grades 5–8	+ 55 points/27%	+ 57 points/28%
	Through Gr. 4	+202 points/—	+207 points/—

(Based on data from the NAEP: J.R. Campbell, K. Voelkl, and P.L. Donahue, *Report in Brief, NAEP 1996 Trends in Academic Progress*, Washington, DC: National Center for Education Statistics, 1997, pp.5-6).

[342] Jo Thomas, "Questions of Excellence In Consortium Ranking," *The New York Times*, April 22, 1998, p.B11.

[343] Harold W. Stevenson and Shinying Lee, "An Examination of American Student Achievement from an International Perspective" in Diane Ravitch (ed.), *Brookings Papers on Education Policy: 1998*, Washington, DC: Brookings Institution Press, 1998, p.8.

[344] "A Nation Still at Risk," *Policy Review*, July-August 1998, p.24.

[345] David W. Breneman, "Remediation in Higher Education: Its Extent and Cost," in Diane Ravitch (ed.), *Brookings Papers on Education Policy: 1998*, Washington, DC: Brookings Institution Press, 1998, p.362.

[346] For more information, one can read the National Association of Scholars' *The Dissolution of General Education: 1914–1993*.

[347] Ethan Bronner, "Long a Leader, U.S. Now Lags In High School Graduate Rate," *The New York Times*, November 24, 1998, p.A1.

[348] While statistics demonstrate that the Black-White graduation rate has shrunk from 11.4 points in 1970 to 0.3 points in 1995 (U.S. Bureau of the Census, *Statistical Abstract of the United States: 1997*, Washington, DC, 1997, p.176-Table 273) some of this progress may be due, not to educational progress, but a lowering of academic standards, social promotion and grade inflation. The role of this weakening of the educational experience as it relates to the narrowing of the Black-White gap and the overall drop in the national dropout rate merits further

study. Charles Sykes observes, "Educationists like to point to high graduation rates as a sign of success, when they often mean that the standards have been lowered to the point where no one could possibly fail to meet them. Dropout rates also can be lowered by making school even less demanding than leisure time" (Charles J. Sykes, *Dumbing Down Our Kids*, New York: St. Martin's Press, 1995, p.62).

[349] U.S. Bureau of the Census, *Statistical Abstract of the United States: 1997*, Washington, DC, 1997, p.176-Table 273.

[350] U.S. Bureau of the Census, *Statistical Abstract of the United States: 1997*, Washington, DC, 1997, p.176-Table 273.

[351] J.R. Campbell, K. Voelkl, and P.L. Donahue, *Report in Brief, NAEP 1996 Trends in Academic Progress*, Washington, DC: National Center for Education Statistics, 1997, pp.13-19.

[352] "A Nation Still at Risk," *Policy Review*, July-August 1998, p.24.

[353] Richard W. Judy and Carol D'Amico, *Workforce 2020*, http://www.hudson.org/wf2020/EXSUMSW.html.

[354] John A. Nidds and James McGerald, "Corporations View Public Education," *The Education Digest*, October 1995, pp.27-28.

[355] Terry Pristin, "In Survey, Business Leaders Criticize New York Schools," *The New York Times*, August 28, 1998, p.A24.

[356] June Kronholz, "High Schools Get Low Grades in Poll of Employers," *The Wall Street Journal*, January 8, 1999, p.B6.

[357] "Grading high-school dipomas," *USA Today*, March 15, 1999.

[358] Terry Pristin, "In Survey, Business Leaders Criticize New York Schools," *The New York Times*, August 28, 1998, p.A24.

[359] Charles J. Sykes, *Dumbing Down Our Kids*, New York: St. Martin's Press, 1995, p.22.

[360] Lowell C. Rose and Alec M. Gallup, "The 30th Annual Phi Delta Kappa/Gallup Poll of the Public's Attitudes Toward The Public Schools," *Phi Delta Kappan*, September 1998, p.46.

[361] One of the most consistent findings of public opinion research "involves optimism about personal life side by side with pessimism about larger society." In general, optimism/satisfaction declines as people move farther way from themselves, their families, and their communities (Everett Carll Ladd and Karlyn H. Bowman, *What's Wrong: A Survey of American Satisfaction and Complaint*, Washington, DC: The AEI Press, 1998, p.24); This fact is important, because it effectively rebuts the argument by some that respondents assign lower grades to schools outside their community largely because urban schools are in very bad shape while their communities' schools are deserving of the high grades they give them. This argument is made in Lowell C. Rose's and Alec M. Gallup's *The 30th Annual Phi Delta Kappa/Gallup Poll of the Public's Attitudes Toward The Public Schools.*

[362] "Dollars to Students, Not Districts," *The Wall Street Journal*, January 18, 1998, p.A14-Review & Outlook.

[363] In national totals, 41% said that public schools were improving in 1998 as opposed to 41% in 1979; 48% said that public schools were worsening in 1998 as opposed to 42% in 1979. Among public school parents 49% said the public schools were getting better in 1998, while 53% felt the same way in 1979; Among this same group, 43% said they were getting worse in 1998 and 39% said the same in 1979 (Lowell C. Rose and Alec M. Gallup, "The 30th Annual Phi Delta Kappa/Gallup Poll of the Public's Attitudes Toward The Public Schools," *Phi Delta Kappan*, September 1998, p.47).

[364] Lowell C. Rose and Alec M. Gallup, "The 30th Annual Phi Delta Kappa/Gallup Poll of the Public's Attitudes Toward The Public Schools," *Phi Delta Kappan*, September 1998, p.49.

[365] Patricia M. Lines, "Homeschooling: An Overview for Educational Policymakers," U.S. Department of Education Working Paper, January 1997, p.4.

[366] Isabel Lyman, "Homeschooling: Back to the Future?" *Policy Analysis*, Washington, DC: The Cato Institute, January 7, 1998, p.7.

[367] A strong case can be made that The National Commission on Excellence in Education's *A Nation At Risk* published in March, 1984 marked the beginning of the school reform effort. Another case can be made that the reform movement came to life in 1977 with publication of the Wirtz (Willard Wirtz) Panel's report addressing the decline in SAT scores.

[368] Sec.401.Findings, H.R. 577: Education Savings and School Excellence Act of 1998: http://thomas.loc.gov/cgi-bin/cpque...hsel=TOC_37812

[369] Ethan Bronner, "In Bilingual-Schooling Setback, Educators See Another Swing of Pendulum," The New York Times, June 10, 1998, p.B11; The tendency for schools to pursue fads of the day is not a new phenomenon. Educational philosopher Boyd Bode, described this situation in the *New Republic* in 1930 writing, "To the casual observer, American education is a confusing and not altogether edifying spectacle. It is productive of endless fads and panaceas..." (Diane Ravitch, The Schools We Deserve, New York: Basic Books, Inc. Publishers, 1985, p.45).

[370] Charles J. Sykes, *Dumbing Down Our Kids*, New York: St. Martin's Press, 1995, pp.12-13.

[371] Ethan Bronner, "In Bilingual-Schooling Setback, Educators See Another Swing of Pendulum," *The New York Times*, June 10, 1998, p.B11.

[372] E.D. Hirsch, Jr., *The Schools We Need*, New York: Doubleday, 1996, p.9.

[373] John E. Chubb and Terry M. Moe, *Politics Markets & America's Schools*, Washington, DC: The Brookings Institution, 1990, p.30.

[374] Heather MacDonald, "The Flaw in Student-Centered Learning," *The New York Times*, July 20, 1998, p.A19.

[375] Charles J. Sykes, *Dumbing Down Our Kids*, New York: St. Martin's Press, 1995, p.10.

[376] E.D. Hirsch, Jr., *Cultural Literacy*, New York: Vintage Books, 1988, p.25; "People have asked the comprehensive high schools to be almost everything to almost everybody," reports Marc Tucker, president of the National Center on Education and the Economy (Tamara Henry, "Higher achievement means setting standards early," *USA Today*, February 23, 1998); Also, Herbert J. Walberg,

"Uncompetitive American Schools: Causes and Cures," in Diane Ravitch (ed.), *Brookings Papers on Education Policy*, Washington, DC: Brookings Institution Press, 1998, pp.183-184.

[377] John E. Chubb and Terry M. Moe, *Politics, Markets, & America's Schools*, Washington, DC: The Brookings Institution, 1990, p.78.

[378] E.D. Hirsch, Jr., *Cultural Literacy*, New York: Vintage Books, 1988, p.25.

[379] Hugh B. Price, "Urban Education: A Radical Plan," *Education Week*, December 8, 1999.

[380] Not surprisingly messages such as "Enter to Learn, Go Forth to Serve," were sometimes carved at the entrances of schools earlier in the 20th Century (Tom Brokaw, *The Greatest Generation*, New York: Random House, 1998, pp.152, 158-159).

[381] Letter to Colonel Charles Yancey, January 6, 1816 (Emily Morison Beck (ed.), *Bartlett's Familiar Quotations*-Fifteenth Edition. Boston: Little, Brown and Company, 1980, p.389).

[382] E.D. Hirsch, Jr., *The Schools We Need*, New York: Doubleday, 1996, p.233.

[383] The National Commission on Excellence in Education, *A Nation At Risk*, Cambridge, Massachusetts: USA Research, March 1984, p.7.

[384] "American Thanksgiving," *The Wall Street Journal*, November 27, 1998, p.A10-Review & Outlook.

[385] David Harmer, *School Choice*, Washington, DC: The Cato Institute, 1994, p.26.

[386] David Harmer, *School Choice*, Washington, DC: The Cato Institute, 1994, p.26.

[387] David Harmer, *School Choice*, Washington, DC: The Cato Institute, 1994, p.27.

[388] Alexis de Tocqueville, *Democracy in America* (edited by J.P. Mayer), New York: Perennial Library, 1988, p.239.

[389] Richard W. Judy and Carol D'Amico, *Workforce 2020*, http://www. hudson.org/wf2020/EXSUMSW.html.

[390] John A. Nidds and James McGerald, "Corporations View Public Education," *The Education Digest,* October 1995, p.27.

[391] The importance of higher education is discussed in substantial detail in the chapter on American Higher Education.

[392] Paul T. Hill, Lawrence C. Pierce, and James W. Guthrie, *Reinventing Public Education*, Chicago: The University of Chicago Press, 1997, p.27.

[393] Peter F. Drucker, *Managing in a Time of Great Change*, New York: Truman Talley Books/Plume, 1998, p.226.

[394] John Taylor Gatto, Dumbing Us Down, Philadelphia: New Society Publishers, 1992, p.75.

[395] Alexis De Tocqueville, *Democracy in America* (Edited by J.P. Mayer), New York: Perennial Library, 1988, p.404.

[396] A wide range of literature documents the disproportionate share of problems plaguing the nation's urban and inner-city schools.

[397] John E. Chubb and Terry M. Moe, Politics, Markets & America's Schools, Washington, DC: The Brookings Institution, 1990, p.ix.

[398] Ben J. Wattenberg, *Values Matter Most*, Washington, DC: Regnery Publishing, 1995, p.24.

[399] Ben J. Wattenberg, *Values Matter Most*, Washington, DC: Regnery Publishing, 1995, p.24.

[400] John E. Chubb and Terry M. Moe, Politics, Markets & Schools, Washington, DC: The Brookings Institution, 1990, p.78.

[401] Jo Thomas, "Questions of Excellence In Consortium Ranking," The New York Times, April 22, 1998, p.B11.

[402] June Kronholz, "Here's Y Americans Have a Big Problem With Algebra," *The Wall Street Journal,* June 16, 1998, p.A15.

[403] June Kronholz, "Here's Y Americans Have a Big Problem With Algebra," *The Wall Street Journal,* June 16, 1998, p.A15.

[404] John E. Chubb and Terry M. Moe, *Politics, Markets, & Schools*, Washington, DC: The Brookings Institution, 1990, p.92. Also see: Anthony S. Bryk, Valerie E. Lee, and Julia B. Smith, "High School Organization and Its Effects on Teachers and Students: An Interpretative Summary of the Research," paper presented at the Conference on Choice and Control in American Education, University of Wisconsin, 1989, pp.55-59; E.D. Hirsch, Jr., *The Schools We Need*, New York: Doubleday, 1996, pp.178-179.

[405] Jo Thomas, "Questions of Excellence In Consortium Ranking," *The New York Times*, April 22, 1998, p.B11.

[406] This result should be looked at with some caution. This study was conducted during the 1980s, and some things may have changed. However, given that only 5 percent of American 8th graders scored in the top 10 percent in math in the TIMSS, the nation's elite math students are not performing as well as their international counterparts (Harold W. Stevenson and Shinying Lee, "An Examination of American Student Achievement from an International Perspective," in Diane Ravitch (ed.), *Brookings Papers on Education Policy*, Washington, DC: Brookings Institution Press, 1998, pp.8-10).

[407] Charles J. Sykes, Dumbing Down Our Kids, New York: St. Martin's Press, 1995, pp.64-65. The incident pertaining to the Avery Coonley School, located in Downers Grove, Illinois, is also documented in Lynne V. Cheney *Telling The Truth*, New York: Simon & Schuster, 1995, p.39.

[408] Charles J. Sykes, *Dumbing Down Our Kids*, New York: St. Martin's Press, 1995, p.65.

[409] Numerous studies point to a rising skill level for the jobs of the future. One of the most comprehensive studies dealing with this issue is the Hudson Institute's Workforce 2020.

[410] E.D. Hirsch, Jr., *Cultural Literacy*, New York: Vintage Books, 1988, p.1. For specific examples, see: Charles J. Sykes, *Dumbing Down Our Kids*, New York: St. Martin's Press, 1995, pp.20-22.

[411] Valerie Strauss, "Boys School In Md. Easing Grading Policy," *The Washington Post*, September 12, 1998, p.B1.

[412] John Silber, "Those Who Can't Teach," *The New York Times*, July 7, 1998, p.A15.

[413] William H. Honan, "S.A.T. Scores Decline Even as Grades Rise," *The New York Times*, September 2, 1998, p.A26.

[414] Valerie Strauss, "Boys School In Md. Easing Grading Policy," *The Washington Post*, September 12, 1998, p.B1.

[415] William H. Honan, "S.A.T. Scores Decline Even as Grades Rise," *The New York Times*, September 2, 1998, p.A26.

[416] Charles Sykes notes that grade inflation seems most widespread in schools with high rates of poverty (Charles J. Sykes, *Dumbing Down Our Kids*, New York: St. Martin's Press, 1995, p.32). Ironically, many of these schools with high rates of poverty are the urban schools that are among the nation's worst performers.

[417] Lowell C. Rose and Alec M. Gallup, "The 30th Annual Phi Delta Kappa/Gallup Poll of the Public's Attitudes Toward The Public Schools," *Phi Delta Kappan*, September 1998, pp.46-47.

[418] Chester E. Finn, Jr., "The Federal Role in Education Reform: First Do No Harm," Testimony prepared for delivery to the Committee on the Budget, U.S. Senate, February 11, 1998, http://www.edexcellence.net/library/frist.html.

[419] "A Nation Still at Risk," *Policy Review*, July-August 1998, p.23.

[420] Joe Mahoney, "U.S. history foreign to CUNY students," *Daily News*, February 16, 2000, p.22.

[421] "Elite College Seniors Flunk Basic American History," Washington, DC: American Council of Trustees and Alumni, Press Release, February 17, 2000.

[422] Jacques Steinberg, "Chancellor Vow to Fail Students Lacking In Skills," *The New York Times*, April 21, 1998, p.A1.

[423] Pam Belluck, "In Chicago, the Story Behind the Rising Test Scores," The New York Times, January 21, 1999, p.A20.

[424] U.S. Government Printing Office, "Strengthening your child's academic future."

[425] Criticism of tests is nothing new. As early as the 1920s "tests were repudiated for belonging to a 'factory model' of education, for introducing competition where it does not belong, for denying the individuality of students' talents and interests, for degrading education by encouraging passivity, mindlessness, and triviality, and for sending the wrong messages about what is valuable in education and in life," observes Hirsch (E.D. Hirsch, Jr., *The Schools We Need*, New York: Doubleday, 1996, p.177). Hirsch deals with various criticisms in detail on pages 196-214.

[426] Diane Ravitch, *The Schools We Deserve*, New York: Basic Books, Inc., Publishers, 1985, pp.172-173.

[427] "'We Know The Situation,'" *The Wall Street Journal*, October 30, 1998, p.A18.

[428] In a 1961 study by Paul Diederich and his colleagues, 300 student papers were evaluated by 53 graders. More than one-third of the papers received every possible grade: A, A-, B+, B, B-, C+, C, C-, and D; 94% of the papers received seven or more grades; every paper received five or more grades. The College Board also instituted multiple choice testing because the student's performance would otherwise depend on who graded the exam and when. The Educational Testing Service found that it could not guarantee that a student who received an A in one year might receive a C in another on the same work. A 1994 study by Daniel Koretz found that a recent large-scale effort based on trained raters evaluating student work was not able to reliably assess performance (E.D. Hirsch, Jr., *The Schools We Need*, New York: Doubleday, 1996, pp.183-186).

[429] Diane Ravitch, *The Schools We Deserve*, New York: Basic Books, Publishers, Inc., 1985, p.173.

[430] E.D. Hirsch, Jr., *The Schools We Need*, New York: Doubleday, 1996, p.177.

[431] Linda Darling-Hammond, "What Matters Most: 21st-Century Teaching," *The Education Digest*, November 1997, p.5.

[432] John E. Chubb and Terry M. Moe, *Politics, Markets & America's Schools*, Washington, DC: The Brookings Institution, 1990, p.88.

[433] Diane Ravitch, *The Schools We Deserve*, New York: Basic Books, Inc., Publishers, 1985, p.89.

[434] U.S. Bureau of the Census, *Statistical Abstract of the United States: 1997*, Washington, DC: 1997, p.168-Table 259.

[435] Ronald J. Alsop (ed.), *The Wall Street Journal Almanac: 1998*, New York: Ballantine Books, 1997, p.125.

[436] In one example, 59 percent of prospective teachers in Massachusetts failed the teaching proficiency exam (Fred Bayles, "In Mass., those who can't (spell or write), teach," **USA Today**, June 24, 1998, p.3A.

[437] Leon Botstein, "Making the Teaching Profession Respectable Again," *The New York Times*, July 26, 1999.

[438] U.S. Bureau of the Census, *Statistical Abstract of the United States: 1997*, Washington, DC, 1997, p.166-Table 255.

[439] Diane Ravitch, "Lesson Plan for Teachers," *The Washington Post*, August 10, 1998.

[440] Diane Ravitch, "Lesson Plan for Teachers," *The Washington Post*, August 10, 1998.

[441] Consortium for Policy Research in Education, "Public Policy and School Reform," *The Education Digest*, December 1996, p.6.

[442] John E. Chubb and Terry M. Moe, *Politics, Markets & America's Schools*, Washington, DC: The Brookings Institution, 1990, p.95. For more information, one can read pages 95-99. For a discussion on the productive use of seatwork by teachers see pp. 170-171 of E.D. Hirsch, Jr's *The Schools We Need*.

[443] Herbert J. Walberg, "Uncompetitive American Schools: Causes and Cures," in Diane Ravitch (ed.), *Brookings Papers on Education Policy*, Washington, DC: Brookings Institution Press, 1998, pp. 185, 187.

[444] Herbert J. Walberg, "Uncompetitive American Schools: Causes and Cures," in Diane Ravitch (ed.), *Brookings Papers on Education Policy*, Washington, DC: Brookings Institution Press, 1998, p.187.

[445] E.D. Hirsch, Jr., *The Schools We Need*, New York: Doubleday, 1996, p.10.

[446] Charles J. Sykes, *Dumbing Down Our Kids*, New York: St. Martin's Press, 1995, pp.101-102. For a further discussion on the benefits of phonics one can read pages 102-106. E.D. Hirsch, Jr., describes the current consensus on "child-centered" principles and the fact that research has found that these principles are more worst practices than best practices in *The Schools We Need*, pp.172-173.

[447] E.D. Hirsch, Jr., *The Schools We Need*, New York: Doubleday, 1996, p.173.

[448] John Taylor Gatto, *Dumbing Us Down*, Philadelphia: New Society Publishers, 1992, p.1.

[449] John Taylor Gatto, *Dumbing Us Down*, Philadelphia: New Society Publishers, 1992, pp.2-4.

[450] The National Commission on Excellence in Education, *A Nation At Risk*, Cambridge, Massachusetts: USA Research, 1984, p.5.

[451] U.S. Bureau of the Census, *Statistical Abstract of the United States: 1997*, Washington, DC, 1997, p.156-Table 238.

[452] Arthur Levine, "Why I'm Reluctantly Backing Vouchers," The Wall Street Journal, June 15, 1998, p.A28.

[453] U.S. Bureau of the Census, *Statistical Abstract of the United States: 1997*, Washington, DC, 1997, p.170-Table 262.

[454] Milton Friedman, *Capitalism and Freedom*, Chicago: The University of Chicago Press, 1982, p.94.

[455] Joseph Sobran, "...and conformity is no longer a vice," *The Washington Times*-National Weekly Edition, December 14, 1997, p.31.

[456] David Harmer, School Choice, Washington, DC: The Cato Institute, 1994, p.82.

[457] 8.7 percent of the schools subject to strong administrative control are private; 55.2 percent of the schools subject to weak administrative control are private (John E. Chubb and Terry M. Moe, *Politics, Markets & America's Schools*, Washington, DC: The Brookings Institution, 1990, p.171.

[458] University of Rochester economist and education researcher Eric A. Hanushek has observed that educational productivity has been falling at 3.5 percent per year relative to low productivity sectors of the economy. For more information see Erik A. Hanushek, "The Productivity Collapse in Schools," Working Paper No. 8, Rochester, NY: W. Allen Wallis Institute of Political Economy, December 1996.

[459] "...we have found that one of the most important influences on student achievement is school organization. We have also found that the strongest influence on school organization is bureaucratic control," write Chubb and Moe (John E. Chubb and Terry M. Moe, *Politics, Markets & America's Schools*, Washington, DC: The Brookings Institution, 1990, p.166).

[460] David Harmer, *School Choice*, Washington, DC: The Cato Institute, 1994, p.57.

[461] For a more detailed discussion of the political activities of teacher unions, one can read pages 66-108 in Myron Lieberman's *The Teacher Unions* (New York: The Free Press, 1997).

[462] John E. Chubb and Terry M. Moe, *Politics, Markets & America's Schools*, Washington, DC: The Brookings Institution, 1990, p.101.

[463] Chester E. Finn, Jr., "The Federal Role in Education Reform: First, Do No Harm," Testimony prepared for delivery to the Committee on the Budget, U.S. Senate, February 11, 1998, http://www.edexcellence.net/library/frist.html.

[464] U.S. secondary schools also spend 54 percent more per student than the international average (Chester E. Finn, Jr. and Herbert J. Walberg, "The World's Least Efficient Schools," *The Wall Street Journal*, June 22, 1998, p.A22).

[465] Paul Ciotti, "Money and School Performance," *Policy Analysis No. 298*, The Cato Institute, March 16, 1998, p.23.

466 Ethan Bronner, "Report Shows Urban Pupils Fall Far Short in Basic Skills," *The New York Times*, January 8, 1998, p.B1.

467 H.R. 577, Education Savings and School Excellence Act of 1998, Sec.401 Findings, http://thomas.loc.gov/cgi-bin /cpque...report=hr577.105sel=TOC_37812; It should be noted that federal dollars are not transferred directly to schools but to state education agencies (SEAs) and local education agencies (LEAs) who then administer the monies (Chester E. Finn, Jr., "The Federal Role in Education Reform: First, Do No Harm," Testimony prepared for delivery to the Committee on the Budget, U.S. Senate, February 11, 1998).

468 H.R. 577, Education Savings and School Excellence Act of 1998, Sec.401 Findings, http://thomas.loc. gov/cgi-bin/cpque...hreport=hr577.105sel=TOC_37812; According to the Statistical Abstract of the United States: 1997 that figure is 55 percent.

469 Jacques Steinberg, "Federal Funds for Teachers Reveal Surprising Hurdles," *The New York Times*, November 14, 1999, p.A18.

470 U.S. Bureau of the Census, *Statistical Abstract of the United States: 1997*, Washington, DC, 1997, p.164-Table 251.

471 U.S. Bureau of the Census, *Statistical Abstract of the United States: 1997*, Washington, DC, 1997, p.168-Table 259.

472 Michael Chapman, "Let 100,000 New Teachers Bloom," *Investor's Business Daily*, December 16, 1998, p.A22.

473 U.S. Bureau of the Census, *Statistical Abstract of the United States: 1997*, Washington, DC, 1997, p.171-Table 263.

474 U.S. Bureau of the Census, *Statistical Abstract of the United States: 1997*, Washington, DC, 1997, p.171-Table 264.

475 Samuel G. Sava, "Maybe Computers Aren't Schools' Salvation," The New York Times, September 6, 1997.

476 Chester E. Finn, Jr. and Herbert J. Walberg, "The World's Least Efficient Schools," *The Wall Street Journal*, June 22, 1998, p.A22.

[477] The nation has been hiring around 2 million new teachers per decade according to the U.S. Bureau of Labor Statistics. Consequently, the National Center for Education Statistics forecasts that the number of new teachers needed will decline over the next decade (C. Emily Feistritzer, "The Truth Behind the 'Teacher Shortage,'" *The Wall Street Journal*, January 28, 1998).

[478] The recent experience in which 59 percent of prospective teachers failed the Massachusetts proficiency exam is one indicator of the competency problem. "The controversy over the test has obscured the real story, which is that so many prospective public school teachers failed a test that a bright 10th grader could pass without difficulty," Boston University chancellor John Silber says (John Silber, "Those Who Can't Teach," The New York Times, July 7, 1998, p.A15).

[479] Brent Staples, "Finding Qualified Teachers for the Dead Zone," *The New York Times*, January 26, 1998.

[480] John Silber, "those Who Can't Teach," *The New York Times*, July 7, 1998, p.A15.

[481] Sheila Schwartz, "Teaching's Unlettered Future," *The New York Times*, August 6, 1998, p.A23.

[482] Randal C. Archibold, "Getting Tough on Teachers," *The New York Times—Education Life*, November 1, 1998, p.22.

[483] John Silber, "Those Who Can't Teach," *The New York Times*, July 7, 1998, p.A15.

[484] This situation is discussed in detail in Chapter 6 on American Higher Education.

[485] Sheila Schwartz, "Teaching's Unlettered Future," *The New York Times*, August 6, 1998, p.A23.

[486] On pages 39-60 of his *Dumbing Down Our Kids*, Charles Sykes details just how pervasive the emphasis on self-esteem has become in the nation's schools.

[487] Heather MacDonald, "Why Johnny's Teacher Can't Teach," *City Journal*, Spring 1998, p.14.

⁴⁸⁸ Carol Innerst, "Reuniting theory and reality in educating teachers," *The Washington Times-National Weekly Edition*, June 8-14, 1998, p.12.

⁴⁸⁹ Dan Haron, *The New York Times*-Letters to the Editor, July 24, 1998.

⁴⁹⁰ Carol Innerst, "Reuniting theory and reality in educating teachers," *The Washington Times-National Weekly Edition*, June 8-14, 1998, p.12.

⁴⁹¹ E.D. Hirsch, Jr., *The Schools We Need*, New York: Doubleday, 1996, p.123.

⁴⁹² Randal C. Archibold, "Getting Tough on Teachers," *The New York Times-Education Life*, November 1, 1998, p.23.

⁴⁹³ Randal C. Archibold, "Getting Tough on Teachers," *The New York Times-Education Life*, November 1, 1998, p.23.

⁴⁹⁴ Randal C. Archibold, "Getting Tough on Teachers," *The New York Times-Education Life*, November 1, 1998, pp.23-24.

⁴⁹⁵ Chester E. Finn, Jr., "The Federal Role in Education Reform: First, Do No Harm," Testimony prepared for delivery to the Committee on the Budget, U.S. Senate, February 11, 1998, http://www.edexcellence.net/library/frist.html.

⁴⁹⁶ John Silber, "Those Who Can't Teach," The New York Times, July 7, 1998, p.A15.

⁴⁹⁷ The American Federation of Teachers has 950,000 members and the National Education Association has 2.3 million members (Steven Greenhouse, "Teachers Reject Merger of Unions By Large Margin," The New York Times, July 6, 1998, p.A1.

⁴⁹⁸ Myron Lieberman, *The Teacher Unions*, New York: The Free Press, 1997, pp.1-2.

⁴⁹⁹ Greg Fossedal/Kevin Pritchett, "The out-of-touch teachers' unions," The Washington Times-National Weekly Edition, July 13-19, 1998, p.33.

⁵⁰⁰ Myron Lieberman, The Teacher Unions, New York: The Free Press, 1997, p.110.

[501] John E. Chubb and Terry M. Moe, Politics, Markets & America's Schools, Washington, DC: The Brookings Institution, 1990, p.49.

[502] Charles J. Sykes, *Dumbing Down Our Kids*, New York: St. Martin's Press, 1995, p.229. In 1991, Gerald Bracey, an NEA research analyst attempted to refute the reports of declining test scores and labeled reports of the decline in America's public schools "the Big Lie" (Sykes, *Dumbing Down Our Kids*, p.235).

[503] Raymond Hernandez, "Teachers To Lose Lifetime Licenses," *The New York Times*, July 17, 1998, p.A1.

[504] John E. Chubb and Terry M. Moe, *Politics, Markets & America's Schools*, Washington, DC: The Brookings Institution, 1990, p.48.

[505] Charles J. Sykes, Dumbing Down Our Kids, New York: St. Martin's Press, 1995, p.231.

[506] Myron Lieberman, *The Teacher Unions*, New York: The Free Press, 1997, pp.31-33; "National Education Association: Convention Delegates Debate Change," *Organization Trends*, Washington, DC: Capital Research Center, September 1997, pp.1-5.

[507] Myron Lieberman, *The Teacher Unions*, New York: The Free Press, 1997, p.34. Interestingly enough, teacher unions blame social ills—and exonerate themselves—such as decline in the two-parent family for problems plaguing the public schools (*The Teacher Unions*, p.219). However, the social agenda embraced by the unions, for example their support for alternative lifestyles exacerbates some of the social problems they blame (*The Teacher Unions*, p.229). Indirectly, at best, and directly, at worst, teacher unions bear some of the blame.

[508] "Asides," *The Wall Street Journal*, June 9, 1999.

[509] Myron Lieberman, *The Teacher Unions*, New York: The Free Press, 1997, p.225.

[510] Anemona Hartocollis, "In School," *The New York Times*, February 24, 1999, p.A21.

[511] John E. Chubb and Terry M. Moe, *Politics, Markets & America's Schools*, Washington, DC: The Brookings Institution, 1990, p.79.

[512] John E. Chubb and Terry M. Moe, *Politics, Markets & America's Schools*, Washington, DC: The Brookings Institution, 1990, p.85.

[513] "In bargaining, school boards have not been a match for nationally organized unions that can bring to bear strong, narrow self interest, statistical research, and specialized expertise to negotiations. Yet according to Harvard University and University of Chicago economists Caroline Minter Hoxby and Samuel Peltzman, respectively, teachers' union success was associated with worse results for students," observes Herbert J. Walberg (Herbert J. Walberg, "Uncompetitive American Schools: Causes and Cures," in Diane Ravitch (ed.), *Brookings Papers on Education Policy 1998*, Washington, DC: Brookings Institution Press, 1998, p.181).

[514] Herbert J. Walberg, "Uncompetitive American Schools: Causes and Cures," in Diane Ravitch (ed.), *Brookings Papers on Education Policy 1998*, Washington, DC: Brookings Institution Press, 1998, p.179.

[515] Paul T. Hill, Lawrence, C. Pierce, and James W. Guthrie, *Reinventing Public Education*, Chicago: The University of Chicago Press, 1997, pp.31-32.

[516] John E. Chubb and Terry M. Moe, *Politics, Markets & America's Schools*, Washington, DC: The Brookings Institution: 1990, p.156.

[517] George H. Wood, Ph.D., Schools That Work, New York: Dutton, 1992, p.xvii.

[518] E.D. Hirsch, Jr., *The Schools We Need*, New York: Doubleday, 1996, p.17.

[519] David Boaz (Ed.), *Liberating Schools*, Washington, DC: Cato Institute, 1991, p.1.

[520] A survey of White parents found that 62% said that they sometimes take U.S. freedoms for granted. In the same survey 37% of African American parents and 35% of Hispanic parents felt the same way. In the same survey, 61% of all parents said that they believed the nation was losing its identity—its beliefs and values (The Thomas B. Fordham Foundation, *A Lot To Be Thankful For*, 1998, pp.16-17.

[521] Thomas Toch, "Outstanding Schools," *U.S. News & World Report*—Special Report, January 18, 1999, p.48.

[522] John E. Chubb and Terry M. Moe, *Politics, Markets, & America's Schools*, Washington, DC: The Brookings Institution, 1990, p.206.

[523] Chester E. Finn, Jr. and Michael J. Petrilli (eds.), "The State of State Standards 2000," Washington, DC: Thomas B. Fordham Foundation, January 2000, p.1.

[524] Chester E. Finn, Jr. and Michael J. Petrilli (eds.), "The State of State Standards 2000," Washington, DC: Thomas B. Fordham Foundation, January 2000, pp.1-2.

[525] Chester E. Finn, Jr. and Michael J. Petrilli (eds.), "The State of State Standards 2000," Washington, DC: Thomas B. Fordham Foundation, January 2000, p.2.

[526] Numerous innovative reforms can be found in: The Thomas B. Fordham Foundation's *Selected Readings on School Reform*, Winter 1999; George H. Wood, *Schools That Work*, New York: Dutton, 1992; John E. Chubb and Terry M. Moe, *Politics, Markets, & America's Schools*, Washington, DC: The Brookings Institution, 1990; Paul T. Hill, Lawrence C. Pierce, and James W. Guthrie, *Reinventing Public Education*, Chicago: The University of Chicago Press, 1997; In addition, characteristics of effective schools that support many of the reforms discussed in the above books can be found in: "Outstanding High Schools," a *U.S. News & World Report* Special Report, January 18, 1999, pp.46-87. This special report has generated controversy. Chester E. Finn, Jr. and Michael J. Petrilli wrote in a *Wall Street Journal* op-ed piece (January 18, 1999, p.A18) that the report "compounds an alarming trend in U.S. education: expecting less of poor and minority youngsters and those who teach them." They reach this conclusion because the special report is not based strictly upon actual test scores but a comparison of actual scores with expected scores generated by a statistical model which takes into consideration "students' family circumstances." Although Finn and Petrilli are quick to dismiss the impact of family on educational performance, the "strongest and most consistent finding in research on student achievement is that family background is a major influence, perhaps even a decisive one," report Chubb and Moe (John E. Chubb and Terry M. Moe, *Politics, Markets & America's Schools*, Washington, DC: The Brookings Institution, 1990, p.101). Clearly, the most effective method of measuring school performance would be on a value-added basis which avoids the contentions that surround considerations of family background and other socioeconomic factors on educational performance. Nev-

ertheless, in the absence of testing to measure the value particular schools add, the *U.S. News & World Report* approach represents a realistic though not necessarily precise assessment of school performance. Finn and Petrilli also criticize the report for excluding "such famously successful institutions as New York's Stuyvesant High School,...the high schools of Brookline and Newton, Mass., and Winnetka, Ill.'s celebrated New Trier..." To be fair, these schools might well have qualified for recognition as outstanding schools in the report, however, many schools, particularly independent ones, opted not to participate. Therefore, their exclusion from the report does not necessarily reflect on their performance.

[527] Mitchell B. Pearlstein, "Strange Brew: Minnesota's Motley Mix of School Reforms," Washington, DC: The Thomas B. Fordham Foundation, January 2000, p.2.

[528] New York City Schools Chancellor Rudy Crew announced that summer school would be mandatory for third, sixth, and eighth graders who perform poorly on citywide reading and math tests and in their regular courses (Randal C. Archibold, "For Some Failing Students, Crew Orders Summer School," *The New York Times*, February 24, 1999, p.A1).

[529] Lynne V. Cheney, "Tyrannical Machines," Washington, DC: National Endowment for the Humanities, 1990, p.7.

[530] West Side High School Principal Fernard M. Williams, Sr. ha been able to dramatically improve school attendance, cut the dropout rate, and also increase some test scores in two years. Maria Newman, "From a Newark Principal, Lessons in Accountability," *The New York Times*, March 21, 1999, p.A44. In one notable example, despite the fact that the "Direct Instruction" teaching method (where teachers operate from detailed scripts teaching children what they need to know and drill home the important lessons) has been found to be highly effective in promoting learning, few teachers employ this technique and colleges of education generally do not teach it to their students who comprise the nation's future teachers (Lynne Cheney, "Effective Education Squelched," *The Wall Street Journal*, May 12, 1999).

[531] Hugh B. Price, "Urban Education: A Radical Plan," *Education Week*, December 8, 1999.

[532] Tamara Henry, "States to tie teacher pay to results," *USA Today*, September 30, 1999, p.1A. "Denver Teachers Accept Plan Linking Pay to Performance," *The New York Times*, September 12, 1999, p.A35.

[533] Daniel Golden, "Penatagon-Run Schools Excel in Academics, Defying Demographics," *The* Wall Street Journal, December 22, 1999, pp.A1, A6.

[534] In New York City which releases school board election voter turnout figures, the numbers have ranged between 5% and 12.5% of eligible voters with an average of 7% in recent years. Considering that the City's voter turnout is not significantly different from the nation's turnout in national elections, this lack of turnout is likely representative of school board elections. Lynette Holloway, "Turnout Is Decidedly Tepid in Schools Vote," *The New York Times*, May 19, 1999, p.B3.

[535] State governments should, however, be cautious in ensuring that their efforts to improve schools do not lead to counterproductive mandates and controls. Setting higher standards is one thing. Telling schools how to achieve them is another. For dangers associated with expanded controls one can refer to pages 194-198 in Chubb's and Moe's *Politics, Markets & America's Schools.*

[536] Florida will be implementing a plan that will enable children in the state's poorest performing public schools to use state funds to transfer to private schools. Rick Bragg, "Florida Will Award Vouchers for Pupils Whose Schools Fail," *The New York Times*, April 28, 1999, pp.A1, A22.

[537] For a discussion on "educational enterprise zones" see Pete du Pont, "Education Enterprise Zones" in David Boaz (ed.), *Liberating Schools*, Washington, DC: Cato Institute, 1991, pp.207-212.

[538] Today 26 states employ such exams and the White House is now encouraging all states to implement such exams. But the effort will be controversial and litigious. Ben Wildavsky, "Achievement testing gets its day in court," *U.S. News & World Report*, September 27, 1999.

[539] Already a number of states are rolling back or watering down their standards in light of rising public criticism of the new standards. "Realistic School Standards," *The New York Times*, March 20, 1999, p.A14. Jacques Steinberg, "Academic Standards Eased As a Fear of Failure Spreads," *The New York Times*,

December 3, 1999, pp.A1, A26. "Dismal test scores impede move to boost academic standards," *USA Today*, December 7, 1999.

[540] Maria Newman, "New Jersey Finds No Simple Solutions in School Takeovers," *The New York Times*, March 21, 1999, pp.37,44.

[541] Jacques Steinber, "Academic Standards Eased As a Fear of Failure Spreads," *The New York Times*, December 3, 1999.

[542] Anemona Hartocollis, "Ignoring State Curriculum Caused Poor Scores," *The New York Times*, November 9, 1999.

[543] Shaming of bad schools has shown some promise. In Alabama, 24 schools were placed on "academic alert" in Alabama with a majority of their students performing below the 23rd percentile of the Stanford Achievement Test. The results were dramatic. In just one year, 2 schools were removed from the list, while 13 others were upgraded to "academic caution" (Jacques Steinberg, "Public Shaming: Rating System for Schools," *The New York Times*, January 7, 1998, p.B7).

[544] Leo Klagholz, "Growing Better Teachers in the Garden State," Washington, DC: The Thomas B. Fordham Foundation, January 2000, pp.5-6.

[545] Arizona has such an open-enrollment law (June Kronholz, "Charter Schools Begin To Prod Public Schools Toward Competition," *The Wall Street Journal*, February 12, 1999, p.A2).

[546] Harvard University Professor Caroline Hoxby predicts that public school districts would have to lose between 6% and 9% of their students to charter schools to begin to feel pressure to compete (June Kronholz, "Charter Schools Begin To Prod Public Schools Toward Competition," *The Wall Street Journal*, February 12, 1999, p.A1). Presently, charter schools enroll 0.5% of public school students in charter states with a high of 2.3% in Arizona (U.S. Department of Education, "A National Study of Charter Schools," July 1998, pp.35-37).

[547] Median enrollment in charter schools opened during the 1994–95 school year or earlier is 180 as opposed to those opened in 1996–97. Older charter schools are generally larger. Median public school enrollment is 505. Should the average charter school grow to half the size of the average public school, 17,600–26,600 charter schools would be required. Should the average charter school become comparable in size to the average public school, 8,800–13,300 charter schools

would be required (U.S. Department of Education, "A National Study of Charter Schools," July 1998, pp.38-39 and U.S. Bureau of the Census, Statistical Abstract of the United States: 1997, Washington, DC, 1997, p.163-Table 250).

[548] Hugh B. Price, "Urban Education: A Radical Plan," *Education Week*, December 8, 1999.

[549] Daniel L. Duke, "The Future of High School," *The Education Digest*, January 1999, p.50.

Chapter 5

[550] Stephen D. Krasner, "The Day After," *Foreign Policy*, January/February 2005, p.68.

[551] Stephen D. Krasner, "The Day After," *Foreign Policy*, January/February 2005, p.68.

[552] Stephen D. Krasner, "The Day After," *Foreign Policy*, January/February 2005, pp.68-70.

[553] William Strauss and Neil Howe, *The Fourth Turning*, New York: Broadway Books, 1997, p.3.

[554] Paul Johnson, "America's New Empire for Liberty," *Hoover Digest*, 2003 No. 4, p.8.

[555] In an address to a joint session of Congress on September 20, 2001, President Bush declared of the terrorists, "We have seen their kind before. They are the heirs of all the murderous ideologies of the 20th century. By sacrificing human life to serve their radical visions—by abandoning every value except the will to power—they follow in the path of fascism and Nazism, and totalitarianism." (http://www.whitehouse.gov/news/releases/2001/09/20010920-8.html).   On May 23, 2002, in a speech to Germany's Bundestag while on a state visit, President Bush termed the terrorist threat the "new totalitarian threat." (http://www. whitehouse.gov/news/releases/2002/05/20020523-2.html).

[556] President Bush told the Bundestag, "Together, we oppose an enemy that thrives on violence and the grief of the innocent. The terrorists are defined by their hatreds: they hate democracy and tolerance and free expression and women

and Jews and Christians and all Muslims who disagree with them...These ene-mies kill in the name of a false religious purity, perverting the faith they claim to hold. In this war...we are defending civilization, itself." (http://www. whitehouse.gov/news/releases/2002/05/20020523-2.html). In February 1995, NATO Secretary General Willy Claes stated, "Islamic militancy has emerged as perhaps the single gravest threat to the NATO alliance and to Western security" and suggested that the scale of danger was perhaps greater than the threat posed by communism. Daniel Pipes, "Who Is the Enemy?" *Commentary*, January 2002, p.22.

[557] Josh Meyer and Bob Drogin, "Resilient Al Qaeda Resumes Plotting," *Los Angeles Times*, June 11, 2002.

[558] "Al-Qa'ida Commander in Iraq: 'A Terror Attack Against the U.S. With 100,000 Deaths is Imminent,'" Memri.org, November 14, 2003.

[559] Rex A. Hudson, *The Sociology and Psychology of Terrorism: Who Becomes a Ter-rorist and Why?* Washington, DC: Library of Congress, September 1999, pp.10-13.

[560] Bruce Hoffman, "Terrorism and Counterterrorism After September 11th," U.S. Department of State website, http://usinfo.state.gov/journals/itps/1101/ijpe/pj63hoffman.htm.

[561] Rex A. Hudson, *The Sociology and Psychology of Terrorism: Who Becomes a Ter-rorist and Why?* Washington, DC: Library of Congress, September 1999, p.10.

[562] Palestinian terrorists attempted to blow up the huge Pi Glilot petroleum and gas depot near Herzliya, Israel in May 2002. David Rudge, "Security boosted at strategic sites, Pi Glilot closure continues," *Jerusalem Post*, May 28, 2002.

[563] Barton Gellman, "Cyber-Attacks by Al Qaeda Feared," *The Washington Post*, June 27, 2002, p.A1.

[564] "New York Terror Targets," ABC News.com, May 21, 2002 (http:// abcnews.go.com/sections/us/DailyNews/warning020521.html).

[565] Ali A. Mohamaed, a former Green Beret sergeant and one of six men indicted for the bombings of the U.S. embassies in Kenya and Tanzania in 1998 tied his assaults to Osama Bin Laden and linked Bin Laden to Hezbollah security chief

Imad Mughniya. Milt Bearden and Larry Johnson, "A Glimpse at the Alliances of Terror," *The New York Times*, November 7, 2000.

[566] Milt Bearden and Larry Johnson, "A Glimpse at the Alliances of Terror," *The New York Times*, November 7, 2000.

[567] Dana Priest and Douglas Farah, "Terror Alliance has U.S. Worried," *The Washington Post*, June 30, 2002, p.A1.

[568] David von Drehle, "U.S. Fears Use of Belt Bombs," *The Washington Post*, May 13, 2002, p.A1.

[569] Transcript of Testimony by Secretary of Defense Donald H. Rumsfeld, Defense Subcommittee of the Senate Appropriations Committee, May 21, 2002 (http://www.defenselink.mil/speeches/2002/s20020521-secdef.html).

[570] http://www.whitehouse.gov/news/releases/2002/01/20020129-11.html.

[571] *Comprehensive Report of the Special Advisor to the DCI on Iraq's WMD*, September 30, 2004, p.1.

[572] *Comprehensive Report of the Special Advisor to the DCI on Iraq's WMD*, September 30, 2004, p.1.

[573] Henry Kissinger, *Diplomacy*, New York: Simon & Schuster, 1994, pp.311-314.

[574] President Reagan's March 8, 1983 speech before the National Association of Evangelicals at http://reagan.webteamone.com/speeches/empire.cfm.

[575] http://www.cnn.com/SPECIALS/cold.war/episodes/14/documents/debate/.

[576] John L. Esposito (ed.), *The Oxford History of Islam*, Oxford: Oxford University Press, 1999, p.ix.

[577] St. Martin's College, Overview of World Religions: Online Encyclopedia of Islam at http://philtar.ucsm.ac.uk/encyclopedia/islam.

[578] Desmond Stewart and the Editors of Time-Life Books, with an Introduction by Philip K. Hitti, *Early Islam*, New York: Time-Life Books, 1975, p.7.

[579] Michael Scott Doran, "Somebody Else's Civil War," *Foreign Affairs*, January/February 2002, p.25.

[580] Michael Scott Doran, "Somebody Else's Civil War," *Foreign Affairs*, January/February 2002, p.26.

[581] St. Martin's College, Overview of World Religions: Online Encyclopedia of Islam at http://philtar.ucsm.ac.uk/encyclopedia/islam.

[582] Michael Scott Doran, "Somebody Else's Civil War," *Foreign Affairs*, January/February 2002, p.27.

[583] Michael Scott Doran, "Somebody Else's Civil War," *Foreign Affairs*, January/February 2002, pp.26-27.

[584] Dr. Muqtedar Khan, "A Memo to American Muslims," October 5, 2001 at http://www.ijtihad.org/memo.htm.

[585] Ralph Peters, "A Remedy for Radical Islam," *The Wall Street Journal*, April 29, 2002, p.A18.

[586] Barbara Crossette, "A Challenge to Asia's Own Style of Islam," *The New York Times*, December 30, 2001.

[587] Graham E. Fuller, "The Future of Political Islam," *Foreign Affairs*, March/April 2002, p.58.

[588] "Jews, Zionism, and Israel in Syrian Textbooks," the Center for Monitoring the Impact of Peace, http://www.edume.org/reports/6/toc.htm.

[589] "The Palestinian Authority School Books and Teacher's Guide," the Center for Monitoring the Impact of Peace, http://www.edume.org/reports/1/toc.htm.

[590] Dr. Arnon Gross, "The Significance of the New Palestinian Textbooks," Hebrew University symposium, January 16, 2001, http://www.israelemb.org/articals/2001011604.html.

[591] The Hamas Covenant, August 18, 1988.

[592] Neil MacFarquhar, "Anti-Western and Extremist Views Pervade Saudi Schools," *The New York Times*, October 19, 2001, p.B1.

[593] Neil MacFarquhar, "Anti-Western and Extremist Views Pervade Saudi Schools," *The New York Times*, October 19, 2001, p.B3.

[594] Thomas F. Friedman, "War of Ideas," *The New York Times*, June 2, 2002.

[595] Neil MacFarquhar, "Anti-Western and Extremist Views Pervade Saudi Schools," *The New York Times*, October 19, 2001, p.B3.

[596] Thomas L. Friedman, "Arabs at the Crossroads," *The New York Times*, July 3, 2002, p.A19.

[597] Saad Mehio, "How Islam and Politics Mixed," *The New York Times*, December 2, 2001.

[598] Memri.org, "Arab Progressive: 'Tell Me One Arab University That can Stand Side by Side with Oxford, Cambridge, Harvard…'" November 24, 2004.

[599] Memri.org, "Arab Progressive: 'Tell Me One Arab University That can Stand Side by Side with Oxford, Cambridge, Harvard…'" November 24, 2004.

[600] United Nations Development Program, *Arab Human Development Report 2003: Building a Knowledge Society*, October 2003, pp.1-8.

[601] Irshad Manji, *The Trouble With Islam*, New York: St. Martin's Press, 2003, pp.30-32.

[602] Irshad Manji, *The Trouble With Islam*, New York: St. Martin's Press, 2003, pp.2, 56.

[603] http://www.cpj.org/attacks01/mideast01/mideast.html.

[604] United Nations Development Program, *Arab Human Development Report 2003: Building a Knowledge Society*, October 2003, p.3.

[605] Tim Golden, "Crisis Deepens Impact of Arab TV News," *The New York Times*, April 16, 2002, p.A16.

[606] David Hoffman, "Beyond Public Diplomacy," *Foreign Affairs*, March/April 2002, p.85.

[607] Thomas L. Friedman, "Listening To the Future," *The New York Times*, May 5, 2002.

608 Dennis Ross, *The Missing Peace*, New York: Farrar, Straus and Giroux, 2004, pp.15-45.

609 Nicholas Wade, "In DNA, New Clues to Jewish Roots," *The New York Times*, May 14, 2002.

610 The Balfour Declaration, November 2, 1917.

611 The Feisal-Weizmann Agreement, January 3, 1919.

612 The Peel Commission Report, July 1937.

613 Library of Congress, Country Study on Israel.

614 "A Year After the War," The Pew Research Center for the People & the Press," March 16, 2004.

615 "A Year After the War," The Pew Research Center for the People & the Press," March 16, 2004.

616 "A Year After the War," The Pew Research Center for the People & the Press," March 16, 2004.

617 "A Year After the War," The Pew Research Center for the People & the Press," March 16, 2004.

618 "A Year After the War," The Pew Research Center for the People & the Press," March 16, 2004.

619 "A Year After the War," The Pew Research Center for the People & the Press," March 16, 2004.

620 Erica Goode, "Finding Answers in Secret Plots," *The New York Times*, March 10, 2002.

621 Erica Goode, "Finding Answers in Secret Plots," *The New York Times*, March 10, 2002.

622 Thomas L. Friedman, "Eastern Middle School," *The New York Times*, October 2, 2001, p.A25.

[623] Gerald P. O'Driscoll, Jr., Kim R. Holmes, and Mary Anastasia O'Grady, *2002 Index of Economic Freedom*, Washington DC: The Heritage Foundation, 2002; *Freedom in the World*, Washington, DC: Freedomhouse, 2002; *The World Factbook 2001*, Washington DC: The Central Intelligence Agency, 2001.

[624] Daniel Pipes (edited by Wladyslaw Pleszczynski), "A New Round of Anger and Humiliation: Islam after 9/11," from http://www.danielpipes.org/pf.php?id=417.

[625] Brink Lindsey, "The New Totalitarians," *Navigator*, December 2001, p.8.

[626] Daniel Pipes (edited by Wladyslaw Pleszczynski), "A New Round of Anger and Humiliation: Islam after 9/11," from http://www.danielpipes.org/pf.php?id=417.

[627] Bernard Lewis, "What Next?", Lecture at the Greenwich Library at Greenwich, Connecticut, September 14, 2003.

[628] Gilles Kepel, *Jihad: The Trail of Political Islam*, Cambridge, MA: The Belknap Press, 2002, p.69.

[629] Gilles Kepel, *Jihad: The Trail of Political Islam*, Cambridge, MA: The Belknap Press, 2002, p.71.

[630] Roy Mottahedeh, "Arabs and America: Education Is the Key," *The Washington Post*, February 12, 2002, p.A25.

[631] Roy Mottahedeh, "Arabs and America: Education Is the Key," *The Washington Post*, February 12, 2002, p.A25.

[632] United Nations Development Program, *Arab Human Development Report 2003: Building a Knowledge Society*, October 2003, p.9.

[633] The United Nations Development Programme's *Human Development Report 2001*, the Heritage Foundation's *The Index of Economic Freedom*, the Cato Institute's *Economic Freedom of the World: 2001*, Freedomhouse.org's *Freedom in the World 2000–2001*, and Donald Sutherland, *Does Freedom Matter?*, White Plains, New York: The Institute for SocioEconomic Studies, 2002.

[634] The United Nations Development Programme's *Human Development Report 2001*, the Heritage Foundation's *The Index of Economic Freedom*, the Cato Insti-

tute's *Economic Freedom of the World: 2001*, Freedomhouse.org's *Freedom in the World 2000–2001*, and Donald Sutherland, *Does Freedom Matter?*, White Plains, New York: The Institute for SocioEconomic Studies, 2002.

635 Richard Roll and John Talbott, *Why Many Developing Countries Just Aren't*, Los Angeles: UCLA, November 20, 2001, pp.25-30.

636 Freedomhouse.org's *Freedom in the World 2001–2002*.

637 The United Nations Development Programme's *Arab Human Development Report 2002*.

638 United Nations Development Program, *Arab Human Development Report 2003: Building a Knowledge Society*, October 2003, p.4.

639 United Nations Development Program, *Arab Human Development Report 2003: Building a Knowledge Society*, October 2003, p.5.

640 Christopher M. Blanchard, "Al Qaeda: Statements and Evolving Ideology," Congressional Research Service, November 16, 2004, p.1.

641 Christopher M. Blanchard, "Al Qaeda: Statements and Evolving Ideology," Congressional Research Service, November 16, 2004, pp.1-6.

642 Christopher M. Blanchard, "Al Qaeda: Statements and Evolving Ideology," Congressional Research Service, November 16, 2004, p.6.

643 Thomas Kean and Lee Hamilton, Prepared Statement to the Committee on International Relations, U.S. House of Representatives, August 24, 2004.

644 Melana Zyla Vickers, "World's Youth Movement Colored by Red, White and Blue," *USA Today*, December 15, 2004.

645 Advisory Group on Public Diplomacy for the Arab and Muslim World, *Changing Minds, Winning Peace*, October 1, 2003.

646 Dimitri K. Simes (President of the Nixon Center), "America's Imperial Dilemma," *Foreign Affairs*, Nov/Dec 2003, pp.91-94.

647 Helena K. Finn, "The Case for Cultural Diplomacy," *Foreign Affairs*, Nov/Dec 2003, p.15.

[648] K. Alan Kronstadt, "Education Reform in Pakistan," Congressional Research Service, December 23, 2004, pp.4,6.

[649] K. Alan Kronstadt, "Education Reform in Pakistan," Congressional Research Service, December 23, 2004, pp.4,6.

[650] Jeffrey Gedmin, "Axis of Weakness," *The Weekly Standard*, October 18, 2004, p.19.

[651] David Blankenhorn, "Propositions," New York: Institute for American Values, 2001.

[652] David Blankenhorn, "Propositions," New York: Institute for American Values, 2001.

[653] David Hoffman, "Beyond Public Diplomacy," *Foreign Affairs*, March/April 2002, p.83.

[654] Alan Cowell, "British Police Revise Time Span of Subway Bombs: 3 Blasts Within 50 Seconds," *The New York Times*, July 10, 2005, p.8.

[655] http://www.whitehouse.gov/news/releases/2003/03/20030317-7.html.

[656] Amy Hawthorne, "Middle Eastern Democracy: Is Civil Society the Answer?" Carnegie Endowment for International Peace, March 2004.

[657] Bernard Lewis, "What Went Wrong?" *The Atlantic*, January 2002.

[658] Jessica Tuchman Mathews, "Now for the Hard Part," *From Victory to Success: Afterwar Policy in Iraq*, Carnegie Endowment and Foreign Policy, July 24, 2003, p.53.

[659] "President Outlines Steps to Help Iraq Achieve Democracy and Freedom," May 24, 2004, http://www.whitehouse.gov.

[660] Robert F. Worth, "Iraqi Civilians Fight Back Against Insurgents," *The New York Times*, March 22, 2005.

[661] Reuel Marc Gerecht, "The Struggle for the Middle East," *The Weekly Standard*, January 3/10, 2005, p.23.

662 Dexter Filkins, "Iraq's Sunnis Voted in Larger Numbers This Time, Officials Say," *The New York Times*, October 21, 2005.

663 Dexter Filkins, "Iraq's Sunnis Voted in Larger Numbers This Time, Officials Say," *The New York Times*, October 21, 2005.

664 "RPT-UN Official Says Iraq Constitution Vote Accurate," *Reuters AlertNet*, October 25, 2005.

665 Dexter Filkins, "3 Sunni Parties Form Bloc to Take part in Iraq Vote," *The New York Times*, October 27, 2005.

666 Dr. Nimrod Raphaeli, "The Elections in Iraq—The Roots of Democracy," MEMRI.org, December 21, 2005.

667 "Iraq's Election Result," *The Washington Post*, December 22, 2005.

668 "Iraq's Election Result," *The Washington Post*, December 22, 2005.

669 Dr. Nimrod Raphaeli, "The Elections in Iraq—The Roots of Democracy," MEMRI.org, December 21, 2005.

670 Dr. Nimrod Raphaeli, "The Opportunity Before Kurdistan: A New Model for a Middle East Democracy," Memri.org, September 7, 2005.

Chapter 6

671 Henry Kissinger, *Does America Need a Foreign Policy?* New York: Simon & Schuster, 2001, p.283.

672 Niall Ferguson, *Colossus: The Price of America's Empire*, New York: The Penguin Press, 2004, p.125.

673 U.S. Census Bureau, *Global Population Profile: 2002* and U.S. Central Intelligence Agency, *World Factbook: 2003*.

674 U.S. Census Bureau, *Global Population Profile: 2002* and Thomas P.M. Barnett, "The Pentagon's New Map," *Esquire*, March 2003.

675 U.S. Census Bureau, *Global Population Profile: 2002* and Thomas P.M. Barnett, "The Pentagon's New Map," *Esquire*, March 2003.

[676] U.S. Census Bureau, *Global Population Profile: 2002* and U.S. Central Intelligence Agency, *World Factbook: 2003.*

[677] U.S. Census Bureau, *Global Population Profile: 2002.*

[678] U.S. Census Bureau, *Global Population Profile: 2002.*

[679] U.S. Census Bureau, *Global Population Profile: 2002.*

[680] U.S. Census Bureau, *Global Population Profile: 2002.*

[681] U.S. Declaration of Independence.

[682] Henry Kissinger, *Does America Need a Foreign Policy?* New York: Simon & Schuster, 2001, p.283.

[683] "Wallace Attacks Our Russian Policy," *The New York Times*, January 11, 1947; "Truman Betraying U.S., Wallace Says," *The New York Times*, March 14, 1947; "Wallace Sees U.N. As Sole Peace Hope," *The New York Times*, April 1, 1947; "The Text of Wallace's Speech on Foreign Policy to American Veterans in Paris," *The New York Times*, April 24, 1947; "Wallace on Tour Hits Truman Plan," *The New York Times*, May 3, 1947.

[684] Henry Kissinger, *Does America Need a Foreign Policy?* New York: Simon & Schuster, 2001, p.286.

[685] Niall Ferguson, *Colossus: The Price of America's Empire*, New York: The Penguin Press, 2004, p.302.

[686] U.S. Declaration of Independence.

[687] George C. Marshall—Nobel Lecture, December 11, 1953.

[688] Diane Ravitch, *Left Back: A Century of Failed School Reforms*, New York: Simon & Schuster, 2000, p.459.

[689] Henry Kissinger, *Does America Need a Foreign Policy?* New York: Simon & Schuster, 2001, p.286.

[690] Diane Ravitch, *Left Back: A Century of Failed School Reforms*, New York: Simon & Schuster, 2000, p.466.

691 Department of Defense Information Report, October 2001.

692 Chester A. Crocker, "Engaging Failing States," *Foreign Affairs*, September/October 2003, p.34.

693 Chester A. Crocker, "Engaging Failing States," *Foreign Affairs*, September/October 2003, p.36.

694 Chester A. Crocker, "Engaging Failing States," *Foreign Affairs*, September/October 2003, pp.37-38.

695 Vice Admiral Lowell E. Jacoby, U.S. Navy, "Current and Projected National Security Threats to the United States," Testimony before the U.S. Senate Select Committee on Intelligence, February 24, 2004.

696 Thomas P.M. Barnett, "The Pentagon's New Map," *Esquire*, March 2003.

697 Thomas P.M. Barnett, "The Pentagon's New Map," *Esquire*, March 2003.

698 Chester A. Crocker, "Engaging Failing States," *Foreign Affairs*, September/October 2003, p.35.

699 Chester A. Crocker, "Engaging Failing States," *Foreign Affairs*, September/October 2003, p.36.

700 Thomas P.M. Barnett, "The Pentagon's New Map," *Esquire*, March 2003.

701 Thomas P.M. Barnett, "The Pentagon's New Map," *Esquire*, March 2003.

702 Eliot Cohen, "History and the Hyperpower," *Foreign Affairs*, July/August 2004, p.63.

703 Niall Ferguson, "A World Without Power," *Foreign Policy*, July/August 2004, p.34.

704 Niall Ferguson, "A World Without Power," *Foreign Policy*, July/August 2004, pp.38-39.

705 The National Security Strategy of the United States, September 2002.

706 The National Security Strategy of the United States, September 2002.

[707] The National Security Strategy of the United States, September 2002.

[708] Congressional Research Service, "Foreign Aid: An Introductory Overview of U.S. Programs and Policy," April 15, 2004, pp.30-31.

[709] Congressional Research Service, "Foreign Aid: An Introductory Overview of U.S. Programs and Policy," April 15, 2004, pp.30-31.

[710] President Woodrow Wilson's Fourteen Points.

[711] "The 'Truman Doctrine,'" *The New York Times*, March 23, 1947.

[712] "Truman Betraying U.S., Wallace Says," *The New York Times*, March 14, 1947.

[713] "Wallace Sees U.N. As Sole Peace Hope," *The New York Times*, April 1, 1947.

[714] "The Text of Wallace's Speech on Foreign Policy to American Veterans in Paris," *The New York Times*, April 24, 1947.

[715] "Wallace Sees U.N. As Sole Peace Hope," *The New York Times*, April 1, 1947.

[716] "Wallace On Tour Hits Truman Plan," *The New York Times*, March 3, 1947.

[717] "Wallace Returns, Decries Our 'Road,'" *The New York Times*, April 28, 1947.

[718] "Pravda Calls Rise in U.S. Friends Soviet Blessing on Eve of May Day," *The New York Times*, May 1, 1947.

[719] "China Reds Hail Wallace," *The New York Times*, April 28, 1947.

[720] "Chilean Reds Praise Wallace," *The New York Times*, April 19, 1947.

[721] "Churchill's Views Criticized," *The New York Times*, April 20, 1947.

[722] "Churchill Fears Appeasement," *The New York Times*, April 21, 1947.

[723] "Poll Shows New England Strongly Behind Truman," *The New York Times*, March 23, 1947.

[724] "Truman's Appeal for Action Backed on Pacific Coast," *The New York Times*, March 23, 1947.

[725] "Opinion Is Cautious Among Many in Upper South," *The New York Times*, March 23, 1947.

[726] "Opinion Is Sharply Divided Over Our New Policy," *The New York Times*, March 23, 1947.

[727] Jeremy A. Rabkin, *The Case for Sovereignty*, Washington, DC: AEI Press, 2004, p.12.

[728] Jeremy A. Rabkin, *The Case for Sovereignty*, Washington, DC: AEI Press, 2004, pp.14-15.

[729] Jeremy A. Rabkin, *The Case for Sovereignty*, Washington, DC: AEI Press, 2004, pp.19.

[730] President Bush's Inaugural Address, January 20, 2005.

[731] President Bush's Inaugural Address, January 20, 2005.

[732] President Bush's Inaugural Address, January 20, 2005.

[733] Richard Roll and John Talbott, "Why Many Developing Countries Just Aren't," UCLA: November 20, 2001, p.27.

[734] Richard Roll and John Talbott, "Why Many Developing Countries Just Aren't," UCLA: November 20, 2001, p.50.

[735] Richard Roll and John Talbott, "Why Many Developing Countries Just Aren't," UCLA: November 20, 2001, p.50.

[736] International Monetary Fund, "World Economic Outlook," April 2003, pp.105-106.

[737] International Monetary Fund, "World Economic Outlook," April 2003, pp.108-109.

[738] International Monetary Fund, "World Economic Outlook," April 2003, pp.112-113.

[739] President Wilson's Fourteen Points, January 8, 1918.

[740] Colin Powell, "No Country Left Behind," *Foreign Policy*, January/February 2005, p.30.

[741] National Intelligence Council's *Mapping the Global Future*, December 2004.

[742] Steven Erlanger, "Abbas Declares Victory in Vote by Palestinians," *The New York Times*, January 10, 2005, p.A1.

[743] Steven Erlanger, "9 Die in Palestinian Attack in Gaza Strip," *The New York Times*, January 14, 2005, p.A14.

[744] Greg Myre and Steven Erlanger, "Abbas Deploys Forces in Gaza to Prevent Attacks on Israel," *The New York Times*, January 22, 2005, p.A3.

[745] Alan Cowell, "In A Lift for Abbas, Fatah Backs a New Palestinian Cabinet," *The New York Times*, February 24, 2005, p.A3.

[746] Kenneth Katzman, "Iraq: U.S. Regime Change Efforts and Post-Saddam Governance," Congressional Research Service, March 15, 2005.

[747] Dexter Filkins, "Defying Threats, Millions of Iraqis Flock to Polls," *The New York Times*, January 31, 2005, p.A1.

[748] Dr. Nimrod Raphaeli, "Iraqi Elections (III): The Islamist and Terrorist Threats," MEMRI.Org, January 18, 2005 and "Zarqawi and other Islamists to the Iraqi People: Elections and Democracy are Heresy," MEMRI.org, February 1, 2005.

[749] Dexter Filkins, "Defying Threats, Millions of Iraqis Flock to Polls," *The New York Times*, January 31, 2005.

[750] Hamza Hendawi, "Iraq's New Government Expected to Use Sunni Members to Reach Out to Insurgents," *The Boston Globe*, May 10, 2005.

[751] Hassan M. Fattah, "Last Syria Force Leaves Lebanon," *The New York Times*, April 27, 2005, p.A1.

[752] "Lebanon's Youth Electrifies Hope For A New Beginning," *The Daily Star*, March 1, 2005.

753 U.S. Department of State, "Middle East: 'Peaceful Intifada' Soars on 'Wind of Change', March 3, 2005.

754 U.S. Department of State, "Middle East: 'Peaceful Intifada' Soars on 'Wind of Change', March 3, 2005.

755 U.S. Department of State, "Middle East: 'Peaceful Intifada' Soars on 'Wind of Change', March 3, 2005.

756 U.S. Department of State, "Middle East: 'Peaceful Intifada' Soars on 'Wind of Change', March 3, 2005.

757 Thomas H. Kean, Lee H. Hamilton, et. al., "Final Report on 9/11 Commission Recommendations," December 5, 2005, pp.1-3.

A Look Forward

758 "A Year After the War," The Pew Research Center for the People & the Press," March 16, 2004.

759 "A Year After the War," The Pew Research Center for the People & the Press," March 16, 2004.

760 Robert Kagan, "Power and Weakness," *Policy Review*, June 2002.

761 Robert Kagan, "Power and Weakness," *Policy Review*, June 2002.

762 Gary Shapiro, "Intellectuals Debate Anti-Americanism," *The New York Sun*, December 16, 2004.

763 George Neumayr, "The River of No Return," *The American Spectator*, November 2004, p.36.

764 Leon T. Hadar, "Mending the U.S.-European Rift over the Middle East," Cato Institute, August 20, 2003.

765 Ahto Lobjakas, "EU: Leaders Fight to Salvage Union Constitution After French 'Non,'" Radio Free Europe/Radio Liberty, May 30, 2005.

766 "Dutch resoundingly defeat EU constitution bid," MSNBC, June 1, 2005.

[767] "France Votes 'Non,'" *The International Herald Tribune*, June 1, 2005.

[768] http://www.whitehouse.gov/news/releases/2002/09/20020912-1.html.

[769] "The UN's relevance does not stand or fall on its conduct on any one issue. When the crisis has passed, the world will still be left with, to use Annan's phrase, innumerable 'problems without passports'—threats such as the proliferation of weapons of mass destruction (WMD), the degradation of our common environment, contagious disease and chronic starvation, human rights and human wrongs, mass illiteracy and massive displacement. These are problems that no one country, however powerful, can solve alone. The problems are the shared responsibility of humankind and cry out for solutions that, like the problems themselves, also cross frontiers. The UN exists to finds these solutions through the common endeavor of all states. It is the indispensable global organization for a globalizing world," in Shashi Tharoor, "Why America Still Needs the United Nations," *Foreign Affairs*, September-October 2003, p.76.

[770] Vita Bite, "U.N. System Funding: Congressional Issues," Congressional Research Service, November 15, 2001.

[771] CNN, December 1, 2004: http://www.cnn.com/2004/ALLPOLITICS/12/01/annan.coleman/.

[772] "The majority staff estimates that Saddam generated personal profits of over 21.3 billion in contravention of UN sanctions from 1991–2002," Opening statement of Senator Norm Coleman, Permanent Senate Subcommittee on Investigations, November 15, 2004.

[773] Opening statement of Senator Norm Coleman, Permanent Senate Subcommittee on Investigations, November 15, 2004.

[774] Opening statement of Senator Norm Coleman, Permanent Senate Subcommittee on Investigations, November 15, 2004.

[775] Opening statement of Senator Norm Coleman, Permanent Senate Subcommittee on Investigations, November 15, 2004.

[776] Statement of Congressman Henry Hyde, Committee on International Relations, November 17, 2004.

[777] Statement of Everett Schenk on behalf of BNP Paribas, Committee on International Relations, November 17, 2004.

[778] United Nations, "A More Secure World: Our Shared Responsibility," December 2004, p.1.

[779] United Nations, "A More Secure World: Our Shared Responsibility," December 2004, p.1.

[780] United Nations, "A More Secure World: Our Shared Responsibility," December 2004, pp.4-5.

[781] United Nations, "A More Secure World: Our Shared Responsibility," December 2004, p.32.

[782] United Nations, "A More Secure World: Our Shared Responsibility," December 2004, p.32.

[783] United Nations, "A More Secure World: Our Shared Responsibility," December 2004, p.3.

[784] United Nations, "A More Secure World: Our Shared Responsibility," December 2004, p.47.

[785] United Nations, "A More Secure World: Our Shared Responsibility," December 2004, pp.47-48.

[786] United Nations, "A More Secure World: Our Shared Responsibility," December 2004, pp.49-50.

[787] United Nations, "A More Secure World: Our Shared Responsibility," December 2004, p.51.

[788] United Nations, "A More Secure World: Our Shared Responsibility," December 2004, p.52.

[789] Source: Jeremy A. Rabkin, "The Case for Sovereignty," AEI, June 2004.

[790] Dick K. Nanto and Emma Chanlett-Avery, "The Rise of China and Its Effect on Taiwan, Japan, and South Korea: U.S. Policy Choices," Congressional Research Service, April 12, 2005, p.1.

[791] Office of the Secretary of Defense, "The Military Power of the People's Republic of China," July 2005, Executive Summary.

[792] Office of the Secretary of Defense, "The Military Power of the People's Republic of China," July 2005, p.3.

[793] Office of the Secretary of Defense, "The Military Power of the People's Republic of China," July 2005, p.11.

[794] Office of the Secretary of Defense, "The Military Power of the People's Republic of China," July 2005, p.8.

[795] Office of the Secretary of Defense, "The Military Power of the People's Republic of China," July 2005, p.8.

[796] Thomas Lum and Dick K. Nanto, "China's Trade With The United States And The World," Congressional Research Service, April 29, 2005, p.2.

[797] Dick K. Nanto and Emma Chanlett-Avery, "The Rise of China and Its Effect on Taiwan, Japan, and South Korea: U.S. Policy Choices," Congressional Research Service, April 12, 2005, p.30.

[798] Dick K. Nanto and Emma Chanlett-Avery, "The Rise of China and Its Effect on Taiwan, Japan, and South Korea: U.S. Policy Choices," Congressional Research Service, April 12, 2005, pp.30-33.

[799] Dick K. Nanto and Emma Chanlett-Avery, "The Rise of China and Its Effect on Taiwan, Japan, and South Korea: U.S. Policy Choices," Congressional Research Service, April 12, 2005, p.37.

[800] Kishore Mahbubani, "Understanding China," *Foreign Affairs*, September/October 2005, p.49.

[801] Stuart D. Goldman, "Russia," Congressional Research Service, May 24, 2005, p.2.

[802] Stuart D. Goldman, "Russia," Congressional Research Service, May 24, 2005, Introduction.

[803] Sharon Squassoni, "Iran's Nuclear Program: Recent Developments," Congressional Research Service, November 23, 2005, p.5.

804 A. Savyon, "The 'Second Islamic Revolution' in Iran: Power Struggle at the Top," MEMRI.org, November 17, 2005.

805 "Ahmadinejad Denies Holocaust, Again," *Jerusalem Post*, December 14, 2005.

806 "Iranian TV Blood Libel," MEMRI.org, December 22, 2005.

807 Wickham Steed, "Hitler's Aim Is Conquest, Steed Warns the British," *The New York Times*, June 11, 1933.

About the Author

Mr. Tell graduated from Dartmouth College with a Bachelor of Arts degree in government in 1956 and earned his juris doctor degree from the University of Michigan in 1959. He retired as a Senior Vice President from Texaco Inc. on January 1, 1998 after 34 years of service with responsibility for the company's worldwide government affairs, public relations, advertising and sales promotion.

From 1982–97, Mr. Tell also managed Texaco's relationship with the New York Metropolitan Opera including sponsorship of the live radio and television broadcasts. During the 1990–91 50th Anniversary season of these broadcasts, Mr. Tell arranged with the BBC and the European Broadcast Union to carry these broadcasts live to over 15 countries in Europe. Countries in Asia and Latin America have also joined the network for these broadcasts in more recent years.

Mr. Tell serves on the Executive Committee and Board of Governors of the Foreign Policy Association, is a Trustee of the Manhattan Institute and is a member of the National Council of the American Council of Trustees and Alumni. He also serves on the Board of Directors of the Institute for American Values.

978-0-595-67620-0
0-595-67620-0

Printed in the United States
48577LVS00003B/199-219